THE
100 BEST
GREAT LAKES

SHIPWRECKS

VOLUME I
LAKE ONTARIO • LAKE ERIE • LAKE HURON

Books by Cris Kohl:

DIVE SOUTHWESTERN ONTARIO!

SHIPWRECK TALES: THE ST. CLAIR RIVER (TO 1900)

DIVE ONTARIO! THE GUIDE TO SHIPWRECKS AND SCUBA DIVING

DIVE ONTARIO TWO! MORE ONTARIO SHIPWRECK STORIES

TREACHEROUS WATERS: KINGSTON'S SHIPWRECKS

THE 100 BEST GREAT LAKES SHIPWRECKS, VOLUME I

THE 100 BEST GREAT LAKES SHIPWRECKS, VOLUME II

THE
100 BEST
GREAT LAKES

VOLUME I
LAKE ONTARIO • LAKE ERIE • LAKE HURON

BY
CRIS KOHL

ILLUSTRATED WITH PHOTOGRAPHS,
MAPS, AND DRAWINGS

THE 100 BEST GREAT LAKES SHIPWRECKS, VOLUME I

ISBN 0-9681437-2-5

LIBRARY OF CONGRESS CARD CATALOG NUMBER: 98-90679

Published by
SEAWOLF COMMUNICATIONS, INC.,
P.O. BOX 66,
WEST CHICAGO, IL 60186
U.S.A.

DISCLAIMER: Although the author and publisher have tried to make the information as accurate as possible, they accept no responsibility for any loss, injury, death, or inconvenience sustained by any person using this book.

NOTE: Photo credits are shown in terms of the author's source for the photograph rather than a specific photographer who might have taken it, except where the photographer is known and specifically named. Photos © photographers as indicated (excluding Cris Kohl). Artwork © artists as indicated. Text, maps of the individual Great Lakes, and Cris Kohl photos © Seawolf Communications, Inc.

Printed in Hong Kong

FIRST EDITION: NOVEMBER, 1998

03 02 01 00   5 4 3 2

COVER PHOTOGRAPH: *Man's nautical handiwork, here the sunken remains of the steamer,* JOYLAND, *off Lake Huron's Manitoulin Island, rests silently frozen as but one of the many Great Lakes' underwater museums. Freshwater seaweed waves with languid sensuality at planking mounted to frames, while defeated iron bolts take hollow aim at the water which they can no longer frustrate or foil.* PHOTO BY CRIS KOHL.

DEDICATION

TO JOAN FORSBERG---

THE BEST PARTNER

ACKNOWLEDGEMENTS

The author sincerely thanks the following individuals and organizations, listed alphabetically, for their assistance during the writing of this book:

INDIVIDUALS: Josh Barnes of Charlevoix, MI; Kent Bellrichard of Milwaukee, WI; James Brotz of Sheboygan, WI; Steve Carrigan of Aurora, IL; Dale Currier of Oswego, NY; Dr. Roger Dean of Port Sanilac, MI; Don Edwards of Thunder Bay, ON; Paul Ehorn of Elgin, IL; Dr. Gary Elliott of Madison Heights, MI; Darryl Ertel of Flint, MI; Tom Farnquist of Sault Ste. Marie, MI; Chuck & Jeri Feltner of Drummond Island and Dearborn, MI; Joan Forsberg of High Lake, IL; Gary Gentile of Philadelphia, PA; Robert Graham of the Center for Archival Collections, Bowling Green State University, Ohio; Capt. Jerry Guyer of Milwaukee, WI; Dennis Hale of Dayton, OH; Joyce Hayward of Bellevue, OH; Adam Henley of Ajax, ON; Capt. Jim Herbert of Barcelona, NY; Capt. Bill Hoey of Detroit, MI; Capt. Jim Jackman of Calumet, MI; Tim Juhl of Carsonville, MI; C. Patrick Labadie, curator, Canal Park Museum, Duluth, MN; Dani Lee of Montreal, Quebec; Daniel Lenihan, Principal Investigator, National Park Service, Submerged Cultural Resources Unit, Santa Fe, New Mexico; Capt. Peter Lindquist of Munising, MI; Barb & Ian Marshall of Stevensville, ON; Marcy McElmon of Trenton, ON; Robert McGreevy of Grosse Point Woods, MI; David & Sue Millhouser of Cape Ann, Massachusetts; Valerie Olson-van Heest of Holland, MI; David Ostifichuk of Smiths Falls, ON; Doug Pettingill of Picton, ON; Capt. Roy Pickering, of Blenheim, ON; Steve Radovan of Sheboygan, WI; Tom Rasbeck of Oswego, NY; Peter Rindlisbacher of Amherstburg, ON; Ralph Roberts of Saginaw, MI; Spencer Shonicker of Kingston, ON; Mark Standfield of Toronto, ON, for initially planting the idea for a book like this into my head; Capt. Jim and Pat Stayer, of Lexington, MI; John Steele of Waukegan, IL; Frederick Stonehouse of Marquette, MI; James Taylor of Picton, ON; Peter Tomasino of St. Charles, IL; Dave Trotter of Canton, MI; Frank Troxell of Davisburg, MI; Sharon Troxell of White Lake Twp, MI; Matt Turchi of Flint, MI; Rev. Peter van der Linden, Marysville, MI; Georgann & Michael Wachter of Avon Lake, OH; George West of Sheboygan, WI; Erika Wetzel, of Windsor, ON; Paul Woehrmann of the Milwaukee Public Library, WI; Susan Yankoo & George Wheeler of Point Traverse, ON; Jon Zeaman of Milwaukee, WI; and Dean Ziegler of Bloomville, OH.

ORGANIZATIONS AND THEIR HELPFUL STAFFS: The Center for Archival Collections (formerly the Institute for Great Lakes Research) Bowling Green State University, OH; the Great Lakes Historical Society, Vermilion, OH; the Great Lakes Marine Collection of the Milwaukee Public Library/the Wisconsin Marine Historical Society, Milwaukee, WI; the Lake Carriers' Association, Cleveland, OH; the Marine Museum of the Great Lakes at Kingston, Ontario; the Metropolitan Toronto Public Library, ON; and the U.S. National Park Service, Submerged Cultural Resources Unit, Santa Fe, New Mexico.

Special thanks to David Bondy for holding the fort while I chased the rainbows.

I apologize to anyone I may have inadvertently overlooked. Finally, I wish to acknowledge and thank the people who have read my previous books and magazine articles on the Great Lakes, and especially to those many who took the trouble to write to me some of the most interesting, informative, and inspiring letters that I have ever read.

CONTENTS

FOREWORD TO VOLUME I BY JOYCE HAYWARD........................x

INTRODUCTION...xii

CHAPTER ONE: LAKE ONTARIO SHIPWRECKS........................1
    Comet 5
    Falconer, Annie...9
    Frontenac 15
    Manola 19
    Marsh, George A. 23
    Munson 31
    Olive Branch... 36
    Sheboygan, City of... 41
    St. Peter.. 47
    Wolfe Islander II 53

CHAPTER TWO: LAKE ERIE SHIPWRECKS 61
    Admiral... 65
    Boland, John J., Jr.. 69
    Brunswick 73
    Carlingford 76
    Clarion 78
    Dundee... 84
    Gale, Steven F. 88
    Little Wissahickon.. 91
    Merida 96
    Morning Star 105
    Nimrod 111
    Passaic..115
    Queen of the West..117
    Richmond, Dean...119
    Tonawanda..122
    Two Fannies..124
    Willis...126

CHAPTER THREE: LAKE HURON SHIPWRECKS 129
    Arabia...135
    Atlantic...139
    Barnum, William H. 143
    Cedarville...145
    Cleveland, City of...149
    Goshawk..152

Grecian 156
India...158
Joyland 160
Mapledawn 165
Marquette 170
Mary Alice B. 174
Merrill, John B. 179
Montana...181
New York...184
Nordmeer...187
North Star 190
North Wind..194
Philadelphia..196
Price, Charles S. 200
Regina..207
Sport..215
Sweepstakes...219
Thompson, Emma E. 222

APPENDIX A: VESSEL TYPES 227

APPENDIX B: VESSEL PARTS.................................233

APPENDIX C: 100 DEEP GREAT LAKES SHIPWRECKS FOR TECHNICAL
            DIVING...239

INDEX TO VOLUME I 261

IMPORTANT CONTACTS...265

ABOUT THE AUTHOR..266

Continued in Volume II:

Foreword to Volume II by C. Patrick Labadie..................x

Introduction..xii

CHAPTER FOUR: Lake Michigan Shipwrecks 267

CHAPTER FIVE: Lake Superior Shipwrecks...................351

APPENDIX D: 100 Most Hunted Great Lakes Shipwrecks.......463

APPENDIX E: Over 100 Shipwrecks in Great Lakes Parks and Preserves..475

APPENDIX F: 100 More Great Lakes Shipwrecks 495

Bibliography 513

Index to Volume II 527

Important Contacts...531

About the Author...532

FOREWORD

TO VOLUME I

by

Joyce Hayward

TEACHER,
EXECUTIVE MEMBER OF THE ASSOCIATION FOR GREAT LAKES MARITIME HISTORY,
GREAT LAKES REGIONAL COORDINATOR OF THE ATLANTIC ALLIANCE FOR MARITIME
HERITAGE CONSERVATION,
PRESIDENT OF THE OHIO CHAPTER OF SAVE ONTARIO SHIPWRECKS,
PAST PRESIDENT OF THE BAY AREA DIVERS SCUBA CLUB OF TOLEDO, OHIO.

As you slip beneath the surface, sinking effortlessly along the down-line towards the bottom, it happens,...the form of a shipwreck materializes before your eyes. What a thrill! What an adventure --- diving Great Lakes shipwrecks!

Whether you are drawn by the recreational experience or by the desire to visit history, it is commonly recognized that certain shipwrecks have greater appeal to the visiting divers.

With his background and experience as a photographer, historian, author, explorer, and avid scuba diver, Cris Kohl certainly has the experience and qualifications to select the best of the best of Great Lakes shipwrecks.

In this book, Cris has completely described the shipwreck site, providing a brief history of the ship in service, cause of loss, and a preview of what you will see during a visit. The ship's location, conditions surrounding the site, as well as topside information provide valuable knowledge.

The sites that Cris has chosen represent a cross-section of our maritime history: sailing vessels, paddlewheelers, steamers, tugboats, and ore carriers. Lying within sport diving recommended maximum depth, these sites were chosen because of their unique qualities, ship features and artifacts, ship integrity, and photographic qualities. Many were nominated by divers who repeatedly visit their favorite site due to the special qualities the site provides.

Whether you are new to Great Lakes shipwreck diving, or a well-traveled diver, this guide is a valuable resource and a must for your collection. Written in the excellent informative style of this popular author, the book invites and entreats you to visit the sites featured.

Cris Kohl has provided the diving public with a unique, well-written resource.

I know you will enjoy and value *The 100 Best Great Lakes Shipwrecks, Volume I.*

Joyce Hayward,
Bellevue, Ohio,
July, 1998

INTRODUCTION

Five immense bodies of fresh water form a unique and highly conspicuous natural feature near the middle of the North American continent. Known collectively and historically as the Great Lakes, a deserved appellation not the least bit guilty of exaggeration, these vast entities of water --- Lakes Ontario, Erie, Huron, Michigan, and Superior --- have a combined area of 94,560 square miles, making them the largest surface of fresh water in the world.

The Great Lakes region, running 860 miles in an east-west direction and 690 miles in a north-south direction, covers an area larger than France.

Geographically, the Great Lakes drain from west to east, emptying eventually through the St. Lawrence River into the Atlantic Ocean. Lake Superior lies at an altitude of 600 feet above sea level; Lakes Michigan and Huron are at the same 579-foot level; Lake Erie sits at 570 feet above sea level, while Lake Ontario, after the waters' dramatic drop over Niagara Falls as it enters this lake, rests at 245 feet above sea level.

Lake	Area in sq. mi.	World rank	Max. depth	Vol. in cu. mi.	World rank
Ontario	7,840	14th	802'	393	11th
Erie	9,910	11th	210'	116	15th
Huron	23,000	5th	750'	849	7th
Michigan	22,300	6th	923'	1,180	6th
Superior	31,700	2nd	1,333'	2,935	4th

Politically, the five Great Lakes are shared by eight U. S. states (east to west: New York, Pennsylvania, Ohio, Michigan, Indiana, Illinois, Wisconsin, and Minnesota), and one Canadian province (Ontario). About 60% of the Great Lakes surface waters lie within the United States, while approximately 40% are contained within Canada. Lake Michigan is the only one of the Great Lakes lying totally within the United States.

Environmentally, all the Great Lakes except Superior have witnessed increased concentrations of most chemicals since the year 1900. Lakes Ontario, Erie, and Michigan have suffered a four-fold increase of chloride, sodium, and sulfate in that time span, while Lake Erie's nitrogen content has increased five times what it was in 1900 and its phosphorus level tripled between 1945 and 1975. These components are significant because they stimulate algae and zebra mussel growth which, for scuba divers, affect visibility and aesthetics with regards to shipwreck exploration. What these elements do to the overall scheme of things in the Great Lakes is even more devastating.

Lake	Max. depth	Mean depth	Length in miles	Width in miles	Retention time of water
Ontario	802'	283'	193	53	8 years
Erie	210'	58'	241	57	3 years
Huron	750'	195'	206	101	20-22 years
Michigan	923'	276'	321	118	90-100 years
Superior	1,333'	487'	383	160	110-190 years

Environmentally, humans as a species have acted unthinkingly about the Great Lakes' future. Atlantic salmon were once naturally plentiful in these waters, but the polluting and damming of rivers which flow into these lakes caused their extinction by 1880. Whitefish, once thriving in huge numbers, were seriously restricted by the late 1800's for the same reasons. Great Lakes sturgeon were greedily overfished and are now on the edge of extinction. Introduced into the Great Lakes were carp, smelt, sea lamprey, alewives, zebra mussels, and the ruffe, all originally foreign to these waters. On the other hand, lake trout and salmon have been re-introduced to the Great Lakes, with varying degrees of success. The struggle to maintain an acceptable balance is ongoing.

Historically, the Great Lakes provided the first means of easy transportation, with First Nation canoes and, later, European vessels plying these natural highways into the continent's heartland. The first of the lakes to be viewed by a European was Lake Huron in 1609 or 1610, when the French explorer, Étienne Brûlé, arrived. Brûlé and Samuel de Champlain are credited with being the first white men to visit Lake Ontario, in 1615. Brûlé and Grenoble reputedly were, in 1622, the first Europeans to see Lake Superior. In 1634, Jean Nicolet became the first white man to reach Lake Michigan, while much later, in 1669, the first European to gaze over Lake Erie was Louis Jolliet. Europeans quickly discovered this area's resource treasures, such as lumber, fertile farmland, freshwater, and minerals like coal, copper, iron, and limestone.

Surface area of the Great Lakes in square miles:

	Ontario	Erie	Huron	Michigan	Superior
Canada	3,880	4,930	13,900	none	11,100
United States	3,460	4,980	9,100	22,300	20,600
Boundary length:	174.6 mi	253 mi.	261 mi.	none	282.8 mi.

Industries and huge urban populations quickly developed because of these resources. In the year 1800, about 300,000 people lived in the Great Lakes region; in 1970, the population had risen to 37,000,000, an increase of 12,000%. Most of this dense, modern settlement extends from Milwaukee-Chicago around southern Lake Michigan, across to Detroit, then around the southern shore of Lake Erie through Toledo-Cleveland-Buffalo, culminating in the "Golden Horseshoe" area along western Lake Ontario running from Niagara Falls to Hamilton to Toronto in Canada.

This incredibly large megalopolis continues to place increasing pressures upon our limited Great Lakes resources, whether these be fresh water, lumber stands, mineral deposits, or the recreational exploration of shipwrecks.

Scuba diving is one activity which this book addresses. The cold, fresh waters of the Great Lakes yield no tropical characteristics, such as colorful coral and exotic fish, but they do contain the best preserved shipwrecks in the world!

That is a powerful, world-renowned claim, not to be taken lightly. A letter I received in 1988 from a marine museum curator in Fremantle, Western Australia, contained the statement, "I have, of course, heard about your amazingly well-preserved [Great Lakes] shipwrecks...." People in the rest of the world are aware that the "submerged cultural resources" in the Great Lakes are definitely unique. Unfortunately, some people in the Great Lakes take our shipwrecks for granted, stealing artifacts and depriving us of chances to view remnants of another era frozen in time in these underwater museums.

Historians surmise that, of the approximately 15,000 vessels that plied Great Lakes waters in recorded history, about 4,000 became permanent residents known as shipwrecks, numbers which always stymie and impress the imaginations of locals and visitors alike. That so much maritime commerce could be sustained on these inland seas in the middle of the North American continent is one of the least-known facts in the overall scheme of world history.

These facts should give an idea of the intense shipping traffic on the Great Lakes in earlier years:

- By 1845, there were 60 steamships and 270 sailing vessels on the Upper Great Lakes alone (that is, upstream of Niagara Falls, namely Lakes Erie, Huron, Michigan, and Superior).

- By 1860, there were over 1,450 commercial ships of all types plying the waters of the five Great Lakes.

- By 1870, there were over 2,000 commercial sailing ships listed on the Upper Great Lakes alone. This was the peak year for sailing vessels.

- In the year 1882, Chicago Harbor recorded 26,000 commercial vessel arrivals and clearances (departures).

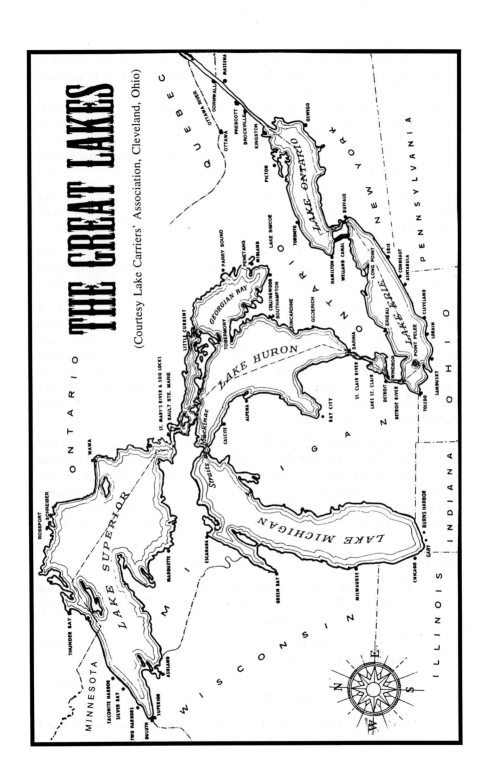

THE GREAT LAKES

(Courtesy Lake Carriers' Association, Cleveland, Ohio)

- One 1892 photograph of Harbor Beach, MI (on Lake Huron) shows 110 crowded commercial steamers, schooners, barges, and tugs taking refuge from a bad lake blow. Talk about tight rafting off!

- As late as 1916, there were 1,837 steamships and 162 sailing vessels working commercially on the Great Lakes.

With numbers like these, it is little wonder that many of these thousands of ships ended up on the bottom of our inland seas.

Fewer than half of these 4,000 shipwrecks have been located to date, but the rate of discovery is changing geometrically with refinements and cost reductions in electronic detection or positioning devices, such as sidescan sonar and the global positioning system. Since these natural shipwrecks in the Great Lakes are a limited, nonrenewable resource, what we have must be treated with the greatest of respect so we do not greedily devour or destroy these resources for the immediate gratification of our own generation's limited time frame.

These books will tell you about the 100 best shipwrecks in the Great Lakes. The criteria for establishing some idea of "bestness" were straightforward:

1. a maximum depth of 130', since this is the safe sport diving limit recommended by training agencies;

2. positive identification of the shipwreck. There are many excellent "mystery" shipwrecks in the Great Lakes, such as the coal schooner in Lake Erie off Port Stanley, Ontario, and numerous unidentified schooners in Lake Huron which have somehow ended up as highlights at scuba or shipwreck shows, but the true challenge lies in identifying them. Without a name, there can be no opportunity to research and appreciate that vessel's history;

3. intactness of the hull (does the shipwreck still look like a ship?);

4. the presence of nautical components or artifacts;

5. the reliability of fairly good underwater visibility at the site;

6. an acceptable lack of zebra mussel coverage of the shipwreck and its components.

That said, let me make it clear that these criteria were not "carved in granite." Had they been, shipwrecks in Lake Erie, lower Lake Michigan, and some parts of Lake Ontario would not have made the list simply because of their camouflaged condition due to cyclical zebra mussel encrustation, or steel ships that were dynamited and no longer have intact hulls, such as the *Sevona* or the *Mapledawn,* would have been eliminated in spite of their absolutely fascinating site characteristics. Also not taken into account in deciding "The 100 Best" were accessibility of the shipwreck (it didn't matter if it was a shore dive or well off shore), or the supposed degree of historical significance of the wreck (every shipwreck has a story to tell, and a valuable history).

Let me explain the headings found in the box that accompanies each shipwreck:

- VESSEL NAME: The was the ship's name at the time of sinking. The launching name is also given if it was different.

- RIG: This refers to the type of vessel it was at the time of loss (see Appendix A for "Vessel Types").

- DIMENSIONS: The first number represents the length of the vessel, followed by a number showing the ship's beam, followed by a number showing the vessel's draft, or depth. All numbers are in feet (e.g. 206') and inches (e.g. 6"). All dimension figures given are those at the time of the ship's loss, since the vessel may have had major alterations or size-changing rebuilds in its history.

- LAUNCHED: Wherever possible, the exact date, as opposed to just giving the year in which a ship was launched, is given. This is for the sake of those researchers who may wish to delve into local archives in quest of contemporary accounts describing the ship's launching. This date is followed by the launch location.

- DATE LOST: This is the date that the ship sank, ending its active career on the Great Lakes and beginning its passive career as a scuba dive site.

- CAUSE OF LOSS: Ships sank for a number of reasons, mainly foundering (filling with water and sinking), burning, colliding (usually with another ship), stranding (running aground and often breaking up), exploding (boilers on steamships were notorious for this), scuttling (purposely being sunk to discard a vessel no longer considered useful), and abandoning.

- CARGO: The vast majority of Great Lakes vessels were workhorses which usually carried heavy loads of lumber, coal, iron ore, or grain. Sorry, no gold-and-silver-laden ships traversed these waters. "In ballast" means the ship carried no cargo at the time of sinking.

- LIVES LOST: This is the number of persons who perished when that ship sank. If known, the number of the entire crew is also given.

- LOCATION: This gives a very general idea of where that shipwreck is located, e.g. 4.5 miles off Milwaukee, WI.

- DEPTH: Once again, this is given in feet. If only one number is given, or the higher number of a range, it is where the deepest part of that sunken vessel rests. Some shipwrecks rise 30' from the bottom!

- ACCESS: Most shipwrecks can be reached only by means of a boat; a few, however, are accessible from shore.

- DIVING SKILL LEVEL: Each shipwreck site is identified as suitable for novice, intermediate, or advanced divers, or midway points in between each of these designations. I thank Joyce Hayward and the Bay Area Divers of Ohio for their assistance in these categories:

A novice dive: a) is less than 60' in depth, b) is suitable for a newly-certified diver or infrequent diver, c) has no or very little current, d) has good visibility, e) may include shipwreck diving with no penetration.

An intermediate dive: a) is suitable for more experienced divers, b) may reach depths between 60' and 100', c) may include wreck diving with no penetration, d) may involve waves or some current, e) may involve open water sites with boat entries, f) has good to moderate visibility, and g) may have other conditions which may warrant more experience.

An advanced dive: a) may reach depths between 100' and 130', b) is suitable for very experienced divers (may prefer specialty certification), c) may involve limited wreck penetration, swift or variable current diving, cold water, or ice diving, d) may have extremely limited or zero visibility, e) may require special skills such as navigation, rescue, cave or cavern diving training or special equipment.

Regarding safety during scuba diving: use common sense and neither neglect nor forget nor ignore your training and your limitations.

- DIVING HAZARDS: These are given in very general terms and are extremely variable and weather-dependent. Make personal on-site evaluations before you scuba dive in unfamiliar waters.

- CO-ORDINATES: These are the exact locations of each shipwreck, given in either latitude/longitude (GPS, Global Positioning System), or TD's (time differentials) for the older Loran system, or both, if known. Unfortunately, there are variations between even the same brand of electronics, so proceed doing a search pattern with a depth sounder and patience if you don't locate the shipwreck immediately. Most numbers have been verified by the author.

Finally, the author is well aware that compiling a list of "the 100 best" Great Lakes shipwrecks is inviting controversy and debate. However, he does not feel like changing his lifestyle now. The author is also aware that "the 100 best" list will change with future shipwreck discoveries, and these newly-discovered shipwrecks will have the diver education and protective legislation introduced all around the Great Lakes in recent years to protect and conserve their intact states.

These two books about "The 100 Best Great Lakes Shipwrecks" are meant to provide the reader with exciting tales of maritime history, and, for the scuba diver, reveal and describe shipwrecks that are the most interesting in the world to explore.

Have fun!

Cris Kohl
High Lake, Illinois,
August, 1998

1

Lake Ontario Shipwrecks

Geologists refer to present day Lakes Ontario, Erie, and Michigan as the "Ontario basin," which became free of ice from the last glacial period, or Ice Age, (which lasted more than a million years), only about 12,000 years ago. Lake Superior and Georgian Bay cleared of ice a bit more recently.

Lake Ontario is the most easterly of the five Great Lakes, as well as the smallest in surface area (although it contains greater cubic area of water than Lake Erie because of its increased depths).

Europeans first saw and explored Lake Ontario in 1615, when Étienne Brûlé became the first white man to gaze across its waters. He was closely followed that same year by Samuel de Champlain and the Huron expedition on their way to fight the Iroquois nation. By 1668, Lake Ontario's north shore had been completely explored by the French from New France (Quebec), and several mission outposts had been established there.

The Seven Years' War (1756-1763) resulted in the loss of New France (Quebec) to Great Britain. The French general, Montcalm, had captured and burned Fort Oswego, New York (then still very British) early in that war in 1756, burning seven British ships and taking 1,600 prisoners in the process, but British forces under Colonel Bradstreet captured Fort Frontenac (present day

Kingston, Ontario) from the French in 1758, and the French fort at Niagara the following year, thus ending French influence on the Great Lakes.

In the autumn of 1780, the British military ship, *Ontario,* was wrecked with the loss of almost 200 lives while sailing from Niagara to Carleton Island.

Lake Ontario was again the scene of conflict during the War of 1812 between the new country of the United States and the old country of Great Britain. The Americans burned down the Lake Ontario city of Toronto (then called York) in 1813. A year later, the British burned down the White House and other government structures in Washington, D.C. Fortunately, that war ended in late 1814, and Canada and the United States have enjoyed the longest undefended border in the world since then.

Here are some quick facts about the lake:

- Lake Ontario is bordered on the north by the province of Ontario in Canada, and on the south by the state of New York in the U.S.A. The lake is about 193 miles long and 53 miles wide.

- The deepest point in Lake Ontario is 802 feet, or about 134 fathoms at a point 28 miles NE from the pierhead light at Rochester, New York, and NNW 15.5 miles from the main light at Big Sodus, New York. The average, or mean, depth of Lake Ontario is 283 feet.

- The surface area of Lake Ontario is 7,340 square miles, which is only slightly larger than the surface area of Georgian Bay and the North Channel in Lake Huron.

- Lake Ontario's chief water supply is from the upper Great Lakes, namely Lakes Erie, Huron, Michigan, and Superior, through the Niagara River. Niagara Falls thunders the combined energy of four Great Lakes' waters in their downhill sleighride towards sea level at the Atlantic Ocean.

- Passage to the upper Great Lakes from Lake Ontario is made possible by the Welland Ship Canal, which runs parallel to the Niagara River and which accommodates vessels with a maximum draft of 27 feet through eight locks, each 820' long.

- The major communities along Lake Ontario's shoreline are Rochester and Oswego in New York state, and Toronto, Hamilton, Oshawa, Cobourg, Port Hope, and Kingston in Ontario. Lake Ontario is considered the least wild of the Great Lakes, possessing a shoreline which imparts the strongest impression of cultivation and landscaping. Lake Ontario's image is the reverse of Lake Erie's in terms of industry and demography: the south shore (New York state) is thinly populated with little industry, while the north shore (the province of Ontario) is the commercial heartland of the country, boasting Canada's largest city, Toronto, hugging the lakefront.

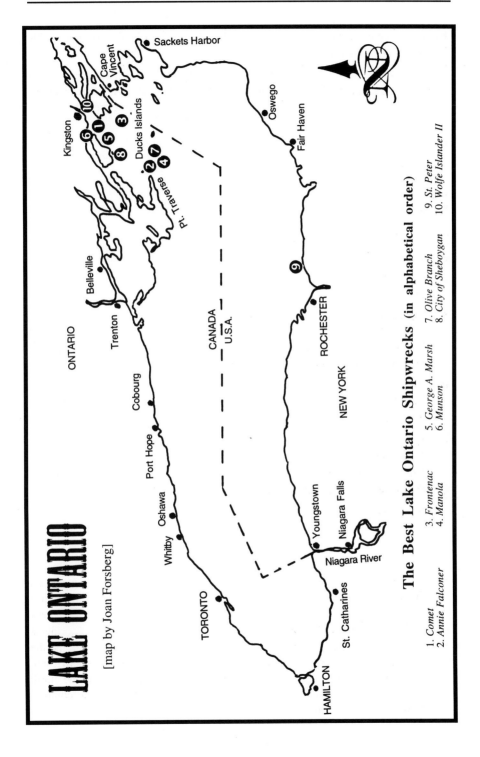

LAKE ONTARIO

[map by Joan Forsberg]

ONTARIO

CANADA
U.S.A.

NEW YORK

Sackets Harbor

Cape Vincent

Oswego

Fair Haven

Kingston

Ducks Islands

Pt. Traverse

Belleville

Trenton

Cobourg

Port Hope

ROCHESTER

Oshawa

Whitby

Youngstown

Niagara Falls

Niagara River

TORONTO

St. Catharines

HAMILTON

The Best Lake Ontario Shipwrecks (in alphabetical order)

1. Comet	5. George A. Marsh	9. St. Peter
2. Annie Falconer	6. Munson	10. Wolfe Islander II
3. Frontenac	7. Olive Branch	
4. Manola	8. City of Sheboygan	

- Lake Ontario was originally named Lake Iroquois by early explorers, after the predominant First Nation tribe in that region.

- The first European-built ships on the Great Lakes were two twin-masted schooners, each about 45' in length and one named the *Frontenac,* built in 1678 by René Robert Cavelier de LaSalle. This was one year before he supervised the construction of his famous ship, the *Griffon,* for upper Great Lakes use. The *Griffon* is often credited with being the first shipwreck in these inland seas. However, LaSalle's *Frontenac* was wrecked near Thirty Mile Point, on the U.S. side of Lake Ontario, on January 8, 1679, thus claiming the record as the first Great Lakes shipwreck.

- The first British ships built on the Great Lakes, sloops named the *Ontario* and the *Oswego,* were launched in 1755 in Lake Ontario.

- The first lighthouse on Lake Ontario, the Isle Forest Light, was established in 1810 at the eastern end of the lake near Kingston.

- The War of 1812 schooners, *Hamilton* and *Scourge,* sank in a sudden storm off present-day St. Catharines, Ontario, on August 7, 1813. They were located in the 1970's in 290' of water, starting endless debate about future use of these historic resources and, more recently, problems of some technical divers possibly damaging/looting the sites.

- The first steamships on the Great Lakes were launched on Lake Ontario in 1816, the *Ontario* at Sackets Harbor on the U.S. side, and the *Frontenac* at Ernesttown, near Kingston, on the Canadian side. Historians continue to debate which vessel was actually first.

- The first commercial, propeller-driven steamer on the Great Lakes, the *Vandalia,* was built at Oswego, New York; her maiden voyage was in November, 1841. This ship was later wrecked in Lake Erie.

- The first U.S. Lifesaving Service on the Great Lakes was established on Lake Ontario in 1876. Canada soon followed suit.

- The worst Lake Ontario marine disaster was the *Noronic,* which burned in Toronto harbor on November 17, 1949, with the loss of 119 passengers.

- Preserve Our Wrecks (P.O.W.), a marine conservation group of mostly scuba divers, was formed at Kingston, Ontario, in 1981 to stop damage to and theft of artifacts from area shipwrecks. Save Ontario Shipwrecks (S.O.S.) was formed in Toronto that same year.

- The first ship purposely scuttled in the Great Lakes for the purpose of creating a scuba dive site was the ferry, *Wolfe Islander II,* at Kingston, Ontario, on September 21, 1985.

Since the Kingston area historically saw the lion's share of maritime traffic on the lake, it is little wonder that most of the lake's finest shipwrecks are near that port. More searching on the U.S. side will certainly bring to light shipwrecks that will be contenders for "the 100 best" in the future.

Comet

(#1 on the map on p. 3)

VESSEL NAME:	COMET
RIG:	wooden sidewheel steamer
DIMENSIONS:	174' 8" x 23' 5" (45' with sidewheels) x 10'
LAUNCHED:	June, 1848; Portsmouth (Kingston), Ontario
DATE LOST:	Wednesday, May 15, 1861
CAUSE OF LOSS:	collision with the schooner, EXCHANGE
CARGO:	farm implements
LIVES LOST:	2 (from about 24 on board)
GENERAL LOCATION:	off Nine Mile Point, eastern Lake Ontario
DEPTH:	65' - 90'
ACCESS:	boat
DIVING SKILL LEVEL:	intermediate-advanced
DIVING HAZARDS:	depth, hypothermia, penetration, silting
CO-ORDINATES:	Lat/Lon: 44.08.350 / 76.35.070
	Loran: 15732.7 / 60036.2

One of the most impressive scuba dive sites in Lake Ontario is the wreck of the combination freight and passenger paddlewheeler named the *Comet,* sitting in about 90' of water.

The elegant, graceful sidewheel steamer, *Comet,* was built by George N. Ault at Portsmouth (Kingston), Ontario, in 1848, utilizing twin, low-pressure engines, built in 1835 and removed from the small steamer, *Unicorn,* formerly *Shannon,* and capable of producing 45 horsepower each. She was not a fast ship, not even for those early times, attaining only ten miles an hour when contemporary steamships were reaching sixteen. She measured 175' in length, 23' in beam, and 10' in draft, with a gross tonnage of 337.

The *Comet* underwent a name change, a sailor's bad luck omen, in 1854, and for the next six years, she plied these waters as the *Mayflower.* Her original name was restored just a year before she sank. Her bad luck, however, started long before her first name change.

The *Comet's* penchant for bad luck began when she struck a shoal and sank in the St. Lawrence River after a few trips. She was raised, repaired, and returned to service and more bad luck. In early November, 1849, the *Comet,* about to enter Toronto harbor, burst a steam pipe, seriously injuring three Irish firemen, two of them fatally. On April 20, 1851, the *Comet's* boiler exploded as she was departing Oswego, New York, tragically killing eight people and ripping an enormous hole in her hull. Eventually raised, the remains of the *Comet* were rebuilt in Montreal, just prior to her name change to *Mayflower*.

Bad luck continued. The *Mayflower* ran ashore at the Scarborough Bluffs, near Toronto, on August 10, 1853; she was pulled off the next day suffering no damage. In the spring following her return to the name *Comet*, powerful winds tore her from her moorings and slammed her against the Cataraqui Bridge on May 7, 1861. A week later, when the *Comet* was fully repaired, she left Kingston for her first trip of the season and steamed right into her final stroke of bad luck.

ART COURTESY OF THE METROPOLITAN TORONTO LIBRARY.

The paddlewheeler, COMET, *lies near Kingston, Ontario.*

On May 14, 1861, Captain Francis Patterson commanded the *Comet*, amidst storm signals and rolling squalls, out of the safety of Kingston harbor. Simultaneously, the Cleveland schooner, *Exchange,* ran frantically before the storm in quest of a safe harbor. In the obscured visibility caused by the foul weather, the bow of the *Exchange* sliced deeply into the hull of the *Comet*. The *Comet* traveled about another eight miles, but it became apparent that the sidewheeler was destined to sink, and Captain Patterson ordered crew and passengers to abandon ship. Two crewmembers were knocked overboard and drowned, while the others quickly jumped into the lifeboat and the yawl and made for the safety of shore.

The massive paddlewheels of the steamer, COMET, *rising about 25 feet above the 90-foot-deep floor of Lake Ontario, impress diver Barb Marshall.*   PHOTO BY CRIS KOHL.

The *Comet* lay undisturbed for over 100 years before Kingston scuba divers Jim McCready and Dr. Robert McCaldon discovered her location after reading a local newspaper article about this wreck and searching with two boats and a depth recorder.

The shipwreck itself is worthy of several visits by experienced divers. The *Comet's* bow and stern have collapsed, but her distinctive paddlewheels are still intact and tower about 25' above the lake floor. The rocker arms and walking beams are also clearly visible. Portions of her railings, doors, and smokestacks rest along the east side of the wreck. Remnants of her cargo of farm implements lie scattered around the wreck.

The wreck lies in deep water (about 90'), so being constantly conscious of bottom time is essential. The slight current is negligible, but silt has built up on and inside the wreck, and it is all too easy for careless or thoughtless divers to stir up the silt and reduce visibility for others who may be diving at that time or shortly thereafter. It sometimes gets dark down there at that depth, so take an underwater light. The paddlewheels are intact, but the rest of the wreck is not.

For trained and experienced divers, limited penetration below deck is possible at the stern to view the engines and twin boilers. Because of the zebra mussel invasion of the Great Lakes since the late 1980's, water visibility has improved, but multi-layers of these pests now camouflage distinctive shipwreck details. Even so, the impressive view of the *Comet's* upright paddlewheels will surely take any visiting scuba diver's breath away!

The wreck of the COMET *is considerably broken and scattered, although penetration into the engine room is still possible by experienced divers. Here, diver Dani Lee studies one of the* COMET'S *ancient boilers below deck.* PHOTO BY CRIS KOHL.

Falconer, Annie (#2 on the map on p. 3)

VESSEL NAME:	ANNIE FALCONER
RIG:	two-masted schooner
DIMENSIONS:	108' x 24' 3" x 9'
LAUNCHED:	Wednesday, May 22, 1867; Kingston, ON
DATE LOST:	Saturday, November 12, 1904
CAUSE OF LOSS:	foundered
CARGO:	coal
LIVES LOST:	1 (from crew of 7)
GENERAL LOCATION:	off Point Traverse, Ontario
DEPTH:	67 ' - 78'
ACCESS:	boat
DIVING SKILL LEVEL:	intermediate-advanced
DIVING HAZARDS:	depth, penetration, occasional current, silting
CO-ORDINATES:	Lat/Lon: 45.58.10 / 76.48.28
	Loran: 15882.20 / 60015.06

In the late 1970's, I first heard talk about the discovery of a fantastic, incredibly intact shipwreck named the *Annie Falconer* at a location just off Point Traverse, Ontario, to the east of Kingston. I was not disappointed when I finally explored "the *Annie,*" as local divers affectionately call the *Falconer*. She was, by far, the most upright, intact, and fully loaded shipwreck I had ever seen.

That the *Annie Falconer* continues to be so to this very day, so many years after her discovery, serves as a strong testimonial to the protective nature of Kingston area scuba divers, and to their education of underwater visitors to the fact that our Great Lakes shipwrecks are a vitally important non-renewable resource. In the short term, shipwrecks are the mainstay of the scuba diving industry in the Great Lakes; remove the shipwrecks, or the parts that make them so interesting to guests visiting the sites, and there will be alarmingly little left to see underwater in the Great Lakes that is of any interest. In the long term, remember that shipwrecks display history: they are ice water museums of a period frozen in time, and as such must be treated with the same respect we give land museums and cemeteries. Lastly, I have had the good fortune to explore shipwrecks in three oceans (Atlantic, Pacific, Indian). I know, through experience and listening, that the freshwater Great Lakes are internationally renowned for having the best preserved shipwrecks IN THE WORLD! Don't mess with that significance, buster. Leave our shipwrecks intact!

Back to the *Annie*. The twin-masted schooner, *Annie Falconer,* measuring 108' in length, 24' in beam, and 9' in draft, was built at Kingston, Ontario, by George Thurston and launched on Wednesday, May 22, 1867, only five weeks before Canada became a country. Mr. Daniel Falconer named this vessel in memory of his late wife, Mary Ann ("Annie") Falconer, nee Baker, (1832-1860), seven years after her death. What a strong and memorable love theirs must have been! Their young daughter, also named Annie, christened the ship and, according to reports, swung the christening bottle, but missed! The vessel glided down the launch ramp anyway. Pessimists viewed this as an ill omen, but the *Annie Falconer* enjoyed a long and virtually problem-free life.

The fore-and-aft schooner, ANNIE FALCONER, *from a painting by Gibbons.*

One accident was almost her undoing when the *Annie Falconer* ran aground at Weller's Bay, Ontario, on October 14, 1893, and spent the winter there high and dry. Fortunately, it was a mild winter, and no devastating storms destroyed the ship before she was pulled off that shore with little damage the following April 21st.

The *Annie Falconer* carried a variety of cargoes during her long life on the Great Lakes: lumber, ice, coal, shingles staves, stone, salt, and grain. According to insurance records, in 1875, the *Annie Falconer* was valued at $8,000; in 1882, $6,000; by 1890, only $4,500. At the time of her demise in 1904, the aging *Annie,* had an estimated value of only $1,000; 37 years is considered old for a wooden ship, even on the Great Lakes. At the time of loss, her coal cargo, appraised at $1,500, was worth considerably more than the ship!

The schooner, Annie Falconer, *is the ship second from right displaying the wide white stripe of paint just above her waterline.*   THE RALPH ROBERTS COLLECTION.

The *Annie Falconer* foundered in a violent storm off South Bay Point about 1.5 miles north of False Duck Island, near Timber Island, 25 miles southwest of Kingston, Ontario, on Saturday, November 12, 1904. At that time, she was underway with a cargo of soft coal bound from Sodus Point, New York, to Picton, Ontario.

The *Annie Falconer* had begun to leak about ten miles off False Duck Island, and the crew pumped frantically while the captain steered the ship towards Timber Island in an effort to purposely run her aground rather than lose her in deep water. They didn't make it. The ship sank about halfway between False Duck Island and Timber Island.

The crew of seven escaped the sinking schooner in the ship's yawl boat at about 2:00 P.M. that Saturday, and landed on Amherst Island to the north at 7:30 P.M. after a frighteningly desperate run. They had nothing but their hats and cupped hands with which to bail out the freezing water from their frail, old yawl. The first mate, James Sullivan, died of exposure shortly after landing on Amherst Island when he wandered away from the rest of the crew in the darkness. The survivors found shelter in a nearby farmhouse and, the next day, Captain Murray Ackerman, the *Annie Falconer's* owner and master, telephoned the results of the disaster to his wife and the mate's family and friends. The captain and crewmembers were local boys, all hailing from nearby Picton.

The schooner, *Annie Falconer*

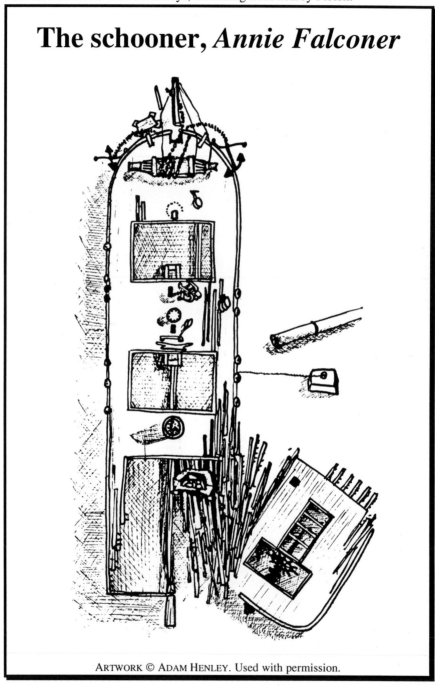

ARTWORK © ADAM HENLEY. Used with permission.

Local marine historians and scuba divers, Barbara Carson, Audrey Rushbrook, and Doug Pettingill, located the wreck of the *Annie Falconer* in 1975. Many of the ship's artifacts, including a kedge anchor and many plates, glassware items, and crockery, were legally salvaged in 1978 and donated to the local marine museum at nearby South Bay, where they are on exhibit for the non-diving population to enjoy. Scuba divers between dives or on bad weather days will also enjoy the large variety of shipwreck exhibits in this museum, which is quite strong in local shipwreck information and displays, both inside and outdoors on the large museum property.

The ship's wheel, or helm, is the focal point of any shipwreck, studied here by diver Marcy McElmon. The absence of a silty patina on the wooden handles of the ANNIE FALCONER'S *wheel indicates that numerous visiting scuba divers have taken turns "steering the* ANNIE." PHOTO BY CRIS KOHL.

The *Annie Falconer* sits upright in 78' of water, on a lake bottom of combined rock and mud. She is uniquely well-preserved, with deadeyes, anchors, the ship's wheel, blocks, a pump, and chains still in place. Her stern section has broken off, but it sits, usually within visible range, at an angle to the main hull. Notched Roman numeral draft markings painted white can still be seen at the stern section. The bowsprit has collapsed in recent years, and the hull is gradually splitting open. In the summer of 1996, the port anchor, which had been hanging precariously on the edge of the bow rail by the steel ball on one end of its crossarm, fell to the lake bottom. The starboard bow anchor hangs by the tip of a fluke, for now. Penetration of this shipwreck is possible at the bow, but only, for the sake of safety, by properly trained and experienced scuba divers. Caution: silt stirs up very easily, particularly below deck.

Water temperatures, as with most shipwreck sites in the Great Lakes, can be pretty low on the *Annie Falconer.* There is frequently a quite noticeable thermocline (a sudden layer of considerably colder water) before you descend to the level of the shipwreck. However, by the end of a warm summer, the temperature on the site at depth can be as much as 56 degrees Fahrenheit (warmer on the surface, of course).

The bowsprit collapsed only recently, showing Mother Nature's determined efforts to break down anything manmade and return it to basic elements.   PHOTO BY CRIS KOHL.

In late 1982, the Kingston-based marine conservation group named Preserve Our Wrecks (P.O.W.), along with the Deep Six Scuba Club of Picton, decided to organize a survey project on the *Annie Falconer.* The actual underwater work ran from May 13 to September 25, 1983, producing a published report of the detailed findings. This was one of the first underwater archaeological surveys done by amateurs anywhere in the Great Lakes. A stone heritage plaque measuring two by four feet, inscribed with the vessel's history, was placed on the hard lake bottom immediately under the *Falconer's* bowsprit. On-going work by Ken Mullings of P.O.W., studying the *Annie Falconer's* slow, natural degradation, has proved to be unique and valuable.

Frontenac

(#3 on the map on p. 3)

VESSEL NAME:	FRONTENAC
RIG:	wooden tugboat
DIMENSIONS:	89' x 22'
LAUNCHED:	1901; Garden Island, Ontario
DATE LOST:	Wednesday, December 11, 1929
CAUSE OF LOSS:	foundered
CARGO:	none
LIVES LOST:	none
GENERAL LOCATION:	between Main Duck Island and Pigeon Island
DEPTH:	100' - 115'
ACCESS:	boat
DIVING SKILL LEVEL:	advanced
DIVING HAZARDS:	depth, hypothermia, darkness
CO-ORDINATES:	Lat/Lon:
	Loran:

The tugboat, *Frontenac,* launched near Kingston and, nearly 30 years later, sunk near Kingston, was discovered by local scuba charter boat captain, Spencer Shoniker, in September, 1995. Acting on a tip from a fisherman, Spencer searched the water west of Kingston using the depth sounder on board his vessel, the *Brooke-Lauren,* named after his two daughters, and came across the historic tugboat, *Frontenac,* which had been submerged for nearly 70 years in a maximum of 115' of water.

The excited first divers exploring this shipwreck were stunned by the sights that are rare on well-explored shipwrecks: porcelain plates, cups, and saucers, all neatly arranged in wooden boxes, the ship's wheel, and the tug's brass compass in a wooden storage box. Other impressive items are the large, four-bladed propeller and the rudder, both still in place and upright; plus the ship's anchors, a huge winch fully loaded with braided steel cable (used by the tug for towing), fallen dorades (air vents), and chain running down the bow.

Spencer Shoniker was careful to keep the *Frontenac's* location a secret, and he took on board only divers he could trust to maintain that secrecy. Most divers emerged from their underwater explorations of this fascinating new site sharing his strong appreciation for the area's maritime history.

One early diver, however, lost control. In what he later described as his snap decision to prevent anyone from stealing the ship's compass, he removed that beautiful artifact from the shipwreck site in a late season dive and swam it about 80' off the wreck. This may indeed have been his true intention, but it disappointed and angered the *Frontenac's* discoverer, who returned the following spring, located the compass, and swam it back to its original position on the hull. In some areas, the practice of removing artifacts from a shipwreck, hiding them underwater off the wreck, and returning to the site at a later date to recover them, has become common, if unscrupulous and, in many waters, illegal, behavior.

The tugboat, FRONTENAC, *seen here in drydock at Kingston to effect some repairs and maintenance upon the vessel's hull, worked in eastern Lake Ontario waters for almost 30 years.*   MARINE MUSEUM OF THE GREAT LAKES AT KINGSTON, #982.2.218.

Researching the story behind the tugboat, *Frontenac,* requires more work than researching a regular ship because secondary sources of information have frequently excluded tugs from their collections of shipwreck stories, wrongly giving the impression that tugboats are inferior vessels of less historic significance than larger commercial ships. Tugboat histories demand that the researcher investigate primary sources of information more intensely than usual.

The 111-ton tugboat, *Frontenac,* constructed by the Calvin Company, slid down the launch ramp at Garden Island near Kingston in 1901. Measuring 89' in length and 22' in beam, the new vessel was built mainly for river and wrecking work, as well as towing log rafts in the summer.

ABOVE: *The tug,* FRONTENAC'S *bow, remains upright, strong, and defiant in 115' of Lake Ontario water. Located in late 1995, this site has become a major goal for visiting scuba divers.* BELOW: *This box of plates and cups from the* FRONTENAC'S *galley is just one of this site's many intact shipboard items.* PHOTOS BY CRIS KOHL.

The Donnelly Wrecking Company, a long-standing and respected Kingston marine salvage business, purchased the *Frontenac* in 1912. A circa-1920 newspaper advertisement for the Donnelly Salvage & Wrecking Co., Ltd., described the technical capabilities of each of their five vessels. According to this ad, the *Frontenac* was "fitted with 100-ton pulling steam winch, two two-ton anchors and 2,500 feet of one and a half inch steel cable. Syphons one six-inch and one four-inch. Steam connections and steel hose for steam pumps."

The *Frontenac* worked for 17 years as a wrecking vessel before the Sin-Mac Lines purchased the tug in early 1929. Little did they, or anyone else, know that this would be the ship's final season afloat.

Late in 1929, when newspapers crackled with the excitement of the opening of the longest suspension bridge in the world, namely the Ambassador Bridge between Windsor, Ontario, and Detroit, Michigan, the new 1,160-ton freighter, *Sarniadoc,* loaded with grain, ran aground in a blizzard near Main Duck Island. The salvage of first, the cargo, and then, the ship, before the long winter set in was uppermost in the minds of local tugboat and salvage vessel operators.

Two Kingston wrecking tugs, the *Frontenac* and the *Rival,* working as a team, cleared Portsmouth harbor at 1:45 P.M. on Wednesday, December 11, 1929, to remove some of the *Sarniadoc's* grain cargo. The *Rival* towed the barge, *Cobourg.* The vessels arrived at the wreck site by 5:00 P.M., only to have the increasing winds and dangerous seas persuade them to change their minds. They wisely retreated towards Portsmouth.

During the return trip, at 8:15 P.M., between Main Duck Island and Pigeon Island, the *Frontenac's* whistle frantically started blowing distress signals. She was taking on water and settling swiftly!

The *Rival* cut her tow and swung back to rescue the *Frontenac's* crew, no easy task considering that the waves were sweeping completely over the sinking ship. The *Rival's* nose had to be run right against the *Frontenac's* hull while the latter's crew jumped onto the former vessel. The *Frontenac* sank within ten minutes. After almost 30 years of hard labor, the wooden hull of the *Frontenac,* in spite of her complete rebuild just a few months earlier, had finally surrendered to the strain of the heavy seas.

By the time the *Rival* picked up the *Cobourg* and returned to Portsmouth, ice covered most of the tug. Captain Mallen, who had come to Kingston specifically to command the *Frontenac,* returned to his home town.

The discovery of the tug, *Frontenac,* poses a dilemma: should the shipwreck and all of its artifacts remain *in situ,* at the site, and run the risk of an errant diver stealing something as unique as the ship's brass compass, or should items like that, which are deemed "at risk," be removed, conserved, and housed in a museum for public display. That debate is long-standing; no satisfactory solution has been forthcoming. The tugboat, *Frontenac,* is an absolute thrill to explore, but the delight of discovery has also become a Pandora's box.

NOTE: Two years later, Spencer Shoniker stopped running charters to the FRONTENAC.

Manola

(#4 on the map on p. 3)

VESSEL NAME:	MANOLA
RIG:	steel steamer (bow half only)
DIMENSIONS:	282' 4" x 40' 3" x 21' 2"
LAUNCHED:	Tuesday, January 21, 1890; Cleveland, Ohio
DATE LOST:	Tuesday, December 3, 1918
CAUSE OF LOSS:	foundered
CARGO:	none
LIVES LOST:	all hands (11)
GENERAL LOCATION:	off False Duck Island, Ontario
DEPTH:	45' - 82'
ACCESS:	boat
DIVING SKILL LEVEL:	intermediate-advanced
DIVING HAZARDS:	depth, hypothermia, penetration, silting
CO-ORDINATES:	Lat/Lon:
	Loran: 15907.5 / 60046.7

The story of the *Manola* is the tale of how one ship became two separate shipwreck sites in two very different Great Lakes!

An enormous bow half of a steel freighter lies upside-down in about 82' of eastern Lake Ontario several miles off Point Traverse 40 miles west of Kingston. How only half a shipwreck managed to exist in the first place is an interesting and, in this case, tragic story.

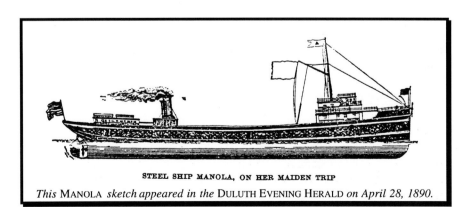

STEEL SHIP MANOLA, ON HER MAIDEN TRIP

This MANOLA *sketch appeared in the* DULUTH EVENING HERALD *on April 28, 1890.*

Built in 1890 by the Globe Iron Works Company of Cleveland, Ohio, the steamer, *Manola,* originally carried a length of 311', a beam of 40', and a draft of almost 25'. The press raved about her being a "magnificent specimen of marine architecture" specially designed for the iron ore trade and capable of cruising at 12 knots fully loaded.

The *Manola* was instrumental in rescuing the crew of the sinking freighter, *Joseph L. Hurd,* on May 10, 1895, after that ship collided with the *Cayuga* (see the Lake Michigan chapter in Volume II for the *Cayuga* story).

After 28 years of faithful service on the Great Lakes, the *Manola* was sold to the Emergency Fleet Corporation of the United States Government on January 25, 1918 for World War I service on the Atlantic Ocean, and, as such, she was cut in half at Buffalo for transit through the old, small, Welland Canal which allows ships to bypass Niagara Falls between Lake Erie and Lake Ontario.

Snowstorm conditions developed while the two halves were being towed across Lake Ontario on December 3, 1918. The towline unexpectedly parted and the bow half of the *Manola* suddenly toppled over and plummeted to the lake depths, taking with it the 11 men who were on board. Tragically, all died, and only one body was ever found. Ironically, World War I, for which the *Manola* was cut in half and towed through the canal and across the open lake, had ended just a few days earlier!

The stern half of the *Manola* was used in a rebuild, the resulting ship being named the *Mapledawn,* which foundered in Georgian Bay in 1924 with, thankfully, no loss of lives, and is today another popular scuba dive site that is among the "100 best" (see Chapter 3 on Lake Huron).

In 1976, local marine historians and underwater explorers Barbara Carson and Doug Pettingill located the remains of the *Manola's* bow half. Many of the ship's artifacts, such as the brass bell and much chinaware bearing the Pittsburgh Steamship Company's name and logo were legally recovered and are exhibited now at the nearby Mariners Park Museum in South Bay, Ontario.

Today, a plastic jug buoy, placed there annually by Kingston's Preserve Our Wrecks, marks the shipwreck site, a fair distance off False Duck Island in open water near the shipping lane. A zesty glide along this huge, overturned half-hull reveals that both bow anchors hang in place impressively, while a spare anchor can be seen in a crawlspace below the shipwreck. Brass portholes still line the lowest portion of the vessel closest to the rocky lake bottom.

The huge, wooden bulkhead where the ship was torched in two in 1918 offers an opening to the interior for very experienced divers with penetration training and proper equipment.

A variety of pulleys and other marine parts litter the lake floor where they spilled when the craft turned turtle. One tank of air is just barely enough to do a single studied circumference of the wreck's exterior, but divers who have ex-

ABOVE: *This photograph of the* MANOLA *was taken just three weeks before the bow half tragically sank in Lake Ontario.* REV. PETER VAN DER LINDEN COLLECTION. BELOW: *Doug Pettingill, co-discoverer of the* MANOLA, *poses with the ship's bell at the Marine Museum at South Bay, Ontario, near Point Traverse.* PHOTO BY CRIS KOHL.

plored this wreck dozens of times are amazed at the interesting items, previously overlooked, that they continue to locate.

Because of its many absorbing items to view, appreciate, and possibly photograph, Point Traverse's half a shipwreck is, in many cases, more fascinating and rewarding than many complete ones in other parts of the Great Lakes!

Doug Pettingill, co-discoverer of the MANOLA *in 1976, hovers below one of the two enormous anchors on the overturned bow at a depth of 75'.*   PHOTO BY CRIS KOHL.

Marsh, George A.

(#5 on the map on p. 3)

VESSEL NAME:	GEORGE A. MARSH
RIG:	schooner
DIMENSIONS:	135' x 27' x 9' 3"
LAUNCHED:	1882; Muskegon, Michigan
DATE LOST:	Wednesday, August 8, 1917
CAUSE OF LOSS:	foundered
CARGO:	coal
LIVES LOST:	11 or 12 (from 14 on board)
GENERAL LOCATION:	between Nine Mile Pt. and Pigeon Island
DEPTH:	70' - 85'
ACCESS:	boat
DIVING SKILL LEVEL:	intermediate-advanced
DIVING HAZARDS:	depth, hypothermia, penetration, silting
CO-ORDINATES:	Lat/Lon: 44.07.690 / 76.36.260
	Lat/Lon: 44.07.37 / 76.36.09 (old system)
	Loran: 15744.2 / 60034.8

The classic, turn-of-the-century, three-masted schooner named the *George A. Marsh* gazes imperiously from its cold water throne in about 85' of eastern Lake Ontario water, an impressive but deadly shipwreck.

What moves most visiting scuba divers is the integral state of this splendid vessel. The ship rests upright and intact, 135' in length, with narrow hatch openings and ladders which sweetly beckon unsuspecting underwater explorers downward into the low, silt-filled holds. One fin kick will raise clouds of silt as thick as Lake Superior fog, making exit for the unprepared an impossibility. This site is not for the rash or the inexperienced.

Rows of eerie deadeyes hang limply like discarded doll heads along both port and starboard railings, while the long bowsprit and various chains point with undiminished dignity towards the *Marsh's* ghostly heading.

The ship's wheel marks the focal point of diver attention at this site, and many a modern romantic has pretended to steer the frozen ship that can be guided today only by a phantom helmsman, on course to infinity. Nearby, the ship's iron stove displays a teapot, a kettle, and various other galley items, spectral cuisine prepared by a culinary banshee. Many blocks, tools, and belaying pins line the shadowy deck, placed conspicuously by early divers who wanted to ensure that others who followed would not miss these stately sights. Also look at and appreciate the ship's rigging, lifeboat, and incredible bowsprit.

In fact, very little has been "salvaged" or stolen since the *George A. Marsh's* discovery by Barbara Carson, Edward Donnelly, and Ted Symonds on October 7, 1967, fifty years after the ship sank. Some small artifacts, such as plates and bottles were removed and placed in the Museum of the Great Lakes at Kingston for public viewing. The graceful bow anchors were removed in October, 1971, the only objects on this shipwreck conspicuous by their absence, leaving the *Marsh* sentenced to sail the silent seas of a spiritual world as a schooner with no anchors.

The *George A. Marsh,* named after Chicago lumber businessman, George Andrew Marsh (1834-1888), slid down the launch ramp at Muskegon, Michigan, in 1882. The ship was owned by its namesake for only the first year of its life, generating several owners over the next few years, who used the ship principally in the lumber trade on Lake Michigan until the vessel was sold to Canadian interests in 1913 and moved to Lake Ontario at the opposite end of the Great Lakes.

Those "Canadian interests" happened to be Captain John Wesley Smith and Jonathon J. B. Flint, both of Belleville, Ontario, near Kingston. Capt. Smith proudly sailed the *George A. Marsh* from Lake Michigan down Lake Huron, across Lake Erie, through the Welland Canal, and eastward the length of Lake Ontario to bring home his new charge. Aware of the bad luck that supposedly accompanies the change of a ship's name, the new owners kept the *Marsh's* designation when their ship was registered as Canadian number 133750.

The local maritime conservation group named Preserve Our Wrecks (P.O.W.), formed in 1981, besides buoying the area's shipwrecks every spring, does a commendable job of educating the diving public about the need to leave Great Lakes shipwrecks as they were found. Anyone caught desecrating any of these Kingston area shipwreck sites, besides being guilty of breaking Ontario laws, would likely have a long swim back to shore --- before being tarred, feathered, and run out of town on a rail by local divers!

Unfortunately, off the wreck of the *George A. Marsh,* mounds of human bones have also been located by scuba divers since the zebra mussel invasion of the southern Great Lakes improved underwater visibility and enticed divers to explore the areas just off the shipwreck, something generally not done prior to 1990. These bones are considered to be the remains of some of the seven bodies which were never recovered. Ideally, these bones should be removed from such easy access, perhaps entombed collectively underwater near the shipwreck, or put to final repose in gravesites on land.

Ironically, since the water cleared up in about 1990, several scuba divers have lost their lives at this site through carelessness and/or lack of experience.

ABOVE: *The schooner,* GEORGE A. MARSH, *was recaulked, freshly painted, and equipped with new sails and lines after Canadian interests purchased the ship in 1913.* BELOW: *The* MARSH *worked on Lake Michigan for the first 31 of her 35 years.* GREAT LAKES MARINE COLLECTION OF THE MILWAUKEE PUBLIC LIBRARY/WISCONSIN MARINE HISTORICAL SOCIETY.

What touches most people who read about the *George A. Marsh* is the sad tale behind this shipwreck. Twelve of the 14 people on board perished in the early morning hours of Wednesday, August 8, 1917, when the vessel foundered in a feverish summer storm while returning to Belleville, Ontario, from Oswego, New York, across the lake, with a load of coal. Around the midnight hour, crewmembers discovered that the *Marsh,* in all the pounding from the heavy seas, had sprung a leak and was rapidly taking on water. Besides a manual pump being used nonstop, the steam pump and siphons were made operational. Everyone on the ship was roused and gathered on deck, just as a precaution in case they needed to abandon ship quickly. Capt. Smith steered the sinking ship towards the nearest land, which happened to be tiny Pigeon Island, in hopes of grounding the doomed vessel. The ship, however, sank at 5:00 A.M. in 85' of water about two miles shy of its destination.

VOL. 53.   BELLEVILLE, ONT

TWELVE LIVES LOST
WHEN SCHOONER SANK

CLER
NOT

SAD TRAGEDY ON LAKE ONTARIO

SCHOONER GEORGE A. MARSH, OF BELLEVILLE, FOUND-ERED YESTERDAY THIRTY MILES FROM KINGSTON—LIFEBOAT CAPSIZED—TWELVE WERE DROWNED—ONLY TWO SURVIVORS—MARSH WAS OWNED IN BELLEVILLE AND WAS TAKING A CARGO OF COAL TO KINGSTON—SEVEN LITTLE CHILDREN AMONG THE VICTIMS.

(Special to The Intelligencer.)

KINGSTON, Aug. 9.—The Sowards Coal Company, of this city, has been officially notified of the sinking of the schooner George A. Marsh, of Belleville, between Nine Mile Point and Pidgeon Island, on Lake Ontario, yesterday morning. The Marsh had on 450 tons of coal from Oswego for the Sowards Company. There were fourteen people on board, and out of that number eleven were drowned and one died from exposure.

resided for years in Kingston, where he followed the occupation of sailor. He was a member of Moira Lodge A. F. & A. M., of this city and a member of Christ church. A widow but no family survives.

Mr. George Cousins, whose home is at the corner of Wharf and Church streets, was born in England 59 years ago, but had lived here for over half a century and had many friends. He had been sailing practically all his life, and was one of the members of the crew of the ill-fated vessel. A widow, one son and two daughters survive. The son, Arthur George, who resides at Sarnia, is by occupation a sailor, being at the present time on one of the upper lakes. The

OTTAWA
rose in the Senator had any dignat. Church wit the exempl This denial result of th Gazette tha his influen ed.

FRENCH

(Can
LONDON
have again
of Bixschoo
endeavored
terday nort
w'th loss b'

The sinking of the GEORGE A. MARSH *with the deaths of many men, women, and children made front page news in their hometown of Belleville, Ontario* [THE DAILY INTELLIGENCER, *August 9, 1917*].

Shock overwhelms us when we learn that Captain John W. Smith, 48 years of age, his second wife, Gertrude Smith, 22 years of age, and five of their children (the first four from the captain's earlier marriage, which had ended with his wife's death in late 1913): Greta (12), Eva (8), John (6), Clarence (4), and Lorraine (1), all died when the *Marsh* sank. Friends, the Neil MacLellan family, had been invited along; the husband survived the sinking, but not so his wife, aged 25 years, their seven-month-old son, and a four-year-old nephew. Two of the three sailors on board also perished (the one who survived was Capt. Smith's brother, William) in this emotionally overpowering tragedy which stirred the community's fervid compassion for a long time afterward.

Five of the 12 bodies were recovered and buried on land: Gertrude and Greta Smith, the two sailors, and the four-year-old nephew. The remains of the other seven who died when the *George A. Marsh* sank are either below deck on the schooner, or scattered around the site just off the shipwreck.

Or so we've been told.

Recent research done by Richard Palmer of New York state indicates that Capt. John Smith, who was mourned for lost when the *George A. Marsh* sank, was known to be a strong swimmer, survived the sinking of his ship, and died in a small town in Oklahoma ten years later!

Shocking New York state newspaper articles, printed in 1927, conjectured that Capt. John Smith, apparently too shaken by the loss of so many of his family members and wishing to avoid having to explain mistakes in judgement which caused the loss of his ship and so many lives, somehow went into hiding after he reached shore when the *Marsh* sank in 1917.

Photographs of the GEORGE A. MARSH'S *tall masts protruding above water at the wreck site were published in* THE DAILY BRITISH WHIG *(Kingston) on Saturday, August 25, 1917, with the heading and cutline, "A Tragedy of Lake Ontario. The picture shows all that remains of the schooner* GEORGE MARSH, *which was lost in a storm near Kingston, with twelve of those on board." Those telltale masts were later dynamited well below the waterline to ensure that they would not be a hazard to navigation.*

Not long afterwards, Capt. Smith strayed into a small town in Oklahoma, penniless and friendless, and far from the waters of the Great Lakes where bad memories abounded. In that town, his candor earned him a loan to start up a business. When he died in 1927, "he was completely out of debt and had his business in first class shape. He ran a flour and feed business, owned an ice dock, and had a freight line to his property and seven trucks on the road."

Capt. Smith left his 1927 estate, valued at $3,000, to his daughter, Margaret, who was 15 years old and at home in Belleville when her father's ship sank and most of her family died in 1917. Coincidentally, the 42-year-old Neil MacLellan, one of the survivors of the *Marsh* sinking (he had incredibly survived two other Great Lakes shipwrecks earlier!), who had sadly lost his wife and baby son in that disaster, married this teenage daughter of Capt. Smith "shortly after the wreck." Life is stranger than fiction.

Capt. John Wesley Smith died and was buried in Oklahoma, but through a Masonic connection, it became known that he was linked with the ill-fated schooner, the *George A. Marsh.*

Diver Dani Lee takes a close look at rows of deadeyes, part of this schooner's standing rigging which was used to maintain the tension on the masts, line both the starboard and the port railings of the George A. Marsh. *Deadeyes resemble skulls, hence the name.* PHOTO BY CRIS KOHL.

Speculation also hints at a German bomb having sent the *George A. Marsh* to the bottom of Lake Ontario near Pigeon Island. After all, World War I

Commercial diver James Taylor examines the GEORGE A. MARSH'S *wheel, the focal point of any shipwreck lucky enough to remain so intact.*   PHOTO BY CRIS KOHL.

was in full tilt, and there were confirmed cases of espionage and sabotage in North America. However, fixing that blame upon the sinking of an aged Great Lakes schooner might be stretching one's imagination a bit too far.

Each successive generation of researchers and writers moves the story of the Great Lakes another step forward. What was written 25 or 50 years ago may seem simplistic today, but it was creditable, innovative, and impressive in its time. We continue to use that knowledge as a springboard to greater details and more information. Now is truly an exciting time to be studying Great Lakes maritime history!

The diminishing light on the ghostly schooner, the *George A. Marsh,* imparts a tinge of respectful fright, while the stillness fills us with strange wonder. The overwhelming tragedy of this shipwreck is still being felt, while the mystery of the vessel's captain is just being unearthed.

The schooner, *George A. Marsh*

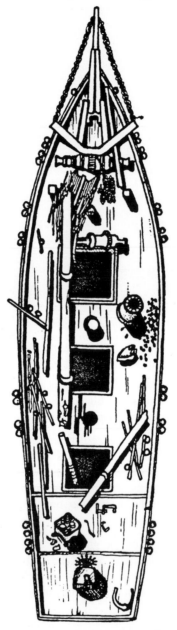

ARTWORK © ADAM HENLEY. Used with permission.

Munson

(#6 on the map on p. 3)

VESSEL NAME:	MUNSON
RIG:	dredge
DIMENSIONS:	
LAUNCHED:	
DATE LOST:	Wednesday, April 30, 1890
CAUSE OF LOSS:	foundered
CARGO:	none
LIVES LOST:	none (from a crew of 3)
GENERAL LOCATION:	6 miles west of Kingston, Ontario
DEPTH:	93' - 111'
ACCESS:	boat
DIVING SKILL LEVEL:	advanced
DIVING HAZARDS:	depth, hypothermia, darkness
CO-ORDINATES:	Lat/Lon:
	Loran: 15701.4 / 60016.0

Scuba divers visiting the deep wreck of the dredge, *Munson,* sitting in 111' of water off Lemoine Point, six miles west of Kingston, Ontario, are consistently astounded at the large number of artifacts at this site. Dishes, bottles, tools, and many other items abound on the upper and lower decks of this unusual vessel.

This shipwreck stands as strong evidence that the education of scuba divers, both local and visiting, has helped enormously in maintaining the integrity of such an historic site. Marine conservation groups have explained to divers that artifacts lose a great deal of their significance when they are removed from their historic surroundings.

The upright *Munson* sits intact, with experienced divers penetrating her basic skeletal layout and twin decks, or appreciating the distinctive crane and bucket features.

Time has left us very few examples of this type of Great Lakes vessel, and the *Munson's* story gives her an edge over other dredges. In April, 1890, the dredge, *Munson,* which was headquartered in Belleville, Ontario, received several work contracts. The most important of these was to ensure that the Montreal Transportation Company's immense, new schooner-barge, the *Minnedosa,* would have adequate launch depth at Kingston on Saturday, April 26, 1890. This connection with the four-masted *Minnedosa,* the largest Canadian sailing vessel ever built on the Great Lakes (she measured an incredible 250' in length) proved to be of lasting historical significance to the *Munson.*

The *Minnedosa* launch project, the little *Munson's* most important job, also turned out to be her last.

This working dredge from the early part of the twentieth century is similar to the MUNSON. *Extracting* MUNSON *documentation is difficult because dredges were not required to be registered.* AUTHOR'S COLLECTION.

On Wednesday, April 30, 1890, her job at Kingston completed, the *Munson* was taken in tow of the tug, *Emma Munson,* along with two scows, and hauled westward to resume construction work on the new Bay of Quinte bridge at the town of Rossmore. A few miles west of Kingston, the dredge appeared to be leaning to one side.

Suddenly the *Munson* tipped over and sank, with crews barely able to cut the towline in time to prevent their being dragged down as well. William Green, the *Munson's* cook, was pulled 30' underwater before he was able to escape from the sinking dredge. The rest of the crew also saved themselves, but all their personal belongings were lost. The *Munson,* valued at about $15,000, likely sank "by the springing of a plank on the bottom of the craft."

Located by a Canadian Hydrographic survey team, the *Munson* is marked on local charts. The shipwreck is usually buoyed by Preserve Our Wrecks members every spring, and numerous charter and private boats visit this site annually, allowing hundred of divers to appreciate this excellent example of the Kingston's area's maritime heritage. The only reason scuba divers can enjoy all of these artifact sights today is because the divers that were there ahead of them did not steal these things. Keep up that tradition!

The dredge, *Munson*

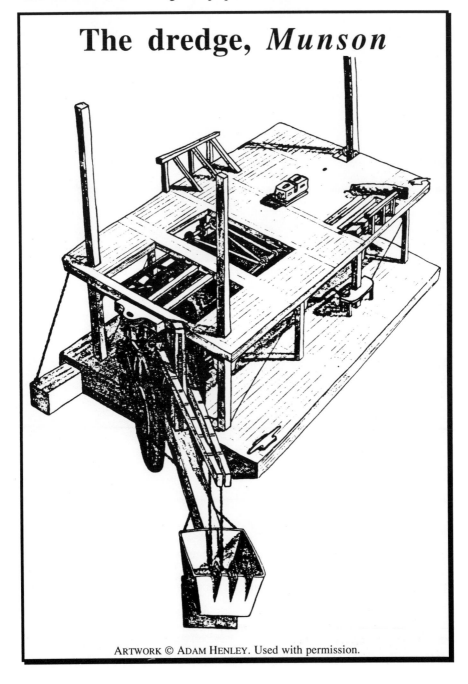

ARTWORK © ADAM HENLEY. Used with permission.

ABOVE: *The* MUNSON'S *gear mechanism for the crane, including the bucket, arm, and chains, impresses scuba diver Marcy McElmon . It is easy to see why this dredge is such a popular site.* BELOW: *Below deck on the dredge,* MUNSON, *a variety of 1890 tools have been neatly placed on a workbench for divers to see . Removing them from the water would quickly turn them into piles of rusting junk; besides, you can rest assured that they are appreciated much more on this site!* PHOTOS BY CRIS KOHL.

Bottles, china, and other kitchen utensils from the dredge, MUNSON, *have been gathered and placed on the upper deck at a depth of about 95' for the enjoyment of visiting divers, such as scuba instructor Marcy McElmon, who otherwise might miss seeing and appreciating them.* PHOTO BY CRIS KOHL.

Olive Branch

(#7 on the map on p. 3)

VESSEL NAME:	OLIVE BRANCH
RIG:	two-masted schooner
DIMENSIONS:	92' x 22' x 8'
LAUNCHED:	1871; Picton, Ontario
DATE LOST:	Thursday, September 30, 1880
CAUSE OF LOSS:	foundered
CARGO:	coal
LIVES LOST:	all hands (5)
GENERAL LOCATION:	between False Duck and Main Duck Islands
DEPTH:	90' - 98'
ACCESS:	boat
DIVING SKILL LEVEL:	advanced
DIVING HAZARDS:	depth, hypothermia, darkness, silting
CO-ORDINATES:	Lat/Lon: 43.56.52 / 76.47.34
	Loran: 15885.11 / 60047.79

A mystery ship succumbed to wild Lake Ontario waves in an early autumn storm on September 30, 1880, sinking between Main Duck Island and False Duck Island. Initial suspicions held the unfortunate vessel to be either the schooner, *Ocean Wave,* the schooner, *Olive Branch,* or the schooner, *Great Western,* but local sailors, better than most people at analyzing a tragic maritime situation, shook their heads and concluded that it had to be the *Olive Branch.*

By October 4th, the schooners, *Ocean Wave* and *Great Western,* had been safely accounted for. To verify the matter, the captain of the schooner, *H.P. Murray,* daringly sailed his ship through immense waves past the topmast of the sunken ship sticking out of the water, and his description of the lost vessel's fly (a small flag on a ship used for the indicating of wind direction) corresponded with that of the *Olive Branch.*

Still, some people were reluctant to believe that evidence. Fishermen on Grenadier Island thought the lost ship could be the schooner, *Volunteer.*

Finally, even though the strong winds and the harsh waves refused to subside, Captain Dix of the *White Oak,* while en route towards Kingston harbor, lowered a boat at the wreck site and approached the mast of the sunken ship at the Ducks. The fly was secured and brought to Kingston, where it was submitted to the inspection of Mrs. Capt. McKee, of the schooner, *Richardson,* who had made the fly for the *Olive Branch*. She recognized it immediately as her handiwork, and the lost ship's identity was confirmed.

ABOVE: *The* OLIVE BRANCH *resembled this vessel, the schooner,* J.H. STEVENS *(built in Milan, Ohio, in 1859 and abandoned in 1908). No photos of the* OLIVE BRANCH *(1871-1880) have come to light yet.* AUTHOR'S COLLECTION. BELOW: *The schooner,* OLIVE BRANCH, *sank near the False Duck Island Lighthouse.* PHOTO BY CRIS KOHL.

Operating primarily as a barley carrier, the *Olive Branch* had been loaded with coal before she left Oswego, New York, bound for Kingston, Ontario. She encountered bitterly severe weather, and sank off False Duck Island. All on board were lost: Captain Aull of Kingston, the cook, Mrs. Minnie Jarvis of Belleville, Ontario, plus two French and one Oswego sailor.

The uninsured (her insurance had expired on September 15, two weeks before her loss!) two-masted schooner, *Olive Branch,* measuring 92' in length, 22' in beam, and 8' in draft, was built in Picton, Ontario, in 1871. At the time of loss, she was rated in the low category of B1 by the underwriters, being valued at only $3,000.

In about 1961, local maritime historian, Willis Metcalfe, met a Kingston scuba diver named Guenter Wernthaler and, with charts in hand, discussed the probable resting place of the *Olive Branch.* A dot was penciled onto the chart, and Mr. Wernthaler, with his depth sounder and his boat set for discovery, excitedly proceeded to the spot and found the shipwreck within a half hour of searching.

A chain still droops from the port bow hawsepipe of the little schooner, OLIVE BRANCH, *which sits in 98' of water at the base of a rocky shoal.* PHOTO BY CRIS KOHL.

The *Olive Branch* is intact, sitting upright at the base of a shoal down which she seems to have slid (the original accounts placed the wreck in about 70' of water, but she now rests in 98'). A sidescan sonar image of the steep slope just off the wreck's stern suggests a skid mark left by the vessel when it slipped down that slope into deeper water.

The schooner, *Olive Branch*

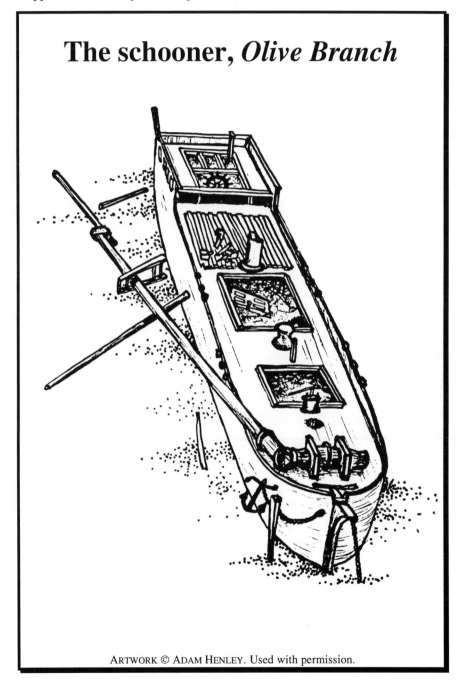

ARTWORK © ADAM HENLEY. Used with permission.

Most of the *Olive Branch's* original artifacts remain on board, including a windlass, the ship's wheel, deadeyes, blocks, a standing capstan near midship, a pump near the bow, hinged catheads (the starboard one still holding a steel-stock fluke anchor), a Quebec stove in an open hold near the stern, a fallen mast complete with a crosstree and wire rigging lying on the vessel's starboard side, and a collapsed bowsprit. Although the *Olive Branch* is situated in an area where drifting silt has been a problem, visibility has ranged from 15' to 40' during the times I visited this site. As with most Great Lakes shipwrecks, this is cold water diving requiring a drysuit, or at least a good wetsuit. Because of the *Olive Branch's* depth, water temperatures rarely reach 50 degrees Fahrenheit at the site.

The physical remains of this terrible tragedy from the past continue to fascinate visiting scuba divers today.

The remains of a crewmember's single shoe, fated to a motionless eternity on the deck of the tragic shipwreck, act as a grim reminder that the schooner, OLIVE BRANCH, *was lost with all hands.* PHOTO BY CRIS KOHL.

Sheboygan, City of

(#8 on the map on p. 3)

VESSEL NAME:	CITY OF SHEBOYGAN
RIG:	three-masted schooner
DIMENSIONS:	135' 2" x 27' 4" x 10'
LAUNCHED:	Wednesday, July 5, 1871; Sheboygan, WI
DATE LOST:	Saturday, September 25, 1915
CAUSE OF LOSS:	foundered
CARGO:	feldspar
LIVES LOST:	all hands (5)
GENERAL LOCATION:	off Amherst Island, Ontario
DEPTH:	90' - 105'
ACCESS:	boat
DIVING SKILL LEVEL:	advanced
DIVING HAZARDS:	depth, hypothermia, penetration, silting
CO-ORDINATES:	Lat/Lon: Loran: 15805.2 / 60016.6

By the summer of 1915, World War I (1914-1918) had been in progress for a year, and, even though most people were proven wrong when they predicted that "the boys" [the Canadian and British soldiers; the U.S.A. did not enter the war until 1917] would be home from the war by Christmas of 1914, spirits remained high. Automobiles were quickly replacing horsedrawn carriages as a means of mobility, and wonderful entertainment was provided by the silent film comedies of Charlie Chaplin and the epic motion pictures of director D.W. Griffith, often to the accompaniment of a live orchestra.

Flying in the face of this optimism, the loss of the *City of Sheboygan* off Amherst Island injected a shot of reality into life around the Great Lakes.

Constructed as a three-masted lumber schooner by Fred Hamilton at Sheboygan, Wisconsin (not to be confused with Cheboygan, Michigan, after which another ship was named), and launched on Wednesday, July 5, 1871, this 261-gross-ton ship enjoyed a long career which spanned almost 45 years on the inland seas.

The *City of Sheboygan's* original dimensions of 135' 3" by 25' 8" by 10' 4" were widened to 30' 1" when she was rebuilt in 1882. Prior to that, she was a canal schooner, bur after 1882, she was too wide for that category of vessel. The ship was owned in Chicago from 1894 to 1897, and in Milwaukee from 1900 until 1915.

The schooner, CITY OF SHEBOYGAN, *built in Sheboygan, Wisconsin, in 1871, and used mainly in the lumber trade, served the Great Lakes for almost 45 years before her tragic sinking on September 25, 1915.* INSTITUTE FOR GREAT LAKES RESEARCH, BOWLING GREEN STATE UNIVERSITY, OHIO.

The schooner, *City of Sheboygan*

ARTWORK © ADAM HENLEY. Used with permission.

Until the spring of 1915, the *City of Sheboygan* was engaged in the lumber-carrying business on Lake Michigan; at that time, however, business slowed down, and Captain Edward McDonald of Toronto purchased the vessel for use on Lake Ontario in the mineral feldspar trade.

In late September, 1915, the old *City of Sheboygan* was loaded with 500 tons of feldspar mined just north of Kingston, Ontario. One local sailor later told the press that he though the ship was "heavily overloaded" when she was towed by a tug out into the open waters of the lake.

The violent storm which sank the *City of Sheboygan* on Sunday, September 25, 1915, also ran the steamer, *Arabian,* ashore a few miles west of Niagara at the other end of Lake Ontario.

Joseph Bray, a resident of Amherst Island, was among those safely on shore observing the struggles of the doomed schooner and incapable of offering any assistance to the drowning crew. He was the man who hastened to the nearby town of Bath, Ontario, to telephone local authorities about the sinking.

Captain McDonald, fearing a bad gale that his overloaded vessel could not handle, had attempted to run into the lee, or protected, side of Amherst Island. He lost the race. The four men and the captain's wife (who worked as cook) were all lost to the powerful wind and waves when their ship slipped out from under them and sank 105' to the bottom of the lake.

After the storm, only a small portion of the tops of the masts remained above the water as silent sentinels marking the site of the tragedy. The first body to be located was that of the captain's wife, Mrs. McDonald, the ship's cook, on Wednesday, October 6, 1915, ten days after the sinking. The badly decomposed body was located by fishermen five miles out in the lake off Long Point. The

SCHOONER WENT DOWN

CITY OF CHEYBOYGAN SANK ON SUNDAY MORNING

Near Amherst Island—It Left Kingston on Saturday With Feldspar For Buffalo.

Newspaper headlines on Tuesday, September 28, 1915, in Kingston's DAILY BRITISH WHIG, *reported the tragic loss of the schooner,* CITY OF SHEBOYGAN. *Even in 1915, press accuracy seemed unimportant: "Cheboygan" should be spelled "Sheboygan."*

Picton diver and marine historian, Doug Pettingill, studies one of several deadeyes on the starboard railing of the schooner, CITY OF SHEBOYGAN, *sitting upright in 105' of water off the southwest side of Amherst Island.*   PHOTO BY CRIS KOHL.

body of one of the sailors, Robert Milne of Port Hope, Ontario, was found about a mile and a half from the scene of the wreck. The other three bodies, and those of the two, white, Pomeranian dogs which Mrs. McDonald had on board, were not located.

Several factors combined to account for the sinking of the *City of Sheboygan.* The nefarious weather conditions were the obvious culprits. However, not to be overlooked was the fact that the schooner was heavily overloaded with feldspar, as witnessed by several people the day she sailed, observing that "her main rail was only three feet above water." Also, Capt. McDonald had sailed only on steamers, and had no experience mastering a schooner. Lastly, the schooner itself had just recently left a drydock where extensive repairs had been made on the ship, indicating an aging frailty which warned loudly against pushing the vessel too far. That warning sign was not heeded.

In the early summer of 1963, three scuba divers named Lloyd Shales, Barbara Carson, and John Birtwhistle, with assistance from James McRady, Peter Ottenhof, and Ronald Hughes, located the remains of the schooner, *City of Sheboygan.* Miss Carson did most of the historical research, which gave the group a general area to search in their 18-foot outboard-powered boat. They found the wreck quickly using a depth sounder, proof that the research was, indeed, sound.

The wreck of the schooner, *City of Sheboygan,* rests in 105' of water, a fair depth, and hence is well-preserved. Much of her rigging and most other shipboard items, including deadeyes, are intact on the wreck. The masts are broken, but identifiable.

The ship's wheel and anchor were donated to the nearby Marine Museum at South Bay, Ontario, where they remain on public display, so that anyone, scuba divers and non-divers alike, can view and appreciate some of this tragic vessel's remains.

St. Peter

(#9 on the map on p. 3)

VESSEL NAME:	ST. PETER
RIG:	three-masted schooner
DIMENSIONS:	135' 7" x 26' x 12' 1"
LAUNCHED:	Saturday, May 24, 1873; Toledo, Ohio
DATE LOST:	Thursday, October 27, 1898
CAUSE OF LOSS:	foundered
CARGO:	coal
LIVES LOST:	6 (from a total of 7)
GENERAL LOCATION:	five miles northwest of Sodus, New York
DEPTH:	98' - 120'
ACCESS:	boat
DIVING SKILL LEVEL:	advanced
DIVING HAZARDS:	depth, hypothermia, silting, penetration
CO-ORDINATES:	Lat/Lon: 43.18.32 / 77.07.70
	Loran:

The romantic notion that "the captain must go down with his ship" when a vessel was in danger of sinking was as idealistic in Queen Victoria's time as it is bizarrely unrealistic today. Indeed, the master of a doomed ship was often the last one to leave the disappearing deck, with varying degrees of success. There are many cases of Great Lakes sinkings where the captain "went down with his ship." The loss of the three-masted schooner named the *St. Peter* ended ironically: the captain was the sole survivor!

But let us turn back the hands of time even more, to the time, 25 years earlier, when this ship was born. The TOLEDO BLADE of Saturday, May 24, 1873, reported that "Messrs. Skidmore's & Abair's new vessel lying on the banks of Swan Creek, near the foot of Smith Street, was announced to be launched at five o'clock this afternoon. The vessel has a length over all of 140 feet, twelve feet depth of hold and 26 feet breadth of beam, and will be christened the *St. Peter*. The craft has been about four months in building and cost $26,000, and will have a capacity of about 18,000 bushels of grain through the canal. The vessel lies parallel with the stream and the launch will be what is known as a side one, the vessel falling some six feet perpendicularly."

The builder of this fine, new schooner was David F. Edwards, the ship measured precisely 135' 7" in length, the launch went without a hitch, and the vessel was given official number 115232 when her first enrollment was issued at Toledo on June 14, 1873.

The *St. Peter* spent the majority of her runs hauling cargoes such as coal between Lake Ontario ports and Lake Erie harbors. She was a reliable workhorse, but her days were numbered because larger and more powerful steamships, with many times more carrying power, were steadily putting the small sailing ships out of business. With her tragic and dramatic demise at the near-retirement age of 25 years, the aging *St. Peter* avoided the fate of so many other sailing ships which, in later years, oozed unseen from semi-active old age to the muddy bottoms of numerous Great Lakes "boneyards" where decrepit, wooden ships were simply abandoned by their owners.

The three-masted schooner, St. Peter, *was a mirror image of her sister ship, the* John Wesley, *pictured in this artist's rendition. Launched at Toledo a few weeks before the* St. Peter, *the* John Wesley *outlived her sister by three years, becoming a total loss on the shores of Lake Huron on September 7, 1901.* Great Lakes Marine Collection of the Milwaukee Public Library/Wisconsin Marine Historical Society.

Over a chilly, five-day period from October 21st to the 26th, 1898, the *St. Peter* docked at the Delaware, Lackawanna & Western Railroad coal trestle at Oswego, New York, taking on a load of 607 tons of chestnut coal due for delivery to Toledo, Ohio. Tugboat Capt. William Scott towed the loaded schooner out of Oswego harbor and into the open waters of Lake Ontario at 7:00

A.M., Wednesday, October 26, 1898, at which time the sails went up and the *St. Peter* became westbound. Capt. Scott returned to Oswego for his next tow, the ten-year-old schooner, *Keewatin*. But the *Keewatin's* crew shook their heads while wrapping covers over her sails, heeding a just-received weather report indicating that an early winter blizzard with 70-mile-an-hour winds had just passed Chicago and, thrust by the prevailing westerlies, was heading east towards Lake Ontario. They were not going to be caught on the open lake in such conditions. The *Keewatin,* because of this caution, survived and worked for another quarter of a century on the Great Lakes before being abandoned and forgotten in some quiet backwater.

On board the *St. Peter,* no one had heard the weather report. In this era before radio (both commercial radio and ship-to-shore or ship-to-ship), Capt. John Griffin, with 40 years of sailing experience on the Great Lakes, and part owner of the *St. Peter,* appeared confident that he could provide for the safety of the five other people on board: his wife, Josephine, first mate John McCrate from Kingston, a 23-year-old seaman named Bosworth, and three Swedish immigrants, doomed forever to be known as the unknown crew, working for passage west.

The western winds steadily increased throughout that day and into the evening and night. Finally, the full power of this storm forced the *St. Peter,* which had reached the mouth of the Niagara River, to turn around, face east, and go wherever the uncontrollable winds pushed the ship. As the schooner passed Charlotte, New York, a tug headed out in response to the *St. Peter's* burning torch signal. The tug, however, could not find the schooner, and spent hours searching for the ship. Off Putneyville, the *St. Peter* was desperately flying distress signals, namely colors at half mast. Things were reaching extremely tense levels on board the schooner when the searching tug finally located the beleaguered ship.

Before the wide eyes of the men aboard the approaching tug, the *St. Peter* suddenly sank. The captain did not go down with his ship. Everyone else did. Capt. Griffin later recounted the sinking of his ship and the subsequent death of his wife:

"...All at once, she [the ship] gave a lurch to port and shipped a heavy sea. At the next wave, she gave another lurch and went down without any warning. I do not know what caused her to go down. It might have been that the coal listed to one side and caused her to careen, or it might have been that force of the waves broke in the cabin doors.

"We were all on the deck when she went down, so none of us was caught in the hold or cabin. I saw my men floating around in the water as they were tossed up by huge waves. I spoke to my wife several times after we were in the water. She seemed to have hold of something that kept her up. I had a hold of two oars and tried to get to her, but just as I would get almost within reach of her, I would be beaten back by a huge breaker.

"At last, she said that she was tired out and could hang on no longer. I called to her to hang on a little while longer and maybe someone would come and pick us up. Finally she said she could not stand it any longer and called to me 'good-bye'. She threw up her hands and went down. I believe she braved the storm longer than the men."

Help was nearby, but neither Captain nor Josephine Griffin was aware of that fact. Capt. Griffin lost consciousness at that point.

The tug, *Proctor's,* lifesaving report, dated October 27, 1898, stated:

"...Steered directly for her, and, when distant about three miles, were horrified to see her give a lee lurch. go over on her beam ends, partially right and then disappear. Steamed ahead as rapidly as possible and soon reached the spot. About 10 feet of the fore and main masts were standing above water, and in the midst of the floating wreckage the life-savers saw a man clinging to a spar. Crew of tug poured a gallon of oil over the side; the surfmen cast off the lifeboat, and, by skillful management, succeeded in rescuing the man in an unconscious condition.

"...The rescued man revived...and proved to be Captain Griffin of the lost vessel, who stated that his wife and four seamen must have perished in the catastrophe, which was entirely unexpected by those on board. Surfmen carefully patrolled the beach, but no bodies were found. At 1 A.M. on the 28th, the weather having moderated sufficiently, life-saving crew returned to station arriving at 5:30 A.M. Captain Griffin was furnished with dry clothing from the stores of Women's National relief Association and succored until evening, when he departed for his home in Toledo."

Contemporary speculation by some newspapers was that Capt. Griffin was drunk while in command, and indeed, several whiskey, champagne, and beer bottles were recovered by scuba divers after the wreck was located in 1971. If Capt. Griffin was profoundly under the influence, then he had a drunkard's luck, similar to the ship's baker on the sinking *Titanic* 16 years later in 1914, who unknowingly timed his gin-drinking just right so as to help him survive the time he spent bobbing in the icy water, rather than hasten his demise.

However, it is unlikely that the captain could have managed to take his ship the length of Lake Ontario and then half a length again while in a state of intoxication. No one lost confidence in him, his abilities, or his sobriety, because in 1899, he was captain of another ship. He continued to sail the inland seas until 1902, when he passed away quietly in his Toledo home after 44 years of sailing the Great Lakes.

The *St. Peter* carried insurance for $2,000 at the time of loss. That she carried insurance at all indicates that she was still considered insurable and of some value by the underwriters, but the low amount proves that her age was a liability against her seaworthiness.

EIGHT SOULS DROWNED FROM THE SCHOONER ST. PETER.

SHE ENCOUNTERED A TERRIBLE GALE ON LAKE ONTARIO.

OFF SODUS THE ANCIENT VESSEL WENT TO THE BOTTOM.

CAPT. JOHN GRIFFIN RESCUED WHEN NEARLY DEAD.

Life-Savers Were Only a Mile Away When She Sank.

Terse, point-form headlines were the norm in late nineteenth-century newspapers. These bits of vital information, which recount the loss of the schooner, ST. PETER, *are from the* DETROIT FREE PRESS, *October 28, 1898.*

An oil slick calms down choppy waves and waters, and the efficacy of oil as a means, at least, of checking the force of the seas has long been recognized. After the loss of the *St. Peter,* one Great Lakes newspaper pontificated: "...Does it not seem that oil would have prevented the *St. Peter* and the *Doty* [the steamer, *L.R. Doty,* had disappeared on Lake Michigan with all 17 hands in the same storm that subsequently sank the *St. Peter*] disasters, with their large loss of life? Trickling from barrels at the most advantageous point on the ship, the stuff would have spread over the lake to sufficient extent as to almost kill the force of the seas and transform the huge bodies of water, with their crested tops, into long rolls which the vessels would have been better able to weather. Neither the *Doty* nor the *St. Peter* could have afforded to be without every means known to man for their own safety, considering their peculiarly unseaworthy condition. The *St. Peter* was an old schooner and of little value.... This is the testimony of vesselmen."

A few ship's captains may have taken this sound advice to heart, but to what extent has not been recorded.

The *St. Peter* was reportedly discovered in about 120' of water in 1971 by a team of divers named Deepstar Enterprises, under the leadership of Robert Bristol, a Kodak employee in nearby Rochester, NY. Some of the artifacts they recovered included a cast iron bread pan, a caulking pot with caulk still in it, cheese crocks with 75-year-old cheese, still edible, in them, the ship's wheel, a 500-pound gearbox, and the 1,800-pound starboard anchor.

The absence of the port anchor and chain indicates that the *St. Peter* was at anchor trying to ride out the storm. The first scuba divers at this site found a hatchet embedded in the wood of the port rail near the port anchor's cathead, indicating that the crew may have desperately cut the port anchor stowing line to allow that anchor to sink. This would have caused the *St. Peter* to swing around with her head into the wind in an attempt to stop her uncontrolled eastward progress. Speculation also considers that the *St. Peter's* rudder cable may have broke, causing the ship to "lurch to port," as the sole survivor stated.

By early 1975, 137 items had been recovered from the *St. Peter;* these items formed the basis of a display in the Rochester (New York) Museum under the research and direction of Richard Kilday, the director of technology.

Ironically, one of the artifacts recovered from the tragic *St. Peter* was a rust-covered horseshoe which had been nailed to the mast for good luck.

Sitting upright and considerably intact, rising a fair distance off the lake bottom, the *St. Peter* offers an excellent divesite for advanced divers. A portion of the bowsprit still extends off the ship's bow, while both port and starboard anchor catheads are still in place. A winch and pump sit on the bow, while another pump lies toppled near midship. A mast, rigging, and other ship items lie off the wreck on the port side. Deadeyes line the *St. Peter's* railings.

The *St. Peter* is an adrenalin-producing divesite coupled with a tragic story, an awareness of which makes any exploration of this material history all the more exciting.

Wolfe Islander II

(#10 on the map on p. 3)

VESSEL NAME:	WOLFE ISLANDER II
RIG:	steel ferry
DIMENSIONS:	144' 3" x 43' 1" x 8'
LAUNCHED:	Thursday, March 21, 1946
DATE LOST:	Saturday, September 21, 1985
CAUSE OF LOSS:	scuttled
CARGO:	none
LIVES LOST:	none
GENERAL LOCATION:	about three miles off Kingston, Ontario
DEPTH:	40' - 85'
ACCESS:	boat
DIVER SKILL LEVEL:	intermediate-advanced
DIVING HAZARDS:	depth, hypothermia, penetration, silting
CO-ORDINATES:	Lat/Lon: 44.13.55 / 76.24.98
	Loran: 15639.2 / 60051.06

The *Wolfe Islander II* ferry, the first vessel sunk in the Great Lakes specifically for the creation of a scuba dive site, is probably the most frequently visited shipwreck in the Kingston area. However, had things been different in China in the 1940's, or had the opponents to her controversial scuttling had their way in the 1980's, this vessel would not be where she is today.

Built at Collingwood, Ontario, in 1946, official number 157269, the 164' ship, with the proposed name, *Ottawa Maybrook,* was intended as a gift from the Canadian government to China to assist her recovery from 15 years of war and civil difficulties. However, when China declared herself a Communist state after World War II, Canada canceled her gift, opting instead to use the vessel at Kingston. Replacing the *Wolfe Islander,* an aging vessel which had been operating since 1905, the renamed *Wolfe Islander II* ferry plied the two-mile route between Wolfe Island and Kingston from 1946 until late 1975, carrying residents, students, tourists, vehicles, and a future shipwreck book writer.

The *Wolfe Islander II* had her dramatic moments during these years. A deckhand was accidentally killed in the spring of 1947 when the rigging holding the lifeboat upon which he was sitting collapsed. Both he and the lifeboat plunged into the water from the third deck, the boat landing on top of him. On the other hand, the *Wolfe Islander II* was the scene of births on two separate occasions in the late 1940's, from island ladies who waited too long before heading to a hospital on the mainland. Both babies were boys, delivered on comfortable bunks in the crew's quarters.

In December, 1975, the *Wolfe Islander III* replaced the *II,* which stayed in the area on standby duty. The semi-retired *Wolfe Islander II* served admirably as a spectator craft during the 1976 Olympic Regatta. After that, she sat idle.

In 1984, the Marine Museum of the Great Lakes at Kingston acquired the *Wolfe Islander II* ferry, with the intention of restoring her as a floating exhibit. However, in the spring of 1985, the museum quite unexpectedly acquired the much larger, newly decommissioned Canadian Coast Guard vessel, the *Alexander Henry*. Display plans for the smaller fish were shelved after catching the big one.

The Museum sold the *Wolfe Islander II* for the sum of $1.00 to the Comet Foundation, which had plans for turning the ship into a scuba dive attraction. The people on Wolfe Island felt betrayed.

The WOLFE ISLANDER II'S *stern displays her name and port.*   PHOTO BY CRIS KOHL.

To raise money to help offset the $8,000 scuttling expense, bits and pieces of the *Wolfe Islander II* ferry, such as a bilge pump, signal flags, mahogany doors, firepails, and life preservers, were sold at auction, raising about $1,700. For a fee of $5.00 each, people could engrave their signatures in one of the ship's 33 portholes, which remained on the vessel when she was sunk.

Unfortunately, a few of these portholes have disappeared since then. Some reportedly headed east; more evidence is being sought.

Eleventh-hour threats from a member of the Wolfe Island council argued that the proposed scuttling showed "a complete disregard for our heritage on Wolfe Island" and contravened provisions in the township's plans, as well as provided potential liability problems, but Kingston diver/lawyer, Wayne Gay, heading the Wolfe Islander Sinking Committee, was satisfied that all zoning bylaws and other legal aspects had been satisfied. Sport shop owners, Steve and Terry Alford, along with Wayne Gay, spearheaded the scuttling project.

The *Wolfe Islander II* was sunk in an "all-weather" area about three miles east of Kingston at 11:48 A.M., Saturday, September 21, 1985, with a flotilla of over 100 horn-sounding boats in attendance. Seacocks had been opened and a pump-equipped boat poured water into the ferry to help sink her faster. Rusty dust burst through vents to the surface as air trapped below deck was forcibly replaced by water. Scuba divers explored her that same day, and the vessel has continued to be a very popular attraction.

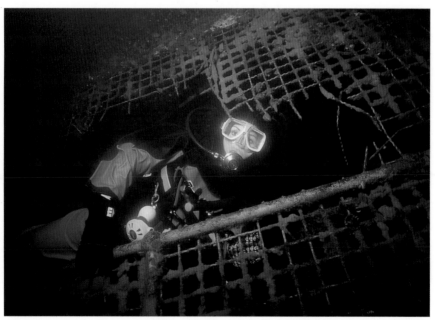

The passenger walkways around the stern half of the WOLFE ISLANDER II *ferry, besides being fitted with iron railings, were enclosed with steel mesh to avoid anyone accidentally falling overboard. Some of this mesh was removed so that divers, such as Marcy McElmon, could access the walkway from its middle.* PHOTO BY CRIS KOHL.

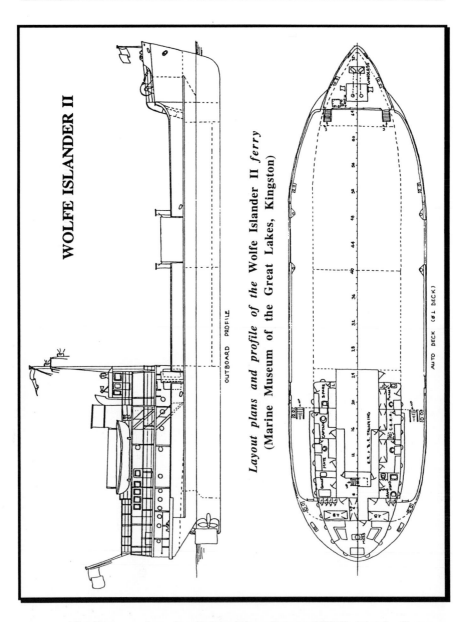

Layout plans and profile of the Wolfe Islander II ferry (Marine Museum of the Great Lakes, Kingston)

The first occasion when I visited the submerged *Wolfe Islander II* was a few months after she was scuttled. A couple of the rooms below deck were airtight and contained air either left over from the scuttling, or from the exhaust ports of visiting scuba divers. In the darkness, we could take our regulators out of our mouths and talk to our dive buddies, at a depth of 65'! Warning: this was still possible to do recently, and likely is so today, but don't breathe that stale air trapped below deck on this vessel. You could start feeling pretty nauseated.

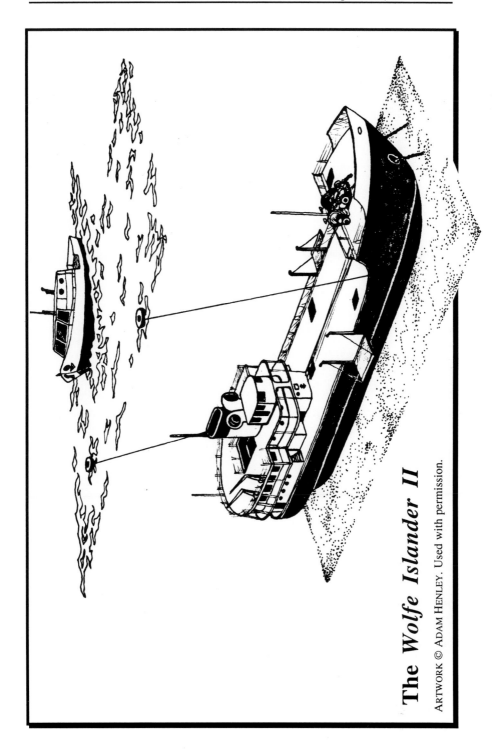

The Wolfe Islander II

ARTWORK © ADAM HENLEY. Used with permission.

Diver Marcy McElmon enters a below-deck room on the WOLFE ISLANDER II *ferry. It is possible to access virtually every room on board this popular 144' steel ship, but cave or wreck penetration training should be taken first. Zebra mussels are beginning to encrust the walls and ceiling, while an easily-disturbed layer of silt sits on the floor waiting to disorient a careless or untrained diver. Even with all doors removed, penetration diving on a shipwreck can be very dangerous.* PHOTO BY CRIS KOHL.

The bronze propeller, slowly losing the battle to avoid encrustation by invading zebra mussels, is another highlight for anyone visiting this shipwreck site. The WOLFE ISLANDER II *ferry plied the waters between Kingston and Wolfe Island for almost 30 years (1946 - 1975) before being scuttled as a scuba dive site on Sept. 21, 1985, thanks to the efforts of area business people and divers.* PHOTO BY CRIS KOHL.

The *Wolfe Islander II* ferry sits upright in 85' of water, with her super-structure rising to about 38' of the surface. Visiting divers can explore her open deck area, complete with davits, bitts, dorades, smokestack, railings, and even a motorcycle, a later addition. More experienced divers can also explore the *Wolfe Islander II's* interior. All doors and hatches have been removed in the interest of diver safety, but it is still possible to get temporarily lost in the below-deck maze of rooms and corridors. One publicized cave diver admitted recently to becoming disoriented due to a "silt-out" below deck on the *Wolfe Islander II.* Use caution and common sense for a fun dive.

Many scuba divers would agree with the KINGSTON WHIG-STANDARD of Tuesday, October 27, 1987, that the *Wolfe Islander II* lives on as "the focal point of one of the greatest inland diving areas on the continent."

"Are we having fun yet?!?!" Scuba diver Marcy McElmon poses inside one of the WOLFE ISLANDER II'S *dorades, or air vents, on the upper deck. This scuttled ship is the most frequently visited divesite in all of Lake Ontario.*   PHOTO BY CRIS KOHL.

2
Lake Erie
Shipwrecks

Geologically, Lake Erie is the oldest of the five Great Lakes, and, ironically, it was the last one discovered by the white man. It was not until the year 1669, when Louis Jolliet dared to travel into the unfriendly Iroquois territory which surrounded Lake Erie, that a European finally saw this huge, shallow lake.

Lake Erie is the eleventh largest body of fresh water in the world. It is the shallowest of the five Great Lakes, having its deepest point at 210 feet, or 35 fathoms, located 6.5 miles SE of Long Point Light, and NNE 24.5 miles from the main light at Erie, Pennsylvania. This deepest part of Lake Erie is just off Long Point, Ontario, a long, narrow spit of land known for the vast number of shipwrecks just off its shores.

The name, "Erie," originated from the Iroquoian word, "Erige," meaning "cat" or "panther," and for that reason, practical French explorers called Lake Erie "Lac du Chat" ("Lake of the Cat") on their early maps. The fierce Erige, or Erie, Indians ("People of the Cat") who lived on the lake's south shore, lived up to their name until 1645, when a war erupted between them and the Iroquois over some insipid athletic event. The proud Erie Indians were decimated to extinction.

Why did it take the early French explorers, who were so hungry for furs and other natural products of this new land, 60 years after their discovery of Lake Huron to first venture into Lake Erie? The French were allies of the friendly Huron Indian tribe further to the north, and Lake Erie was held by the antagonistic Iroquois tribe, who were unfriendly towards the French and the Hurons. The early French fur traders preferred to use the St. Lawrence River-Ottawa River route to Georgian Bay, thereby avoiding both the Iroquois and Lake Erie.

The British, however, allied themselves with the Iroquois in the late 1600's and developed trade with them along Lake Erie's shores. When the Seven Years' War began in 1756, the British already had strong footholds in the Lake Erie area, and took over the French forts at Niagara (1759) and Detroit (1760).

After the American Revolution, many Americans wishing to stay loyal to Great Britain moved to Ontario's Lake Erie and Lake Ontario shorelines. The War of 1812 saw naval action in the form of the Battle of Lake Erie, where U.S. Commodore Oliver Hazard Perry defeated a small British fleet at Put-in-Bay, thus securing the Northwest area for the United States.

Here are some quick facts about Lake Erie:

- Lake Erie forms part of the boundary between Canada (the province of Ontario to the north) and the United States (Michigan, Ohio, Pennsylvania, and New York to the west, south, and east.)

- Lake Erie's length is 241 miles, and its width is 57 miles.

- It is the fourth largest of the five Great Lakes, having a surface area of 9,910 square miles. Only Lake Ontario is smaller.

- Canada has sovereignty over 4,930 square miles of Lake Erie, while the United States edged out slightly more: 4,980 square miles of the lake's surface area. The international boundary length is 253 miles.

- Lake Erie's chief water supply is the Detroit River, which, along with the St. Clair River and Lake St. Clair, carries the discharge of Lake Huron. Lake Erie, in turn, discharges its waters into the Niagara River, over mighty Niagara Falls, and into Lake Ontario on its steady drop towards sea level.

- Lake Erie has a mean depth of only 58 feet, and a maximum depth of only 210 feet. This shallow situation produces the most unpredictable and severe storm conditions known to sailors anywhere.

- The south (U.S.) shore of Lake Erie is heavily industrialized, while the lake's north (Canadian) shore consists chiefly of broad expanses of farmlands and forests. The major communities are Cleveland, Ashtabula, Conneaut, Toledo, Buffalo, Sandusky, Huron, Lorain, Fairport, and Erie in the U.S.A., while Canada's main ports are the small harbors of Port Colborne, Port Dover, Port Burwell, Port Stanley, Erieau, Wheatley, and Leamington.

- The first ship built on the upper Great Lakes was LaSalle's *Griffon* in 1679 along the Niagara River on Lake Erie. This vessel sailed as far west as Green Bay on Lake Michigan, and disappeared with all hands on the return leg of its maiden voyage, the Great Lakes' greatest mystery.

- The city of Detroit was founded in 1701 by French explorer, Antoine de la Mothe Cadillac. Buffalo, at the opposite end of Lake Erie, was founded in 1803. Shipping between these two Lake Erie cities, particularly in the passenger trade bringing immigrants closer to the western lands, peaked from the 1830's until about 1860.

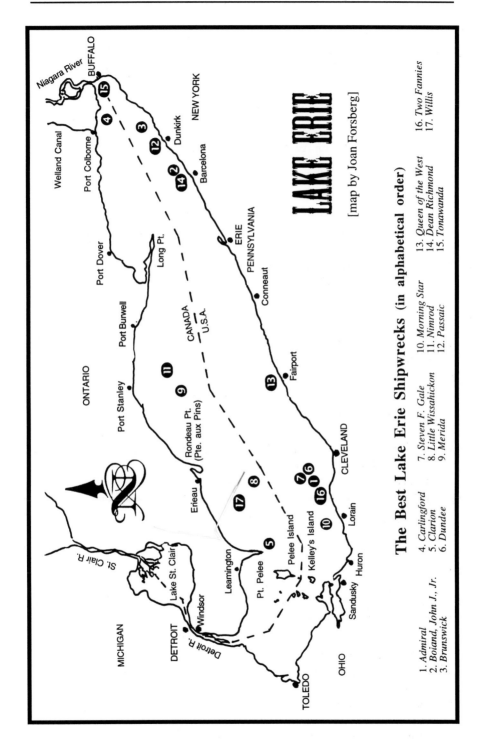

LAKE ERIE

[map by Joan Forsberg]

The Best Lake Erie Shipwrecks (in alphabetical order)

1. Admiral
2. Boiand, John J., Jr.
3. Brunswick
4. Carlingford
5. Clarion
6. Dundee
7. Steven F. Gale
8. Little Wissahickon
9. Merida
10. Morning Star
11. Nimrod
12. Passaic
13. Queen of the West
14. Dean Richmond
15. Tonawanda
16. Two Fannies
17. Willis

- The first steam vessel on the upper Great Lakes was a ship named the *Walk-in-the-Water,* built near Buffalo in 1818. She ran for only three years before a severe Lake Erie storm destroyed her in 1821.

- The first Great Lakes ship with a steeple compound engine, the *Jay Gould*, lies broken at the bottom of Lake Erie off Point Pelee, Ontario.

- The worst disasters on Lake Erie were the burning of the passenger steamer, *Erie,* on August 9, 1841, with the loss of about 150 lives; the burning of the passenger steamer, *G.P. Griffith,* on June 17, 1850, with about 250 lives lost; and the sinking of the passenger steamer, *Atlantic,* after a collision with the steamer, *Ogdensburg,* on August 20, 1852, with about 175 lives lost.

- Lake Erie's notorious affinity for human pollution peaked at two points in the twentieth century, both times having as their main symptom the Cuyahoga River, which discharges into Lake Erie at Cleveland, actually catching on fire! In 1936, that river smoked and smoldered for five days after a spark from a blow torch ignited floating wastes such as oil, paint, and whatever else had been discharged out of the sewers. On June 22, 1969, the heavily-polluted river again caught on fire, and a fire tug was sent to put out the river. Since that time, Lake Erie has returned from the dead due to strong anti-pollution legislation on both sides of the border. Let's hope we can keep it that way!

- Lake Erie is relatively shallow, so most shipwrecks that sank in 60 feet or less were likely dynamited as hazards to navigation, or were destroyed by the elements of nature (ice, wind, waves, current) over the years. Lake Erie, unlike the other Great Lakes, has a soft bottom of mud and silt, so large parts of most shipwrecks have disappeared ten to twenty feet into the lake bottom. Erosion of surrounding farmlands after hefty rainfalls, as well as the gradual, natural retreat of Lake Erie's shoreline, has prompted much soil and mud to pour into the lake before settling on the bottom, helping further to obscure any shipwreck profiles.

One Lake Erie community newspaper article from September, 1939, talked about the lake's vast collection of shipwrecks:

"Rich treasures --- not gold doubloons but everything from cash to whiskey and locomotives --- lie on the bottom of Lake Erie.... The wrecks of ships lie scattered over the bottom of the shallowest of the Great Lakes...but are neglected by treasure hunters who go instead to tropical islands to search for legendary pirates' gold...."

Often have the shipwrecks of Lake Erie and the rest of the Great Lakes been described in terms of "treasure," but the only treasure --- indeed, the truest treasure --- lies in appreciating the stories of the men and women who once trod the decks of these numerous freshwater workhorses, and the human drama involved in the loss of each of these vessels.

Admiral

(#1 on the map on p. 63)

VESSEL NAME:	ADMIRAL (launched as W.H. MEYER)
RIG:	tug
DIMENSIONS:	93' 3" x 22' 1" x 11' 7"
LAUNCHED:	1922; Manitowoc, Wisconsin
DATE LOST:	Wednesday, December 2, 1942
CAUSE OF LOSS:	foundered
CARGO:	none (towing the tanker-barge, CLEVECO)
LIVES LOST:	all hands (14)
GENERAL LOCATION:	8 miles northwest of Cleveland, Ohio
DEPTH:	59' - 74'
ACCESS:	boat
DIVING SKILL LEVEL:	intermediate-advanced
DIVING HAZARDS:	silting, darkness, penetration, hypothermia
CO-ORDINATES:	Lat/Lon: 41.38.243 / 81.54.198
	Loran: 43808.88 / 57412.71

A relatively modern tragedy occurred on Lake Erie in late 1942, while World War II was raging full tilt in Europe and in the Pacific. The tug named the *Admiral* sank in a frightful storm eight miles off Cleveland with the loss of 14 lives, and within 24 hours, the barge it was towing, the *Cleveco,* sank with its entire crew of 18 men; the total loss of 32 lives was staggering!

The 130-gross-ton tug, *Admiral,* was launched in 1922 as the *W.H. Meyer,* hull number 205 of the Manitowoc Shipbuilding Company of Manitowoc, Wisconsin. The vessel's official number was 222239. Sophie Meyer of Milwaukee owned this ship, which measured 93' 3" in length, 22' 1" in beam, and 11' 7" in draft, from 1922 until 1926, at which time ownership went to Henry A. Meyer, also of Milwaukee. In 1935, the Milwaukee Towing Company owned the *W.H. Meyer* until the late summer of 1942, when Cleveland Tankers, Inc. purchased the sturdy little ship, gave her a new pilot house, and changed her name to the *Admiral* for what were to be the final 89 days of her life.

At launch time in 1922, the *W.H. Meyer's* engine and boiler came from the old wooden tug also named the *W.H. Meyer,* official number 81637, which had slid down the launchramp at Benton Harbor, Michigan, in 1898 and had been dismantled at Manitowoc in 1922. The triple expansion steam engine, providing 550 horsepower, was #142 from the Sheriffs Manufacturing Company of

Milwaukee, built in 1898, while the boiler, constructed in 1910, came from the Manitowoc Boilers Works. This old boiler was replaced in 1938 at Manitowoc, but the even older engine remained the same until the vessel's demise.

The tug, *Admiral,* departed Toledo in mid-afternoon on Tuesday, December 1, 1942, carrying a crew of 14 men under the command of 42-year-old Captain John O. Swanson, of River Rouge, Michigan, and towing the 260-foot-long tanker barge, *Cleveco,* which contained 1,000,000 gallons of fuel oil and a full crew. Capt. Swanson had never mastered a tug prior to taking over the Admiral in July, 1942; his lack of experience has been listed among the possible reasons the vessel foundered. The oil barge, *Cleveco,* had been formerly towed by the tug, *Gotham,* at 412 tons, much larger and more powerful than the *Admiral.* Even so, the *Cleveco* had stranded west of Port Colbourne, Ontario, in the summer of 1942, but was released with damage to her steering gear which may not have been completely repaired by December when the ship sank.

Just after midnight, in the very early hours of Wednesday, December 2, 1942, a powerful storm swept across Lake Erie. At approximately 4:00 A.M., Captain William H. Smith on board the *Cleveco* lost sight of the *Admiral's* lights in front of them. With horror, he noticed that the 500-foot-long towline from the *Cleveco* to the *Admiral* descended on an angle into the depths of Lake Erie. The *Cleveco,* no longer making headway, was, in effect, anchored to the sunken tug, *Admiral!*

A strong possibility of what happened is that the barge unexpectedly swung to the port side of the tug and capsized her.

Captain Smith radioed for assistance and ordered the line to the lost *Admiral* cut so that he could drop his own anchor without danger of fouling the tug. The *Cleveco,* although resembling a lake freighter, carried no propulsion, and so she drifted at the mercy of the wind and the waves. Two hours later, the winds had increased to 70 miles an hour, while the waves were reaching 20 feet in height. Captain Smith reported that an aircraft had buzzed his ship's position, that he had the Coast Guard cutter, *Ossipee,* in sight, and that he and his crew were not in danger and had no plans of abandoning their vessel at that point. Icy snow, howling winds, and overtaking seas increased in fury, and the *Ossipee* and the *Cleveco* lost sight of each other in the near-zero visibility. By the time the helpless *Cleveco* was located again, it was too late. The ship had sunk and all 18 men on board had perished.

Ironically, the *Cleveco* carried a cargo of oil which, had any of it been pumped overboard from the struggling barge during the storm, might have calmed the surface waters around the ship enough to ensure her survival.

Coast Guard searching vessels lost radio contact with the *Cleveco* at 4:40 P.M. on Wednesday, December 2, 1942. The next day, searchers found an oil slick, pieces of wreckage, and six bodies from the *Cleveco.*

In late April, 1943, half a year after the double disaster, planes of the Civil Air Patrol conducted a search for the sunken tug, *Admiral*. Three aircraft flew abreast, carrying small buoys to drop should the pilots sight the tug. No buoys were dropped. The *Cleveco* had been located shortly after she sank in relatively shallow water off Euclid Beach. Relatives of the tug's crew protested what they called inadequate attempts to recover their loved ones' bodies.

Seventeen of the 18 bodies from the *Cleveco* were eventually recovered. Not so with the tug, *Admiral;* only three of the 14 people on board were located at the time of loss. The captains of each vessel were never found. Years later, scuba divers found human remains of several crew on board the sunken tug.

All 14 men on board the tug, ADMIRAL, *lost their lives when the ship suddenly sank on December 2, 1942, off Cleveland.* THE GREAT LAKES MARINE COLLECTION OF THE MILWAUKEE PUBLIC LIBRARY/WISCONSIN MARINE HISTORICAL SOCIETY.

An attempt to salvage the *Cleveco's* fuel oil in the summer of 1961 failed, but the wreck was raised and scuttled in slightly deeper water where it no longer posed a threat to navigation. The *Cleveco* lies upside-down in about 75' of water. In 1995, about 500,000 gallons of oil were removed from the leaking shipwreck which had, by then, spent more than half a century underwater.

In October, 1969, commercial diver George Walton, using a magnetometer, located the long-lost tug, *Admiral*. He recovered the bronze bell (with the name *W.H. Meyer* and the year 1898 deeply engraved on it) plus two lights and some tools. Walton reportedly planned to recover artifacts which he had seen in the pilot house, namely the ship's wheel, clock, and "other artifacts that would be valuable items for collectors." He declined to pinpoint the location of the wreck because "he does not want skin-divers racing him to the wreckage." These artifacts are on permanent display at the Great Lakes Historical Society Museum in Vermilion, Ohio.

Walton kept the location secret for years. In the spring of 1981, two groups of scuba divers independently located the *Admiral,* or rather, "relocated" the wreck, rediscovery being a commonly played ego game among some Great Lakes divers, especially when it nets them coverage by gullible media. One team of Cleveland area divers made the news when they located the wreck "after 15 years of looking for it," described human remains on board (a skull and some bones in the captain's cabin, and two more skulls below), and recovered artifacts such as a couple of large, encrusted portholes. The other group of divers, conneced with the Sunken Treasures Maritime Museum of Port Washington, Wisconsin, found the tug in three and a half hours of searching, thanks to information supplied by Great Lakes historian Walter Remick, and a Wesmar sidescan sonar unit. They reportedly explored the wreck for two days, filming on the first day and recovering artifacts for display in the Wisconsin museum on the second.

The human remains were gathered together in about 1982 and buried underwater off one side of this tragic shipwreck, allegedly because some macabre scuba divers visiting the *Admiral* had irreverently played underwater hockey with the bones and skulls of crew members. Also in the early 1980's, Captain Swanson's binoculars and eyeglasses were recovered from the tug and given to his widow, who resided in Cleveland.

The tug, *Admiral,* sits upright, her bow pointing towards Cleveland, sunk to her gunwales in silt in 74' of water. This is a very silty site, with the galley and the crew quarters completely inundated. For trained and experienced divers, the pilot house and the engine room may be penetrated. The *Admiral's* smokestack lies just off the port side in midship.

Early divers at this site noticed that all the rear windows of the pilot house were blown out, indicating that the tug sank very quickly nose first. Later divers argued that the ship's position on the lake floor proves that she sank stern-first, possibly from the weight of ice which had supposedly formed aft. We will likely never know what really happened in the *Admiral's* final moments, since there were neither survivors nor eyewitnesses to the sinking.

All we know for certain is that the tug's towline still stretches out across the muddy lake bottom, reaching out desperately and futilely towards her missing partner, the *Cleveco,* which could save neither the *Admiral's* crew, nor, as it turned out, her own.

Boland, John J., Jr.

(#2 on the map on p. 63)

VESSEL NAME:	JOHN J. BOLAND, JR. (ex-TYNEVILLE)
RIG:	steel, propeller-driven steamer
DIMENSIONS:	252' 9" x 43' 4" x 17' 8"
LAUNCHED:	1928; Newcastle-on-Tyne, England
DATE LOST:	Wednesday, October 5, 1932
CAUSE OF LOSS:	foundered
CARGO:	coal
LIVES LOST:	4 (from a total of 19 on board)
GENERAL LOCATION:	10 miles off Barcelona, New York
DEPTH:	95' - 136' (stay above 130')
ACCESS:	boat
DIVING SKILL LEVEL:	advanced
DIVING HAZARDS:	depth, darkness, penetration, silting
CO-ORDINATES:	Lat/Lon: 42.22.794 / 79.44.000
	Loran:

The 252-foot steel freighter, the *John J. Boland, Jr.,* is one of the newest and most impressive dive sites at the eastern end of Lake Erie. This massive structure, lying on its side in about 136' of water, is still quite intact and penetrable, but only by experienced, properly trained, and prepared divers. The large, four-bladed propeller and rudder at 95' are interesting and photogenic. One anchor is in the hull, while the other one lies on the lake bottom just off the wreck. Railings, ladders, portholes, and the huge cargo holds are still intact. There is usually a sign placed on the outside of the steel hull which warns divers to "STOP. PREVENT YOUR OWN DEATH. DO NOT ENTER UNLESS CAVE OR WRECK TRAINED." Divers should take heed. An exploration around the shipwreck's perimeter, without going inside, will create enough lifelong memories.

This 1,939-gross-ton ship, constructed at the tail end of the boom years of the roaring 1920's by Swan, Hunter & Wigham Richardson, Ltd. as hull number 1282, was launched originally as the *Tyneville* at Newcastle-on-Tyne, Great Britain, in 1928. Times were so good that shipbuilding firms built and launched ships even before they were ordered and paid for by any specific buyer. Hence, the British builders were the ones who named this ship the *Tyneville*.

Captain R. Scott Misener purchased the ship in the spring of 1928 for his firm, the Sarnia Steamship Company, and, ignoring that old sailors' superstition about it being unlucky to change the name of a ship, he renamed the vessel in honor of a business ally. The *Tyneville* became the *John J. Boland, Jr.* (he was a family member of the Boland & Cornelius shipping firm in Buffalo, New York, and lived from 1903 until 1962; yes, he was only 29 years old when the ship named after him sank!). This vessel, which had easily crossed the North Atlantic Ocean, worked on the Great Lakes for only four years before succumbing to one of Lake Erie's notorious squalls.

By 1932, the Great Depression was in its third and worst year, the prosperous times were over for a while, and Great Lakes ships and companies were scrambling to stay afloat economically. The *John J. Boland, Jr.,* which usually hauled cargoes of grain from Port Colborne, Ontario, or Buffalo, New York, to St. Lawrence River harbors, now, in these troubled times, occasionally carried loads of pulpwood and coal as well.

The JOHN J. BOLAND, JR., *built in England during the boom year 1928, sank on Lake Erie in 1932, the Great Depression's worst year; four died.* AUTHOR'S COLLECTION.

The *John J. Boland, Jr.* sailed out of Erie, Pennsylvania, early on the morning of Wednesday, October 5, 1932, loaded with coal for Hamilton, Ontario. Actually, the ship was *over*loaded with coal, since all of her cargo holds were full, and hatch number six was left open and about another 400 tons piled in overflow mode on top of the open hatch and onto the surrounding deck. This short run across Lake Erie, through the Welland Canal, and along the Lake

Ontario shoreline to Hamilton was considered so routine and so safe that ships often engaged in this practice of piling excess cargo onto the deck. The early morning weather looked calm, and most of the 19 crew (one captain, two mates, two watchmen, three deckhands, one Chief Engineer, one Second Engineer, two oilers, three firemen, and two cooks), weary from loading the cargo, went to sleep below deck. The *Boland* carried no passengers and was staffed by an all-Canadian crew.

However, Lake Erie is the shallowest of the five Great Lakes, and as such, produces unpredictable weather. Suddenly, the southwest winds and the pounding waves picked up, and apparent rudder trouble, another unforeseen condition, complemented the ship's instability due to her overloaded state. The struggling crew could not tarp down the open coal pile on the deck; nor could they close the open hatch. Before long, waves washed the deckload off the port side, and the *Boland* took on water. Captain E.C. Hawman, of Collingwood, Ontario, attempted to steer the ship into the wind and run for the protection of the lee shore on the U.S. side. About ten miles off Barcelona, New York, in 40-mile-an-hour winds, the *John J. Boland, Jr.,* rolled over in the trough of the waves at 6:50 A.M. and sank within four minutes.

Four Are Trapped When Ship Sinks

Woman Missing; 15 of Crew Escape

Headline in the DETROIT FREE PRESS, *October 6, 1932, about the* BOLAND *sinking.*

Four lives were lost from the 19 on board: both oilers, S. Brooks of Windsor, Ontario, and Harry Jobes, of St. Catharines, Ontario, an unnamed fireman, and the second cook (sometimes referred to as the assistant stewardess), 24-year-old Miss Jean MacIntyre of Welland, Ontario. All four were reportedly trapped between the decks inside the freighter's hull. The tug, *Betty and Jean,* recovered the floating body of Miss MacIntyre off Barcelona, New York, the day after the sinking. A subsequent Coast Guard search found no more bodies.

The 15 survivors reached shore near Westfield, New York, in the port lifeboat about six hours after the *Boland* sank. Thwarted from landing by a high cliff, the tired crew walked their boat about one mile up the coast before they found access from the lake. At the top of the cliff, the crew crossed a field and followed a road to a gas station, where they telephoned their employer, the Sarnia Steamship Company, which promptly sent a bus to pick them up.

An investigation into the sinking of the *John J. Boland, Jr.,* concluded that Captain Hawman was at fault for the tragedy because he allowed the excess cargo to endanger the safety of his ship and crew. He lost his licence for one year, and the *Boland* became the last vessel on the Great Lakes to sail with deck loads and open hatches.

The Sarnia Steamship Company generously replaced the 15 survivors' clothing.

The steel freighter, JOHN J. BOLAND, JR., *lies intact on her side in about 136' of Lake Erie water. Penetration is very dangerous.*   PHOTO BY DAVID AND SUSAN MILLHOUSER.

Brunswick

(#3 on the map on p. 63)

VESSEL NAME:	BRUNSWICK
RIG:	iron bulk freight steamer
DIMENSIONS:	236' 9" x 36' 4" x 14'
LAUNCHED:	Saturday, May 21, 1881; Wyandotte, MI
DATE LOST:	Saturday, November 12, 1881
CAUSE OF LOSS:	collision with schooner, CARLINGFORD
CARGO:	coal
LIVES LOST:	3 (from a total of 15 on board)
GENERAL LOCATION:	8 miles off Dunkirk, New York
DEPTH:	85' - 115'
ACCESS:	boat
DIVING SKILL LEVEL:	advanced
DIVING HAZARDS:	depth, silting, hypothermia, penetration
CO-ORDINATES:	Lat/Lon: 42.35.431 / 79.24.558
	Loran:

The tragic, single collision between two ships on Lake Erie waters in 1881 inadvertently provided the Great Lakes with a couple of their best shipwrecks for scuba divers to explore over 100 years later.

The four-masted iron steamer, *Brunswick,* slid down the launch ramp of the Detroit Dry Dock Company at Wyandotte, Michigan, on Saturday, May 21, 1881, and sank before her first season was over (similar to another "100 best" shipwreck in Lake Erie, the *Willis,* the final shipwreck in this chapter).

At one o'clock in the morning of Saturday, November 12, 1881, the huge, 1,120-gross-ton steamer, *Brunswick,* sank after colliding with the smaller, 470-gross-ton schooner, *Carlingford,* about eight miles off Dunkirk, New York. The *Brunswick* had just departed Buffalo, New York, with 1,500 tons of coal for Duluth, Minnesota, when the accident occurred. A strong superstition among sailors is that it is bad luck to commence a voyage on a Friday (or launch a ship on a Friday, or do anything major and nautical on a Friday); the *Brunswick* paid a heavy price for ignoring that old supposition.

After the collision, Captain C. Chamberlain of the *Brunswick* headed his vessel back towards the schooner to offer assistance, but, seeing that his own ship was sinking, turned her toward the U.S. shore. The *Brunswick's* bow was burst in, and she sank about 45 minutes after the collision, while steaming towards Dunkirk. The forward portion of the *Brunswick* filled with water, causing her stern to rise high into the cold night air (à la *Titanic,* 31 years later). The captain ordered the two lifeboats lowered, with seven of the crew clambering into the port one, and eight rushing into the starboard. When the *Brunswick* disappeared beneath the waves, the rushing suction of the water dragged down the still-attached starboard lifeboat containing Captain Chamberlain, First Engineer John Francomb, the Stewardess (or cook), Mrs. A.G. Fletcher, her daughter, Millie, and four others. Chamberlain had told everyone to hang onto the lifeboat, as it would surely break free from the sinking ship and bob to the surface. This however, did not happen, as the davit kept a tight grip on the descending lifeboat. Francomb and the two ladies presumably rode the lifeboat to the bottom, as they were never seen again. The captain and four others saved themselves by letting go, surfacing, and clinging to pieces of the wreck before being picked up by the port lifeboat. All 12 in the single lifeboat made their way safely to the New York state shoreline near Dunkirk after several hours. The crew of the *Brunswick,* like the crew of the *Carlingford,* lost all of their personal belongings when the ship sank.

This is the only known photograph ever taken of the short-lived steamer, BRUNSWICK, *in 1881, her only year afloat.* THE GREAT LAKES MARINE COLLECTION OF THE MILWAUKEE PUBLIC LIBRARY/WISCONSIN MARINE HISTORICAL SOCIETY.

The *Brunswick,* measuring 236' 9" in length, was valued at $150,000 when she was launched, but carried insurance for only about one-third of that amount at the time of loss.

A too-close encounter sank the *Brunswick* and the *Carlingford,* but they lie six miles apart, the latter in Canadian waters, the former in U.S. waters. The *Brunswick* rests upright in 85'-115', with the forecastle being the highest part of the shipwreck. Most of the wreck rises 8'-10' off the lake Erie floor. The hole in her bow offers ample evidence of the collision. At the propeller, lake currents have created a 10'-deep hole with sheer walls in the bottom. The starboard side of the *Brunswick* is silted in flush with the bottom, while the port side is starting to give way. There is an enormous steam engine and boiler for visiting divers to appreciate, as well as steam winch machinery in the forecastle. Each of the *Brunswick's* four masts is broken off four or five feet above the deck (in those days, steamers had to carry auxiliary sail power in case of engine failure in order to meet insurance requirements). The iron hull of the *Brunswick* is penetrable, but only by trained and prepared divers utilizing the right equipment.

THE SAD STORY

Of the Collision on Lake Erie Between the

Steamer Brunswick and Schooner Carlingford,

As Related by the Captain of the Former Ill-Fated Craft—A Thrilling Tale.

Headlines from the CLEVELAND HERALD, *November 15, 1881.*

Carlingford (#4 on the map on p. 63)

VESSEL NAME:	CARLINGFORD
RIG:	three-masted schooner
DIMENSIONS:	154' 7" x 31' 1" x 12' 3"
LAUNCHED:	1869; Port Huron, Michigan
DATE LOST:	Saturday, November 12, 1881
CAUSE OF LOSS:	collision with freighter, BRUNSWICK
CARGO:	wheat
LIVES LOST:	1 (from a total of 7 on board)
GENERAL LOCATION:	eastern Lake Erie, off Port Colborne, Ont.
DEPTH:	90' - 105'
ACCESS:	boat
DIVING SKILL LEVEL:	advanced
DIVING HAZARDS:	depth, silting, penetration, hypothermia
CO-ORDINATES:	Lat/Lon: 42.39.274 / 79.28.596 (GPS)
	Lat/Lon: 42.39.49 / 79.28.65 (from Loran)
	Loran:

The schooner, *Carlingford,* and the iron steamer, *Brunswick,* collided in eastern Lake Erie in the early morning hours of Saturday, November 12, 1881, but sank six miles apart, the latter in U.S. waters, the former in Canadian. Both of them rank among the Great Lakes' "100 best" shipwrecks to explore.

The *Carlingford,* loaded with 26,500 bushels of wheat bound from Duluth, Minnesota, on Lake Superior to Buffalo, New York, at the eastern end of Lake Erie, was nearing the completion of her voyage. What caused the disastrous collision was a lack of understanding of proper passing signals. Each ship was aware of the other, and each vessel changed course at least twice in a nervous frenzy to avoid a collision. Their efforts met with failure. The *Brunswick* struck the *Carlingford* on her port side, abeam the foremast.

Captain Homer Durant was temporary master of the *Carlingford* while her usual master/owner, Captain Oscar B. Smith, was on a trip to California (he was surely unhappy upon his return!) After the collision, Durant realized that his charge was doomed to sink, so he and all of the crew of six men, except for one, managed to get into a small boat. They later landed safely near Dunnville, Ontario. The one sailor who failed to survive was Edward Conway, from St. John's, Newfoundland, who had recklessly returned to the sinking schooner to retrieve some of his clothing, only to end up going down with the ship. The *Carlingford* sank within 20 minutes of the collision.

The iron steamer, *Brunswick,* seeing that the *Carlingford's* crew had launched a lifeboat, looked after themselves and steered towards the U.S. shoreline, since their bow was stove in and they, too, were sinking.

No photograph of the three-masted schooner, CARLINGFORD, *seems to exist. The* MINNIE SLAUSON, *seen here under full sail, however, is a reasonable lookalike. The* CARLINGFORD, *built at Port Huron, Michigan, in 1869, measured 154' 7" x 31' 1" x 12' 3"; the* MINNIE SLAUSON, *constructed at Green Bay, Wisconsin, in 1867, measured 156' 3" x 29' x 10'.* AUTHOR'S COLLECTION.

The 470-ton *Carlingford* was constructed at Port Huron, Michigan, by Fitzgerald & Leighton in 1869. She measured 154' 7" in length, with a beam of 31' 1" and a draft of 12' 3". In her first year, she lost a sailor on Lake Erie, and later she broke in two at North Manitou Island in Lake Michigan on November 24, 1869, but was salvaged, repaired, and returned to service.

The *Carlingford,* one of many shipwrecks located in the early 1980's by Gary Kozak in his quest for the *Dean Richmond,* sits upright in water slightly shallower than the *Brunswick,* namely 105' maximum, and this depth is found only inside the hull at the bow, a location requiring special penetration diving training, experience, preparation, and attitude. Divers not doing a penetration dive on this shipwreck will likely not descend deeper than 98'. The hole in the schooner's side offers sufficient proof of the collision. The stern is broken up. Of diver interest are an anchor, rudder, masts, and numerous blocks.

Clarion

(#5 on the map on p. 63)

VESSEL NAME:	CLARION
RIG:	iron package freight steamer
DIMENSIONS:	240' 9" x 36' 1" x 15' 5"
DATE LAUNCHED:	Wednesday, July 27, 1881; Wyandotte, MI
DATE LOST:	Wednesday, December 8, 1909
CAUSE OF LOSS:	burned
CARGO:	mixed (corn, flour, locomotive parts, etc.)
LIVES LOST:	15 (from a total of 21 on board)
GENERAL LOCATION:	off Point Pelee, Canada, western Lake Erie
DEPTH:	58' - 77'
ACCESS:	boat
DIVING SKILL LEVEL:	intermediate-advanced
DIVING HAZARDS:	depth, silting, nets, hypothermia
CO-ORDINATES:	Lat/Lon: 41.57.26 / 82.16.30
	Loran: 43890.08 / 57297.68

"I wish the last trip was over, so I could return home."

Harry Lavis, steward on board the steamer, *Clarion,* spoke those parting words as he left his brother in Milwaukee. Unfortunately, this was indeed the *Clarion's* last trip, as well as Harry's and 14 of his fellow crewmembers'.

On the evening of December 8, 1909, bound from Chicago, Illinois, to Erie, Pennsylvania, with a load of flour, glucose, and general merchandise (and to lay up there for the winter), the *Clarion* encountered fierce winds, normal for this time of year, as she began rounding Point Pelee. Usually this would not have been a problem, but the smoke emanating from one of the cargo holds at about 7:00 P.M. indicated that something was quite amiss.

The *Clarion* was about one mile north of the Southeast Shoal Light Ship off Point Pelee. First Mate James Thompson was overcome by smoke and died in the hatchway while trying to extinguish the fire. A west-southwest gale was blowing, and flames quickly leaped out of control to the superstructure, dividing the crew into two groups. Captain Thomas Belle, from Oswego, New York, one of the group of sailors in the bow half, lost hope in saving his ship, so he ordered one of the iron lifeboats launched. Another man, Joe McCauley, the ship's oiler, perished when the violent waves swept him away from the lifeboat which he was attempting to bail. Thirteen unlucky souls left the flaming *Clarion* in this lifeboat; they were never seen alive again.

The notorious spit of land called Point Pelee has caused the demise of scores of ships in western Lake Erie. The CLARION *sank off this location.*   PHOTO BY CRIS KOHL.

The six crewmembers remaining on the ship's aft half retreated to the far stern, as distant as they could remove themselves from the encroaching flames in order to avoid being roasted. They attempted to launch the ship's other lifeboat, but the sea swiftly swept it out of their control. The first large freighter to arrive at the scene did not dare attempt a rescue, the wind and the waves treacherously dancing around the shallows in that area off Point Pelee. The next steamer, the *Josiah C. Munro,* ran aground in her effort to assist the stricken vessel; after the storm, the *Munro* was released with little damage. By this time, however, it was 8:30 P.M., and the *Clarion* had drifted about a mile to the east of the *Kewaunee,* the South East Shoal Light Ship.

Miraculously, the 524-foot steamer, *Leonard C. Hanna,* downbound with ore, with Captain Matthew Anderson in control of the helm, sighted the burning *Clarion* in the dense fog. In a daring and dangerous maneuver, Captain Anderson positioned the *Hanna* on a course close enough to just brush up against the blazing *Clarion's* bobbing stern. Five of the six men on board the doomed ship were able to jump aboard the *Hanna.* The sixth man, advanced in years and benumbed by the cold, hesitated to leap from the ice-covered, rolling deck, and threw up his arms in despair as the *Hanna* drew away with his five companions.

The CLARION *was a strong vessel of composite (combined iron and wood) construction. However, it could not be fireproofed.*   AUTHOR'S COLLECTION.

Captain Anderson, with calm judgement and nerves of steel, resolved to make another effort to rescue that sole life left aboard the death ship. He turned the *Hanna* around in the smallest possible circle (since time was of the essence), and, again in the howling gale and churning sea, passed under the *Clarion's* stern to within one foot of the ship, and rescued the last man. The blazing ship then drifted away into the dark, stormy night, and eventually sank.

The six rescued men were Chief Engineer A. Welsh, Second Engineer John Graham, Firemen Harry Murray of Milwaukee, Theodore Larson and Joseph Baker of Buffalo, and Second Cook Michael Toomey of Buffalo.

The violent storm which helped sink the *Clarion* also sank the carferry *Marquette and Bessemer #2* with all hands (the location of this wreck is still unknown), and the steamer, *W.C. Richardson,* near Buffalo, New York.

The *Clarion* was valued at $125,000 and her cargo at $150,000, but the appalling forfeiture of 15 lives far overshadowed those losses.

The steamer, *Clarion,* built of a composite (combination) of iron and wood during that transition period when wooden-hulled ships on the Great Lakes were replaced by steel ones, was launched at Wyandotte, Michigan, on Wed., July 27, 1881, by the Detroit Dry Dock Company, official #125937. The 1,712-gross-ton *Clarion,* named after a river in Pennsylvania (because she was owned

The steamer, L.C. HANNA, *in a daring display of incredible seamanship, removed the last six crewmembers from the burning steamer,* CLARION, *near South East Shoal in western Lake Erie on the night of Dec. 8, 1909.* THE MARINE REVIEW, *January, 1910.*

Lake Erie is the shallowest of the five Great Lakes, so storms spring up unpredictably within minutes. They get their worst in November & December; in the darkness of night, the terrors double; add a burning ship, they triple. PHOTO BY CRIS KOHL.

by the Anchor Line, a subsidiary of the Pennsylvania Railroad) and just over 240' in length, carried iron frames with oak decking and superstructure. The *Clarion's* colors were green from the water line to the main deck, with a white hull and superstructure. Her single mast, painted a bright yellow, stood out strong in conjunction with her bright red smokestack.

For 28 years, the *Clarion* toiled in the package freight trade between Chicago, Milwaukee, Buffalo, and Erie as a "line boat,", meaning that she operated in conjunction with a railroad line. The vessel had had some problems early in her career: she displayed a pronounced proclivity for impact with other vessels, namely with the railroad car ferry, *Lansdowne,* on the Detroit River on July 15, 1885, and with the schooner, *Monguagon,* at Milwaukee on May 13, 1888. The *Clarion's* iron stem saved her from any significant damage. However, after 28 years of service, the *Clarion's* time was up on December 8, 1909.

The DETROIT FREE PRESS editorialized on the topic of "Heroes That Brave the Perils of the Lakes" on December 10, 1909: "The bitter fate of the sailors on the *Clarion*...is a reminder to landsmen of the relative insignificance of their own annoyances. We grumbled over the storm here in Detroit. We complained of the freezing cold because it nipped our fingers and made our houses rather uncomfortable. What becomes of these petty annoyances beside the cruel death in icy waves, or the appalling choice of burning or drowning? The season has come when these dismal tales must be told. Every spring brings them and every fall repeats them with added horrors. To a shop-keeper, it must be a matter for wonder why men continue to brave these risks, and why the sailors do not find some other vocation, less full of peril and discomfort. But the world's work must be done, and while commerce calls for transportation there will be men ready to answer. They would scorn the thought that they are heroes. They are earning their livelihood, and that is all, in their estimation. Next year the survivors of this wreck will be at work again on the same waters. There's a great deal of unconscious heroism in this old world. Perhaps it may be well that we should pause to recognize it, since the heroes will not advertise the fact themselves." Hopefully Captain Anderson was also in the writer's thoughts.

The stern section of the *Clarion* is almost totally intact and can be penetrated by experienced, trained divers. In contrast, the bow tipped forward after the sides of the hull collapsed. This site was initially nicknamed "the stern section" because the first scuba divers , in low visibility swimming among many snagged fishing nets, detected only the stern portion of the wreck, in spite of the fact that the entire shipwreck is there. Items found at this site include a four-foot-diameter mushroom anchor in place on the bow, where a windlass with chain is also exposed, the huge propeller, and the steam engine and boiler below deck. Also below deck are locomotive wheels in the hold. There is some mystery to this shipwreck, since the engine on board is a fore and aft triple expansion engine, and not a steeple compound engine which records indicate the *Clarion* carried. Perhaps there was an unrecorded, or, as yet, undetected engine change late in the *Clarion's* career. Most of the decks are gone, but the steel framing is still there, evidence of her composite hull construction.

The First Mate on the CLARION *on December 8, 1909 entered the hold with a fire extinguisher to quell the blaze; he was never seen again.* AUTHOR'S COLLECTION.

Be careful if you are diving this site. Be constantly aware of your depth and bottom time, since anything 60' or deeper is considered a deep dive; this site sits in 77'. Take at least one sharp dive knife with you in case you need to cut yourself out of something, although zebra mussels have weighted down most of the extensive fishnets which once covered this wreck. The silt, especially below deck, stirs up easily and could cause disorientation. Penetration diving is for trained, experienced, and prepared divers only.

Dundee

(#6 on the map on p. 63)

VESSEL NAME:	DUNDEE
RIG:	schooner-barge
DIMENSIONS:	211' x 35' x 16' 6"
LAUNCHED:	1893; West Bay City, Michigan
DATE LOST:	Wednesday, September 12, 1900
CAUSE OF LOSS:	foundered
CARGO:	iron ore
LIVES LOST:	1 (from a total of 7 on board)
GENERAL LOCATION:	13.8 miles north of Rocky River, Ohio
DEPTH:	60' - 77'
ACCESS:	boat
DIVING SKILL LEVEL:	intermediate-advanced
DIVING HAZARDS:	depth, collapsing deck, penetration, silting
CO-ORDINATES:	Lat/Lon:
	Loran: 43841.0 / 57456.5

A huge schooner-barge rises, stern broken and bow collapsing yet still majestic in her grandeur, from the 75-foot depths of eastern Lake Erie off Ohio's shores. Upright, dazzling, and impressive due to her size, this ship features a windlass and a donkey boiler (used for mechanizing the windlass and/or a winch for easier loading of cargo) on the bow, a winch at midship, and six vast holds, each about 14 feet wide and seven feet long, allowing trained and experienced divers to swim below deck from one opening to another, puzzling over what lies beneath the thick silt which is so easily disturbed by even the slightest fin kick. Besides the dangerous, visibility-eliminating silt, the bow and other portions of this vessel, over 100 years old, have started to collapse, making former access and exit points of present-day questionable merit. The turnbuckles, part of the standing rigging for the masts, are part of the nauticalia viewable without dropping below deck.

Use caution when exploring the wreck of the *Dundee*.

The 1,043-gross-ton *Dundee*, launched at West Bay City, Michigan, as a wooden-hulled schooner by James Davidson in 1893, measured 211' in length, 35' in beam, and 16' 6" in draft. Constructed during an economic boom, the *Dundee* soon scrambled for cargoes because of the Panic of 1893, which put a dint for a few years into many markets, including those on the Great Lakes. Just when the economy was starting to look pretty good again, the *Dundee* sank.

The surviving crew of the schooner-barge, DUNDEE, which sank in a cataclysmic storm in the early hours of Wednesday, September 12, 1900 with the loss of their cook, thanked heaven for their ship's tall masts! THE RALPH ROBERTS COLLECTION.

Just prior to midnight on September 11, 1900, the winds picked up and became so powerful that the *Dundee,* downbound in tow of the steamer, *John N. Glidden* with a full load of iron ore for Ashtabula, Ohio, from Marquette, Michigan, was cut loose to fend for herself. On board the *Dundee,* Captain Martin Elven, his five male crew, and one female cook braced themselves for a rough crossing, but they all fully believed their ship would make it.

However, a gigantic, formidable wave suddenly crashed down upon the ship, tearing off the *Dundee's* rudder and carrying away her forward hatch. Water cascaded into the hold. The ship, of course, was unsteerable at this point, the crew, now at the mercy of the wind and waves. Pumping failed to keep the water below deck from rising, and the situation became tense.

When another rogue wave swept Kate Hoffman, the cook, overboard into the churning seas, where she quickly disappeared from view, Captain Elven ordered his crew to take to the rigging. He had no doubt that his ship was going to sink!

Indeed it did. With only the upper portions of the *Dundee's* masts left above water, and with pounding waves threatening to snap them at any moment, the captain and five crew spent several terrifying hours clinging to their flimsy, wooden perches. Fortunately, it was summer's end, and the air and lake waters were still a tolerable temperature. Finally, after daybreak, a passing steamer, the *Charlemagne Tower, Jr.,* rescued the six men and transported them to Cleveland.

The *Dundee,* a duplicate of the schooners *Aberdeen, Paisley,* and *William D. Becker,* was valued at $50,000 in 1894; by the time of her sinking only six years later, when she was owned by the Minch Transit Company, she was appraised at a still high sum of $38,000.

The rescuing steamer, the *Charlemagne Towers, Jr.,* succumbed to an Atlantic Ocean storm 14 years later, off New Jersey's coast, on March 26, 1914. The 260-foot wooden steamer had been launched at Cleveland in 1886.

This storm which sank the *Dundee,* nicknamed "The Galveston Hurricane" since it swept north from that part of Texas where it had left 6,000 people dead, also sank the 19-year-old wooden steamer, *John B. Lyon,* on Lake Erie off Conneaut, Ohio, that same night, with the loss of 11 of her crew of 16. Three men and two women who had lashed themselves to a mast came ashore near Conneaut after spending 15 hours in the water.

The tragic storm of September, 1900, on Lake Erie was the topic of conversation among sailing men and women that entire ensuing winter in the various harbor towns which line both sides of the lake.

The schooner-barge, *Dundee*

ARTWORK BY CRIS KOHL, © SEAWOLF COMMUNICATIONS, INC.

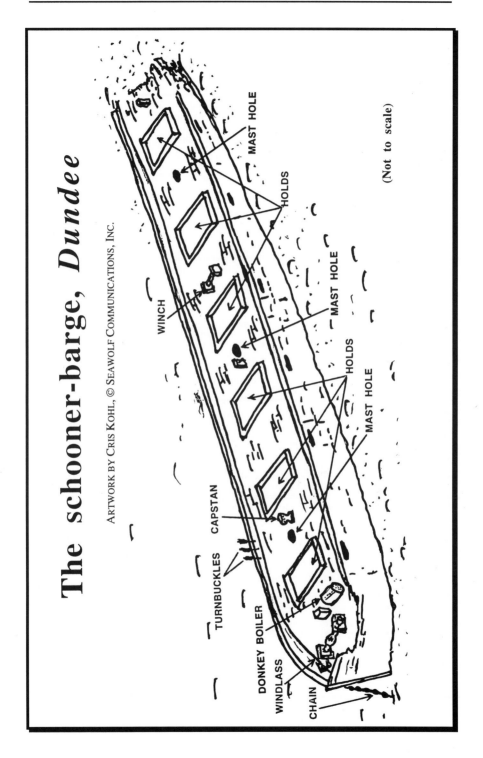

MAST HOLE

HOLDS

MAST HOLE

HOLDS

MAST HOLE

WINCH

CAPSTAN

TURNBUCKLES

DONKEY BOILER

WINDLASS

CHAIN

(Not to scale)

Gale, Steven F. (#7 on the map on p. 63)

VESSEL NAME:	STEVEN F. GALE
RIG:	two-masted schooner
DIMENSIONS:	122' 6" x 24' x 9' 9"
LAUNCHED:	1847; Chicago, Illinois
DATE LOST:	Tuesday, November 28, 1876
CAUSE OF LOSS:	foundered
CARGO:	stone
LIVES LOST:	all hands
GENERAL LOCATION:	17.8 miles northwest of Cleveland, Ohio
DEPTH:	70' - 79'
ACCESS:	boat
DIVING SKILL LEVEL:	intermediate-advanced
DIVING HAZARDS:	depth, silting, hypothermia
CO-ORDINATES:	Lat/Lon: 41.44.451 / 81.52.919
	Loran: 43858.57 / 57449.42

The twin-masted schooner, *Steven F. Gale,* appeared originally as a 266-ton bark when she was built and launched by James Averill at Chicago, Illinois, in 1846. However, the bark rig was not the most versatile for sailing ships toiling on the Great Lakes, and barks virtually disappeared by the end of the 1870's. The *Gale* herself was converted to the more practical schooner rig in 1870.

On Tuesday, November 28, 1876, the *Steven F. Gale,* under Captain Billson, downbound from Kelly's Island, western Lake Erie, to Erie, Pennsylvania, with a cargo of stone, encountered a sudden, violent storm (the kind for which Lake Erie is infamous). The *Gale* foundered with the loss of every person on board.

Several telltale signs indicated that the ship had been lost. Captain Everill of the schooner-scow, Charles Crawford, sighted the doomed vessel's spars rising just above the water. Later reports indicated that the *Steven F. Gale's* cabin, ship's log books, and some trunks containing personal items of clothing washed ashore near Fairport, Ohio.

The wreck of the *Steven F. Gale* sits embedded in Lake Erie mud at a depth of about 79' almost 18 miles northwest of Cleveland, Ohio. Some high-

The schooner, Steven F. Gale

ARTWORK BY CRIS KOHL, © SEAWOLF COMMUNICATIONS, INC.

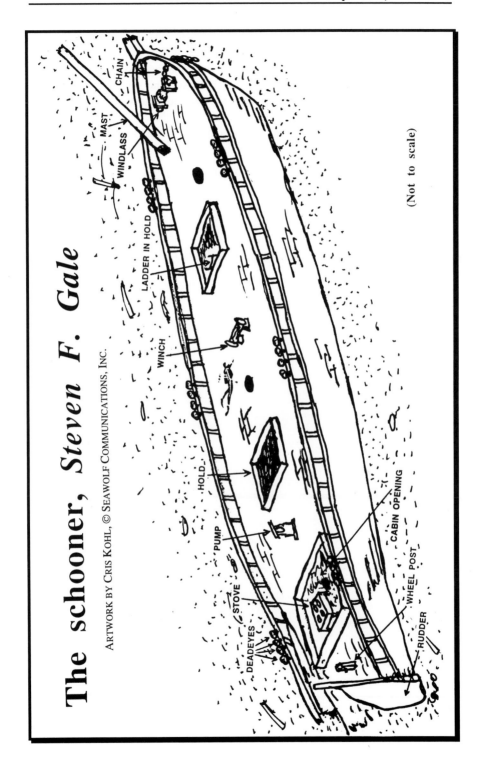

(Not to scale)

CHAIN

MAST

WINDLASS

LADDER IN HOLD

WINCH

HOLD

PUMP

STOVE

DEADEYES

CABIN OPENING

WHEEL POST

RUDDER

highlights of visiting this site are the old stove below deck, but with no overhead danger, in the area near the stern which was once covered by the cabin that the storm had torn off and floated to Fairport. The forward mast lies atop the port bow area, stretching out to the lake bottom. The wreck is lined with deadeyes on both railings, a pump rests on the deck near the stern, while a winch sits near midship. The forward hatch contains a very visible ladder (which scuba divers shouldn't need to descend below deck), and chain and a windlass repose at the very bow.

The schooner, *Steven F. Gale,* is definitely one of the finer shipwrecks for underwater exploration in the Cleveland area.

The schooner, STEVEN F. GALE, *sank in 1876, relatively early in the history of Great Lakes maritime photography. No photograph of her has been found yet. However, the schooner,* KATE LYONS, *above, was quite similar to the* GALE. *The* LYONS *measured 128' 3" x 26' x 8' 3", while the* GALE *was 122' 6" x 24' x 9' 9". The* KATE LYONS, *built in 1866, stranded near Holland, Michigan on October 19, 1905, and broke up from the pounding seas before she could be salvaged.* AUTHOR'S COLLECTION.

Little Wissahickon

(#8 on the map on p. 63)

VESSEL NAME:	LITTLE WISSAHICKON
RIG:	three-masted schooner
DIMENSIONS:	148' x 28'
LAUNCHED:	1869; Marine City, Michigan
DATE LOST:	Friday, July 10, 1896
CAUSE OF LOSS:	foundered
CARGO:	coal
LIVES LOST:	3 (from a total of 7 on board)
GENERAL LOCATION:	middle of Lake Erie, off Erieau, Ontario
DEPTH:	68' - 80'
ACCESS:	boat
DIVING SKILL LEVEL:	intermediate-advanced
DIVING HAZARDS:	depth, slight current, fishing nets, silting
CO-ORDINATES:	Lat/Lon: 41.54.222 / 81.56.786
	Loran: 43919.3 / 57454.8

At noon on a hot summer day, July 10, 1896, two tired sailors left the Lehigh Valley steamer named the *Tuscarora* after she docked at the foot of First Street in Detroit, Michigan. One of the sailors was a ship's mate named George Agans, while the other was a foremast hand named Fred Croft. They were both quite fortunate fellows, happy to have reached solid land. Their ship, the schooner-barge, *Little Wissahickon,* had sunk from under them about ten hours earlier in the middle of Lake Erie.

They had spent six hours being tossed about on their frail life raft before the early morning sun allowed the sailors on the *Tuscarora* to sight them and pick them up. The captain, the cook, and another sailor, less fortunate than themselves, had perished in the sinking.

The 27-year-old *Little Wissahickon* left Buffalo, New York, in tow of the steamer, *James P. Donaldson,* on Thursday, July 9, 1896. The ambitious *Donaldson* was towing three other ships as well, the schooner-barges *T.G. Lester, A.W. Wright*, and *James L. Ketchum.* The five ships headed upbound, all laden with coal for Saginaw, Michigan.

At 8:00 P.M., the *Little Wissahickon*, which had been leaking slowly since the beginning of the voyage, sprang a serious leak. The crew "worked with might and main at the pumps to keep her afloat." By midnight, storm conditions had developed, and, the crew's signals of distress apparently not being comprehended by the other vessels, talk of abandoning ship was directed at Captain George McKay, who was the ill-fated ship's owner as well as master.

Captain McKay seemed to be in a daze, a situation which was never explained. He opted to stay with his ship. Agans and Croft threw a small raft overboard, jumped after it, and, with some hardship, clambered aboard. The strong wind and the waves carried them away from the sinking ship, and in the darkness, they did not see her sink. Nor did they witness two other crewmembers jump overboard, to be picked up by the last tow, the *T.G. Lester*. Remaining on board the *Little Wissahickon* were Captain McKay, the cook named Mrs. Kate Casey of Toronto, and one unidentified sailor. They did not make use of the ship's yawlboat to effect an escape from the sinking barge, and thus the *Little Wissahickon* became their 13-fathom grave. It was estimated that the ship sank at about 2:00 A.M. Captain McKay's son traveled from Bay City, Michigan, and unsuccessfully searched the Canadian shoreline from Erieau to Port Stanley for the remains of his father or the other two victims.

ARE THEY DROWNED?

FOUR OF SCHOONER LITTLE WISSA-HICKON'S CREW MISSING.

THEY ARE HER OWNER, CAPT. McKAY, COOK AND TWO SEAMEN.

SCHOONER FOUNDERED OFF ROND EAU THURSDAY NIGHT.

Headlines from the DETROIT FREE PRESS, *July 11, 1896. Initial reports indicated that four people had died when the* LITTLE WISSAHICKON *sank; it was really three.*

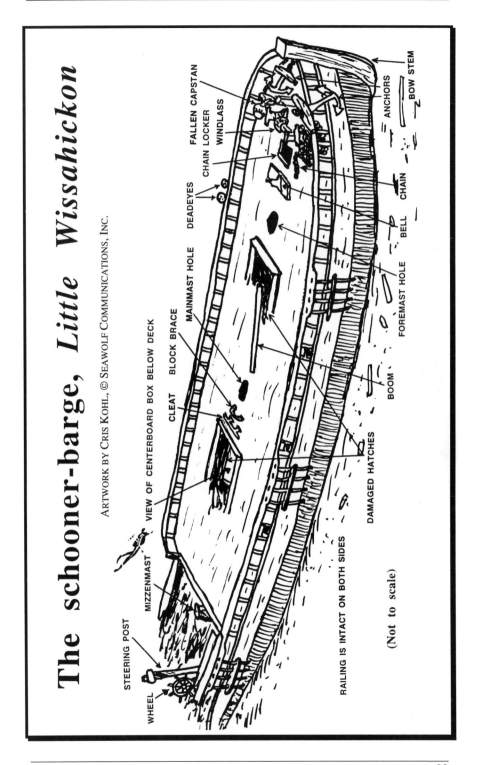

The schooner-barge, Little Wissahickon

ARTWORK BY CRIS KOHL, © SEAWOLF COMMUNICATIONS, INC.

STEERING POST

WHEEL

MIZZENMAST

VIEW OF CENTERBOARD BOX BELOW DECK

CLEAT   BLOCK BRACE

MAINMAST HOLE   DEADEYES

CHAIN LOCKER

FALLEN CAPSTAN

WINDLASS

BOW STEM

ANCHORS

CHAIN

BELL

FOREMAST HOLE

BOOM

DAMAGED HATCHES

RAILING IS INTACT ON BOTH SIDES

(Not to scale)

The three-masted schooner, *Little Wissahickon,* built in 1869 at Marine City, Michigan, by Rogers, measured 148' in length, 28' in beam, and 376 gross tons, and was utilized primarily in the lumber trade. The DETROIT FREE PRESS was not kind to her after her demise, stating that "she was an old craft, not well kept up, and was uninsurable, which means that she was not seaworthy."

Surprisingly, no archival collection has a photograph of the schooner-barge, LITTLE WISSAHICKON, *which sank on July 10, 1896. The vessel pictured here is the* NARRAGANSETT, *at 147' 9" x 26' 10" x 12', quite similar in appearances to the* LITTLE WISSAHICKON *(148' x 28'). The* NARRAGANSETT, *built at Cleveland, Ohio, in 1861, sank in mid-Lake Huron on May 13, 1901.* AUTHOR'S COLLECTION.

Ohio Scuba divers located the *Little Wissahickon* in Canadian waters on July 3, 1987, promptly removed the ship's bell and took it home. They were somewhat disappointed that the bell turned out to be made of cast iron (and not the hoped-for bronze), that it did not have the ship's name emblazoned on it, and that the company which had manufactured that bell in 1886 was still operating (a similarly-sized bell could be purchased new from that company for $185.00).

When news of this bell removal reached Canadian authorities, they were not pleased. In one 1988 letter, it was made clear that "...The Province of Ontario claims ownership to all bottom lands and objects on them, and is prepared to investigate any unauthorized activities or removal of artifacts..." and that "...the removal of artifacts from Ontario waters is illegal, and their transportation across the border is in violation of U.S. and Canadian laws...."

The Ohio divers quickly volunteered to return the bell to the shipwreck site. The bell is now firmly attached to a concrete base near the *Little Wissahickon's* windlass at the bow, along with a plaque provided by the marine conservation group, Save Ontario Shipwrecks, identifying the shipwreck.

The ship's wheel from the schooner-barge, LITTLE WISSAHICKON, *is one of the highlights of an exploration of this Lake Erie shipwreck.*   PHOTO BY CRIS KOHL.

The site of the *Little Wissahickon* boasts a relatively complete shipwreck sitting upright on a sand and silt bottom. At the bow, the visiting scuba diver can appreciate two wooden stock anchors, the ship's bell on a cement block, deadeyes on the rails, and a windlass. The ship's wheel has fallen over at the collapsed stern, where a large rudder post is quite conspicuous. Beware of the occasional slight current, snagged fishing nets which may not be lying flat due to zebra mussel encrustation, and the easily-disturbed, omni-present silt which can easily reduce visibility to an uncomfortable minimum.

If you reach this site at noon on a hot summer day in July, think about the two crewmembers who landed in Detroit on a similar day in 1896, grateful to be alive after their ship sank. Today's undersea explorers are grateful to have such an excellent shipwreck as a divesite.

Merida

(#9 on the map on p. 63)

VESSEL NAME:	MERIDA
RIG:	steel, propeller-driven steamer
DIMENSIONS:	360' x 45' x 25' 8"
LAUNCHED:	Thurs., May 11, 1893; West Bay City, MI
DATE LOST:	October 20, 1916 ("Black Friday" Storm)
CAUSE OF LOSS:	foundered
CARGO:	iron ore
LIVES LOST:	all hands (23)
GENERAL LOCATION:	24.6 miles east of Erieau, Ontario
DEPTH:	65 - 83'
ACCESS:	boat
DIVING SKILL LEVEL:	intermediate-advanced
DIVING HAZARDS:	depth, silt, low visibility, hypothermia, nets
CO-ORDINATES:	Lat/Lon: 42.13.951 / 81.20.786
	Loran: 44160.0 / 57843.9

We swam hesitantly below deck through a hatchway near the stern of the sunken steel steamship and carefully entered the engine room. Beyond the engineworks, the natural light stopped and we had to rely on our limited-angle-of-beam lights to see us through the narrow corridor to an amidship hatch further forward. We were uncomfortably aware that only 21 bodies of the 23 men who had died when this ship sank had been recovered, and that the remains of the other two could conceivably still be below deck, where we were exploring.

Suddenly, a strong movement from the darkened righthand side jolted us. We quickly swung our lights in that direction, to see only a swirling cloud of silt mushrooming from the debris-strewn floor, and the distinctive, eel-like tail of a huge burbot, or freshwater ling, possibly three feet in total length, retreating lightning-like from this unaccustomed intrusion into his darkness.

Below deck in a shipwreck in 13 fathoms (78 feet) and tensed with thoughts of gruesome discoveries, we were caught off guard and frightened by a fish.

That was in 1985, relatively early in this shipwreck's underwater exploration history, and also early in our shipwreck penetration experiences. We returned to this fascinating vessel so many times since then that the *Merida* eventually became our favorite Lake Erie shipwreck for a number of years, partially at least due to an appreciation of her tragic history.

An intensely violent storm sank four ships and claimed the lives of about 50 people on western Lake Erie on Friday, October 20, 1916, an event which became known as the Black Friday Storm of 1916.

The schooner-barge, *D.L. Filer,* became waterlogged and sank near the mouth of the Detroit River with the loss of six of her seven lives (her captain clutched tightly to a protruding mast until rescued.) The wooden steamer, *Marshall F. Butters,* fared better, losing none of her sailors when she sank off Point Pelee near the middle of the lake. An unusually-designed ship, the steel whaleback, *James B. Colgate,* foundered in the middle of Lake Erie off Rondeau Point, with only her captain surviving by clinging to a makeshift raft for over 30 hours before being rescued by a passing vessel. The powerful steamer, *Merida,* however, sank with all hands at an undisclosed location in the lake.

LOSS OF STEAMER MERIDA CONCEDED BY HER MANAGERS

Seven Bodies From Vessel Picked Up; Believed Entire Crew of Twenty-Three Have Perished.

Headlines about the loss of the MERIDA, *from the* DULUTH HERALD, *October 23, 1916.*

A commercial fisherman named Larry Jackson from Port Stanley, Ontario, pulled up an old, steel railing in his torn and rust-stained nets on April 15, 1975. He had accidentally discovered the final resting place of the *Merida,* although it would be several years before scuba divers would finally explore and identify her. A recovered brass capstan cover clearly revealed the ship's name in huge letters. Brass letters on both sides of the vessel's bow spelled out her name. A gold watch was found on the deck close to where the wheelhouse once stood, and a lightbulb from below deck proved to work perfectly on land after 75 years of submergence in Lake Erie!

The *Merida,* built by F.W. Wheeler & Company of West Bay City, Michigan, was launched on Thursday, May 11, 1893, as hull number 95. The *Merida* was, for a while, the longest ship on the Great Lakes, measuring 380' in length, with a beam of 45' and a draft of 26'. Her first enrollment was issued at Detroit, Michigan, on June 17, 1893, with her official number being 92514. Her original owner was D.C. Whitney of Detroit, while her last owner was the Valley Camp Steamship Company of Cleveland, Ohio. A steel freighter with wooden deckhouses, she could make 14 miles an hour, but she failed to outrun the Black Friday Storm of 1916.

MERIDA:
BUILT 1893, at WEST BAY CITY, Mich

Artwork from Samuel Ward Stanton's AMERICAN STEAM VESSELS, *New York: Smith & Stanton, 1895. The* MERIDA'S *engine was still located midship in this early sketch.*

Perhaps being named after a distant city in Venezuela, South America, proved to be unlucky; the *Merida* suffered a fair number of accidents in her career as a Great Lakes bulk carrier. She collided with the barge, *Antrim,* at Duluth, Minnesota, on June 17, 1906, causing damage to both vessels. She damaged herself when she struck an embankment along the St. Mary's River near Sault Ste. Marie on July 8, 1912. She lost her rudder in Lake St. Clair on August 10, 1913, and she crashed into a dock at Chicago, causing substantial damage, on June 19, 1914.

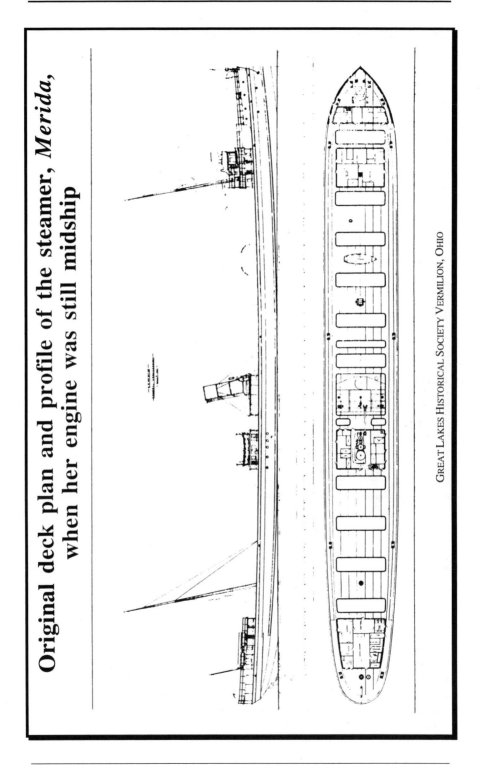

Original deck plan and profile of the steamer, *Merida*, when her engine was still midship

GREAT LAKES HISTORICAL SOCIETY VERMILION, OHIO

However, in mid-October, 1916, while bound from Fort William, Ontario, on Lake Superior, to Buffalo, New York, at the eastern end of Lake Erie, with a load of iron ore, the *Merida* encountered her worst luck of all.

Another freighter, the *Briton,* was trailing the *Merida* from Lake Huron down the St. Clair River, across small Lake St. Clair, down the Detroit River, and into western Lake Erie. The *Briton,* deciding that discretion was the better part of valor, dropped her anchor at about 10:00 A.M. on October 20th on the lee side of Pelee Island to ride out the brewing storm, while the *Merida* poured on the coal and steamed out past Point Pelee into the open lake, showing gutsy determination to make her port of destination on the other side as quickly as possible so commerce could continue and her owners could profit.

The men in the pilothouse of the anchored *Briton* were the last ever to see the *Merida* afloat as she headed east into the eye of the storm.

The steamer, MERIDA, *was lost with all hands on Lake Erie during the Black Friday Storm of October 20, 1916.* AUTHOR'S COLLECTION.

It is believed that the *Merida's* hatch covers were torn off by the storm's force, and that the holds flooded, causing her to sink. Other than 21 dead bodies, little evidence could be found, even though the *Merida's* wheelhouse was towed in by a tug when it was found floating 15 miles south of Port Stanley, Ontario (the wheelhouse bell eventually was installed in the steam tug, *Finglo).* The bodies of Captain Harry L. Jones and crewman Wilfred Austin were never found.

The steamer, *Merida*

ARTWORK BY CRIS KOHL, © SEAWOLF COMMUNICATIONS, INC.

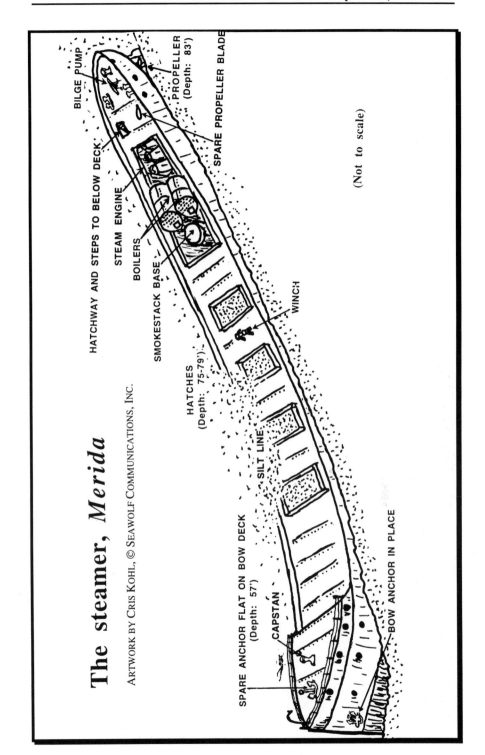

(Not to scale)

BILGE PUMP

PROPELLER
(Depth: 83')

SPARE PROPELLER BLADE

HATCHWAY AND STEPS TO BELOW DECK

STEAM ENGINE

BOILERS

SMOKESTACK BASE

WINCH

HATCHES
(Depth: 75-79')

SILT LINE

SPARE ANCHOR FLAT ON BOW DECK
(Depth: 57')

CAPSTAN

BOW ANCHOR IN PLACE

A marine engineer in Goderich, Ontario, made the accusation that, had the *Merida's* "engines not been shifted so often as they have been, the vessel would have weathered even the tremendous gale of Black Friday." The *Merida's* bad luck was compounded by her engine difficulties. On May 26, 1896, she experienced "an accident unprecedented in the annals of the lake marine" (according to the MARINE REVIEW), when her triple expansion engine began, while underway, to race "with lightning-like rapidity" before going to pieces, fortunately without injury to anyone on board. A new steam engine from the Frontier Iron Works in Detroit was placed into the original midship compartment, but in 1904, for some unexplained reason, her engine and three boilers were moved to the aft end of the vessel.

The wreck of the *Merida* sits upright and intact, with much railing and many stanchions in place. Visibility usually runs from 10' to 40' in waters that require a drysuit, or a full seven millimeter wetsuit at the least. On the bow lies an unusual anchor with hinged flukes, mounted flat on the deck. Brass portholes and a large capstan also adorn the bow area, with thick links of steel anchor chain running down the bow's starboard side, and an anchor in place on the portside equivalent.

If exploring from one end of the wreck to the other, begin at the bow and follow the port (left) rail, as the starboard (right) one disappears completely into the mud and silt bottom before rising again at the stern. Divers have been known to lose this huge steamer underwater by following the starboard rail!

The vessel's spine seems to have snapped, possibly from the weight of her iron ore cargo, and most of the hull at midship is buried in Lake Erie's soft bottom. The bow and stern rise up at tortured angles.

The stern area yields an impressive four-bladed propeller at a depth of about 83', with access to the engine room from the deck near the stern railing. Many more nautical devices and artifacts can be located on the stern deck.

Beware that the silt on this shipwreck is very easily stirred up, causing visibility and orientation problems. Forget about seeing the sights clearly or obtaining good underwater photographs if your buddy is a mud-shoveler. Practise neutral buoyancy. Do not enter this shipwreck unless you have been properly trained in penetration diving, have all the necessary equipment, and are taking all of the precautions.

Since our first aquatic exploration of the *Merida* years ago, we have returned dozens of times to this freshwater museum draped tragically in the silty robes of Great Lakes maritime history. We have not encountered any human remains, but the burbot no longer make us jump nervously when they flit away as we explore their domain in the middle of Lake Erie.

Diver Roy Pickering examines the MERIDA'S *bow capstan, sitting at a depth of about 60' in the middle of Lake Erie.* PHOTO BY CRIS KOHL.

ABOVE: *Burbot, a fish with an eel-like tail, abound on Great Lakes shipwrecks, but there seem to be more of them on the* MERIDA. BELOW: *As you explore the* MERIDA, *you may encounter burbots jealously guarding the shipwreck's brass portholes. These fish may attack you if you try to remove anything.*   PHOTOS BY CRIS KOHL.

Morning Star

VESSEL NAME:	MORNING STAR
RIG:	sidewheel steamer
DIMENSIONS:	248' 2" x 34' x 14' 7"
LAUNCHED:	Saturday, June 7, 1862; Trenton, Michigan
DATE LOST:	Sunday, June 21, 1868
CAUSE OF LOSS:	collision with the bark, COURTLAND
CARGO:	cheese, nails, pig iron, mowing machines
LIVES LOST:	31 (from a total of 90 on board)
GENERAL LOCATION:	off Pt. Pelee, 8 miles north of Lorain, Ohio
DEPTH:	59' - 68'
ACCESS:	boat
DIVING SKILL LEVEL:	intermediate
DIVING HAZARDS:	silting, hypothermia, leaning timbers
CO-ORDINATES:	Lat/Lon: 41.36.812 / 82.12.530
	Loran: 43752.7 / 57246.5

Few things so fascinate the imagination as a disaster at sea. The story of the sinking of the *Morning Star* is a truly tragic and dramatic tale.

Launched on Saturday, June 7, 1862, at Trenton, Michigan, on the shores of the Detroit River, the 1,265-gross-ton passenger and freight sidewheel steamer, *Morning Star,* made her first official run, from Detroit to Cleveland on August 31, 1862 after her interior was completed. On this run, she carried a portion of the 20th Regiment Michigan Volunteers, off to join the fighting in the Civil War. The press said she was "splendidly furnished for the comfort of her passengers."

The Detroit to Cleveland run was the only route the *Morning Star* ever covered. One reason for its popularity was that it was 170 miles between Detroit and Cleveland by land, but only 108 miles by water, scant hours by ship.

The *Morning Star's* lifespan was destined to be only six years and two weeks, during which time she was plagued by mechanical problems and incompetent arsonists. The *Morning Star* fractured her walking beam on November 25, 1866, and cracked one of her piston heads in May, 1868 (a 64-inch cylinder went into the *Morning Star* at this time). These engine problems could very well have been the result of placing the old, 1851 engine from the steamer, *Ocean*, into the new *Morning Star.* On each of these occasions, she was towed to Detroit by her team-mate and sister ship, the *R.N. Rice.* On November 20, 1866, she was almost torched by a bungling pyromaniac who was hired by the swindler who had placed his over-insured cargo on board the steamer in hopes of collecting royally after his loss.

This photograph of the R.N. RICE, *the* MORNING STAR'S *sister ship, is the closest this researcher has come to a picture of the tragic steamer. The* RICE, *built in 1866 at Detroit, burned in 1877, yet returned to service as a barge. On October 3, 1888, a storm drove her ashore four miles north of Holland, Michigan, where she was abandoned in place.* THE GREAT LAKES MARINE COLLECTION OF THE MILWAUKEE PUBLIC LIBRARY/WISCONSIN MARINE HISTORICAL SOCIETY.

On Saturday, June 20, 1868, the *Morning Star's* departure from Cleveland to Detroit was delayed by the last-minute loading of about 20 tons of scrap iron. As a result, the ship left the dock late, not until 10:30 P.M., after dark, and propelled into the night driven by her huge paddlewheels.

Simultaneously, the bark, *Courtland,* under the command of Captain James W. Loudon and laden with 891 tons of iron ore bound from Escanaba, Michigan, to Cleveland, approached from the opposite course.

On board the *Morning Star,* mastered by Captain Edward R. Viger, were 39 cabin passengers, 13 immigrants, and 38 crew, for a total of 90 people. In the cargo holds were 779 bars of iron, 312 barrels (about 20 tons) of scrap iron, 244 kegs of nails, four boxes of glass, 25 boxes of cheese, 65.25 tons of chill metal,

33 mowing machines, seven barrels of oil, 137 kegs of sundries, and two propeller wheels for tugs.

At about midnight, the *Courtland's* mate noticed lights, which he first assumed were those of the Cleveland pier, but later realized they were those of an approaching steamer. He also noticed that his own vessel's green starboard lantern appeared quite dim, so he removed it from the mizzen rigging, took it below to his cabin, and cleaned it.

Ironically, at the precise moment that the bark's mate was replacing the green lantern, the *Morning Star* plowed headstrong into the *Courtland's* starboard side near the mizzen rigging. The *Courtland's* mate was killed instantly. The *Morning Star's* engine room had been alerted to "STOP" just when the two ships collided. It was about 1:30 A.M. on Sunday, June 21, 1868.

This artist's concept of the COURTLAND-MORNING STAR *collision is fairly detailed. However, the steamer struck the bark on her other (starboard) side, not her port.* INSTITUTE FOR GREAT LAKES RESEARCH.

Below deck on the *Courtland,* John Kayne, the second mate, was asleep in his berth at the time of the collision. The splintering timbers struck his face, carrying away a portion of his lower jaw, his teeth, and part of his tongue, a truly terrible injury. The press predicted he would probably not live, but he did.

Some 20 feet of the steamer's bow on the cabin deck, including a portion extending two or three feet below the waterline, were torn off by the impact, while the *Courtland* was swept into one of the *Morning Star's* paddlewheels, which ground it into hundreds of tiny pieces. The steamer was desperately doomed to sink, yet some hysterical passengers hesitated to board lifeboats. One newspaper reporter, after interviewing a survivor, wrote, "Women, half-dressed and completely wild with excitement were running hither and thither, deaf to the entreaties of those who were beseeching them to be composed and crying for the very assistance they were in reality neglecting."

The *Morning Star* sank within ten minutes, while the *Courtland*, whose crew manned the pumps vigorously, went to the bottom after about an hour. The latter's two lifeboats were useless, having been destroyed in the collision. When the *Courtland* finally sank, the crew raced for the rigging. All survived except the mate, who died in the impact of the collision, and the helmsman, who drowned.

At about 3:00 A.M., the steamer, *R.N. Rice,* the *Morning Star's* partner, under Captain William McKay, on her run from Detroit to Cleveland, heard cries emanating from the darkness off the starboard side just before steaming into a floating wreckage field consisting of life jackets, furniture, mattresses, and other debris obviously from some ship. The *R.N. Rice* had sailed into the midst of tragedy.

Terrible Disaster on Lake Erie.

Collision Between Steamer Morning Star and Brig Courtland.

Over Twenty-five Lives Lost

Sixty-five Passengers Saved by the Steamer R. N. Rice.

Headlines of the tragedy in the TOLEDO BLADE, *June 22, 1868.*

The first survivors the *Rice* picked up were Charles F. Newman and Mrs. Chittington, of Chicago, who were clinging to a large box. They told everyone on board about the catastrophic sinking of the *Morning Star*. For several hours, until well into daylight, the *Rice* scoured the area picking up survivors. By then, the wind had spread the debris field over several miles of water. Two tugboats, the *S.S. Coe* and the *Levi Johnson,* also scoured the area in search of more bodies.

Two of the 13 people on board the *Courtland* died, while 31 from the 90 aboard the *Morning Star* perished. Owned by the newly-formed Detroit and Cleveland Navigation Company, which operated from 1868 until 1951, and which also owned the *R.N. Rice,* the *Morning Star* worked for them for only a few weeks before her demise. A hearing in Detroit after the collision placed blame upon the captain and officers of the *Courtland* for failure to display the green light.

The two propeller wheels for tugs were salvaged a few days after the sinking. On July 28, 1868, the tug, *S.S. Coe,* salvaged the *Morning Star's* two anchors and 270' of chain. On September 11, 1868, the wreck was raised and towed about 12 miles from the actual collision site, to within eight miles of Vermilion, Ohio, where the *Morning Star* was accidentally sunk in approximately 55' of water when the hoisting chains slipped. That is where she remains to this day.

Jump to the year 1925. The DETROIT FREE PRESS of Wednesday, February 18th that year reported: "A tombstone in memory of three of the victims of the 'Morning Star tragedy,' which horrified the nation in 1868, was uncovered Tuesday afternoon by excavators at the foot of West Grand boulevard. The marble tablet was found by workers of the Birmingham Sand & Gravel Company. Inscribed on it were the names of three of the victims of the Lake Erie tragedy. The tablet reads:

> 'Helen Peri, Aged 34 Years,
> Florence Yale, Aged 12 Years,
> Cora I. Peri, Aged 6 Years,
> who died in the disaster of the
> Morning Star June 31 [sic], 1868.

> Remember youth, as you pass by,
> As you are now, so once was I,
> As I am now, you soon shall be,
> Prepare for death and follow me.

The newspaper article went on to say that the tablet "is believed to have been erected by the parents of the three who lost their lives in the disaster. The tablet is believed to have been buried when the waterfront, where the tablet was placed, was converted to a railroad yard."

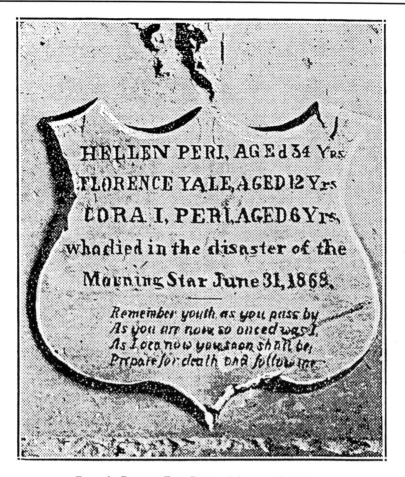

HELLEN PERI, AGEd 34 Yrs

FLORENCE YALE, AGED 12 Yrs

CORA I, PERI, AGED 6 Yrs,

who died in the disaster of the

Morning Star June 31, 1868.

Remember youth as you pass by
As you are now so onced was I,
As I ora now you soon shall be,
Prepare for death and follow me.

From the DETROIT FREE PRESS, *February 18, 1925.*

Today, the *Morning Star* rests in 60 to 70 feet of water. The entire vessel has sunk into the soft, muddy bottom of Lake Erie, but the engine and the boiler are intact, with the walking arm sticking straight up and a paddlewheel reasonably intact. Her immense boiler towers about 30' off the lake bottom. The decks have collapsed over time. Reportedly some of the mowing machines which once comprised part of the *Morning Star's* cargo ended up off her starboard side, but they have apparently broken down and faded into the mud. Water temperatures are in the low 40's in May, rising to a comfortable, almost too warm, 70's by late summer. As with all scuba diving in the Great Lakes, the minimum exposure protection is a wetsuit. This shipwreck abounds with perch, burbot, and the occasional walleye (pickerel), so beware of anglers at the site.

Only a 15-minute boat ride out of Lorain, Ohio, the tragic wreck of the *Morning Star* is one of the most popular scuba dive sites in western Lake Erie.

Nimrod

(#11 on the map on p. 63)

VESSEL NAME:	NIMROD
RIG:	three-masted schooner
DIMENSIONS:	184'
LAUNCHED:	late summer, 1873; Toledo, Ohio
DATE LOST:	Sunday, November 8, 1874
CAUSE OF LOSS:	collision with the schooner, MICHIGAN
CARGO:	corn
LIVES LOST:	none
GENERAL LOCATION:	off Port Burwell/Port Stanley, Ontario
DEPTH:	56' - 70'
ACCESS:	boat
DIVING SKILL LEVEL:	intermediate-advanced
DIVING HAZARDS:	depth, silting, hypothermia
CO-ORDINATES:	Lat/Lon:
	Loran: 44279.7 / 58053.2

In the one, short year that she was afloat such a long time ago, the large schooner, *Nimrod,* seems not to have been photographed by anyone, but today's underwater explorers have taken so many pictures of the wreck that they have endeared themselves to the film manufacturers.

Launched in the late summer of 1873 at Toledo, Ohio, and given official number 18773, the 559-ton schooner *Nimrod's* hull measured 184' in length and, with the addition of her 28' 6" bowsprit, she took on the impressive overall length of 212' 6". Appraised at $37,000, the *Nimrod* entered the Great Lakes bulk freight trade.

On the cold, foggy, dark early morning of Sunday, November 8, 1874, the *Nimrod's* active career ended. Downbound from Chicago to Buffalo with 37,000 bushels of corn, and opposite Port Stanley on Lake Erie, the *Nimrod's* crew panicked when they suddenly saw the dark form of the larger, newer, double-decked schooner, *Michigan,* loaded with coal from Buffalo to Chicago, emerge from the foggy darkness bearing down upon them at full speed! They had only 15 seconds of warning, and could not change their course in that brief time. The *Michigan* glanced off the *Nimrod's* hull and continued on her course, disappearing into the mist. The *Nimrod,* meanwhile, filled with water and sank, according to the crew, in 12 fathoms (a relatively accurate 72') within an hour. The *Nimrod's* crew, which had scrambled for the rigging when the ship sank, recovered their yawl boat after sunrise and headed towards the Canadian shore. The schooner, *Grantham,* picked them up and took them to Port Colborne, Ontario. The *Nimrod*, owned by J.C. Lockwood and Capt. F.H. Wilcox of Milan, Ohio, was partially insured. It was considered too late in the season to attempt a salvage, and the TOLEDO BLADE on Nov. 13, 1874, wrote the ship's final epitaph: "There were few finer modeled vessels on the lakes." The *Michigan* sailed for many more years, finally sinking in Lake Superior on Oct. 2, 1901.

A lookalike to the 184' NIMROD: the three-masted schooner, A.C. MAXWELL (175' in deck length), which sank in a collision in the St. Mary's River on November 5, 1908. Like the NIMROD, the MAXWELL carried an incredibly long bowsprit which yielded additional speed from the jibsails, or headsails. AUTHOR'S COLLECTION.

Captain Robert Hamilton, a commercial fisherman from Port Burwell, Ontario, snagged his nets on the wreck of an unidentified schooner in the fall of 1978. Local diver Mike Verbrugge assembled a team of divers who completed an archaeological survey from 1979 to 1982. Still, the wreck's identity eluded them. A 3,000-pound anchor from this wreck was raised on Sept. 15, 1979, preserved, and placed near the Port Burwell lighthouse as a mariners' memorial. In 1982, divers found a set of numbers, 18773, carved into the deck beam at the bow side of number four hatch. This was the *Nimrod's* official number.

The *Nimrod* shipwreck is sitting upright in 70' of Lake Erie water several miles out of Port Stanley, Ontario. There may be some modern fishing nets snagged along portions of this wreck which the zebra mussels haven't forced flat yet, so take at least one sharp dive knife with you. The silt stirs up easily and reduces visibility dramatically.

The *Nimrod* is the victim of shifting sands and soft lake bottom. The keel and the lower half of the hull have sunk into the sand and silt; the rudder is also buried, and the hull is impenetrable due to the accumulation of sediment. The superstructure, however, is well worth exploring. Only 18' of her bowsprit remain, but this is not bad news, since the bowsprits of most shipwrecked schooners have long collapsed or broken off in their entirety. There is the additional spectacle of a large anchor off her bow. Divers gliding over the deck will notice three large, dark, round holes; these were for the masts, which are missing except for part of one. There are numerous belaying pins and plenty of chain to conjure up a diver's fantasy about the sailing life aboard a Great Lakes schooner over a century ago.

A fine example of a bowsprit cap on the wreck of the NIMROD *in 70' of Lake Erie water frames former U.S. Navy diver Frank Troxell.* PHOTO BY CRIS KOHL.

The schooner, *Nimrod*

ARTWORK © ADAM HENLEY, Used with permission.

Passaic

(#12 on the map on p. 63)

VESSEL NAME:	PASSAIC
RIG:	wooden propeller (steamer)
DIMENSIONS:	198' 3" x 27' 7" x 11' 4"
LAUNCHED:	Saturday, May 24, 1862; Buffalo, New York
DATE LOST:	Sunday, November 1, 1891
CAUSE OF LOSS:	foundered
CARGO:	lumber; towing lumber barges
LIVES LOST:	none (from 15 on board)
GENERAL LOCATION:	off Dunkirk, New York
DEPTH:	74' - 84'
ACCESS:	boat
DIVING SKILL LEVEL:	advanced
DIVING HAZARDS:	depth, silting, hypothermia
CO-ORDINATES:	Lat/Lon: 42.28.733 / 79.27.776
	Loran:

The remains of the package freighter, *Passaic,* lying in about 84' of eastern Lake Erie water about three miles off Van Buren Point, New York, were dynamited by accident in the late 1960's/early 1970's. The "salvager" thought he was working on the *Dean Richmond!*

In spite of that damage, the shipwreck has a vast array of artifacts and structure greeting subaquatic visitors. The sides of the *Passaic* have collapsed outwardly, revealing the large boiler and the entire steam engine, including the crankcase and connecting rods, right to the keel. Also at the stern are her rudder, propeller, and propeller shaft. The bow displays an anchor and an anchor windlass. The wreck of the *Passaic* is usually buoyed by Captain Jim Herbert.

May 24th, 1862, was the *Passaic's* launch date. Built by Bidwell and Mason, the wooden ship slid down the launch ramp at Buffalo, New York, into the Lake Erie waters which would cause her demise almost 30 years later. Her gross tonnage at that time was 654.66, but she was remeasured at Dunkirk on April 8, 1865 as 844.81, and again at Detroit on May 7, 1883 as 531.61.

This old-style package freight propeller with wooden arches (or "hog frames") to strengthen the hull, an ornate, wooden pilot house at the bow, and several upper deck cabins for a limited number of passengers measured 198' 3" x 27' 7" x 11' 4", and could carry 600 tons of cargo in her holds. Her vertical direct-acting engine could produce 504 horsepower of strength. The *Passaic's* first owner (1862-1868) was the New York & Erie Railroad Company, sailing mainly between Dunkirk or Buffalo, New York, and Chicago on Lake Michigan, transporting manufactured goods to the west and carrying grain and other commodities back to the east. The ship's second owner (1868-1877) was the Union Steamboat Company, which sold the *Passaic* to Captain C.C. Blodgett of Detroit in 1877 for $17,500 to replace the *Tioga*, which had recently burned on Lake Erie. Captain McFarlane, last master of the *Tioga*, took command of the *Passaic*. Blodgett owned the ship until her loss 14 years later. The *Passaic's* 1866 value of $36,000 had dropped to $12,000 in her final year, 1891.

The steamer, PASSAIC, *1862-1891.* DRAWING BY ERIC HEYL.

On Saturday, October 31, 1891, the *Passaic* towed the four schooner-barges, *Hattie, Elma, Superior,* and *B.W. Jenness,* all heavily loaded with lumber, downbound towards Buffalo. In an increasing gale, the struggling steamer made no headway, so she cut her tows off Erie. The damage, however, had already been done, and the *Passaic's* seams opened under the strain. Rising waters killed the boiler fires, the crew took to the yawl, and the *Passaic* sank, bow first, at 12:30 A.M. on Sunday. With great difficulties and not until 9:00 A.M., the crewmembers boarded the tow, *Hattie.* By Monday, when the wind subsided, two Buffalo tugs, the *Hebard* and the *Gee,* sailed to the rescue of the anchored, distressed, and pummeled towbarges, each tug bringing in two of them. Mr. Blodgett refused to pay salaries to *Passaic's* crew for the Sunday and Monday, and declined to compensate them for their lost clothing and other effects. It is not known whether the old *Passaic* was insured or not when she sank, but if her owner's actions speak louder than words, we know the answer.

Queen of the West

(#13 on the map on p. 63)

VESSEL NAME:	QUEEN OF THE WEST
RIG:	wooden propeller (steamer)
DIMENSIONS:	215' x 32' 6" x 16' 4"
LAUNCHED:	Wed., March 16, 1881; West Bay City, MI
DATE LOST:	Thursday, August 20, 1903
CAUSE OF LOSS:	foundered
CARGO:	iron ore
LIVES LOST:	none (from 17 on board)
GENERAL LOCATION:	8 miles north of Fairport, Ohio
DEPTH:	60' - 71'
ACCESS:	boat
DIVING SKILL LEVEL:	intermediate-advanced
DIVING HAZARDS:	depth, silting, hypothermia, fish nets
CO-ORDINATES:	Lat/Lon: 41.50.769 / 82.23.133
	Loran: 43986.0 / 57735.1

The oak-hulled bulk freight steamer, *Queen of the West,* was 22 years old, an average lifespan for a Great Lakes ship, when she sprang a leak and foundered in heavy seas eight miles north of Fairport, Ohio, on Aug. 20, 1903.

Built by William Crosthwaite at West Bay City, Michigan, for John Kelderhouse of Buffalo and launched on Wednesday, March 16, 1881, the 818-gross-ton ship measured 215' x 32' 6" x 16' 4". From the time she was built and over the course of her career, the *Queen of the West* received hand-me-downs. Her fore & aft compound engine, rated at 675 horsepower, was an old engine which came from some other ship (INLAND LLOYDS of 1882 describes it as "old machinery"). The MARINE REVIEW states that the *Queen of the West* received one of the boilers from the *Calumet,* which was wrecked in a Lake Michigan storm on November 28, 1889. A 1901 rebuild in Cleveland prompted a tonnage change to 876 gross tons. The *Queen of the West* worked in the coal and iron ore trade.

At the midnight hour just when the new day of Thursday, August 20, 1903 started, the *Queen of the West,* upbound from Escanaba, Michigan, to Erie, Pennsylvania, delivered her consorts, the *H.W. Sage* and the *May Richards,* to Cleveland. All were laden with ore. Continuing towards Erie on her own, she steamed into building seas roughed up by a northeast wind. By 3:00 A.M., massive waves broke over the vessel, and an hour later, her crew began pumping out the water that was seeping into the hull. By the time the ship was off Fairport, Ohio, she was rolling heavily. Captain S.B. Massey had turned the *Queen of the West's* head into the wind, but the water in the hold rose faster than it could be pumped out. Massey ordered the lifeboat launched, but heavy seas tore it from the mother ship and carried it away. Deck hardware loosened and broke with every huge wave. The ship was indeed in jeopardy.

In a *deus ex machina* situation, the steamer, *Codorus,* happened to be passing at that dark hour and responded to the *Queen of the West's* distress signals. All 15 crewmembers (plus the engineer's two daughters) were removed from the sinking ship. Wheelsman Patrick Maloney nearly lost his life when he tried to jump to the *Codorus* and fell between the two rolling ships. He was rescued, but sustained three broken ribs. The lights of the *Queen of the West* disappeared not long after her crew sailed away.

Cleveland diver Joseph Suchy identified this shipwreck as the *Queen of the West* in the summer of 1986.

Subsequent cargo salvage work destroyed most of the decking, but many interesting items remain at the site in 71' of water. At the bow, where the decking is mostly intact, a windlass, some chain, and a winch form the major items of interest. At the stern, the engine and the huge boiler cannot be overlooked. The middle of the shipwreck is mostly open hull, while her railing has fallen off and lies on the lake bottom along the port side.

The bulk freight steamer, QUEEN OF THE WEST. THE GREAT LAKES MARINE COLLECTION OF THE MILWAUKEE PUBLIC LIBRARY/WISCONSIN MARINE HISTORICAL SOCIETY.

Richmond, Dean

(#14 on the map on p. 63)

VESSEL NAME:	DEAN RICHMOND
RIG:	wooden propeller (steamer)
DIMENSIONS:	238' x 35' x 13' 5"
LAUNCHED:	1864; Cleveland, Ohio
DATE LOST:	Saturday, October 14, 1893
CAUSE OF LOSS:	foundered
CARGO:	zinc ingots
LIVES LOST:	all hands (18 lives)
GENERAL LOCATION:	6 miles north of 16-Mile Creek, PA
DEPTH:	100' - 120'
ACCESS:	boat
DIVING SKILL LEVEL:	advanced
DIVING HAZARDS:	depth, darkness, silting, hypothermia
CO-ORDINATES:	Lat/Lon: 42.18.05 / 79.55.56 (old system)
	Lat/Lon: 42.18.436 / 79.55.857 (GPS)
	Loran: 16524.4 / 58602.8

"Lake Erie Heads in the Loss of Life" was the headline which appeared in several Great Lakes newspapers in December, 1893, summarizing the shipping season's losses for that year. A total of 123 lives were lost on the Great Lakes: 59 on Lake Erie, 33 on Lake Huron, 10 on Lake Superior, 12 on Lake Michigan, 4 on Lake Ontario, and 5 on the Detroit River. One reason that Lake Erie's total was so high was due to the loss of the *Dean Richmond.*

On October 15, 1893, a newspaper in Detroit printed a local article which contained this information: "OLD ERIE AROUSED....The storm on Lake Erie was by far the worst of the year. At noon the wind registered sixty miles an hour from the southwest at Buffalo and was increasing....The gale blew out the water in the west end of Lake Erie to such an extent that Toledo harbor is entirely closed to vessels, the water being so low that craft cannot get in or out. The steamer *City of Naples* [later renamed the *Frank O'Connor* and wrecked in Lake Michigan; see Volume II] lay at anchor three miles off Cleveland harbor all day unable to make port...."

The next day's headlines were quite different: "The *Dean Richmond* Goes Down Near Dunkirk," "Of her Crew of Eighteen Not One Was Saved," "Several of the Bodies Have Already Washed Ashore." The steamer, *Dean*

Richmond, lost with all hands in a violent Lake Erie autumn storm, became a mystery shipwreck which remained lost for almost a century.

The *Dean Richmond* was 29 years old when she foundered off Dunkirk, New York, on Saturday, October 14, 1893. The ship departed Toledo on Friday, October 13, 1893 (superstitions were apparently ignored) to Buffalo with a load of bagged meal, flour, and either zinc, copper, or lead. All three metals frequently saw ink in stories about this steamer. The *Dean Richmond* was reportedly seen off Erie, Pennsylvania, struggling heavily against the wretched weather and with one of her smokestacks gone. Almost at dusk on that Saturday, the upbound schooner, *Helen,* sighted the steamer in the trough of the sea with both stacks missing, but the extremely adverse conditions prevented any rescue attempt.

By 7:00 A.M., Sunday, October 15, 1893, wreckage and bodies from the *Dean Richmond* littered the shore near Dunkirk for miles.

Several of the *Dean Richmond's* crew apparently reached shore, only to be dashed to death by the pounding surf on the inhospitable rocks. The press reported that "had the beach been a sandy one, some of them might have survived, but there was little hope for any survivors on the rocky shore at Dunkirk." E. Wheeler, in his early 20's, a lookout on the *Dean Richmond*, apparently survived the waves and rocks, came ashore two miles west of Dunkirk, removed his lifejacket, staggered inland a bit, and died of exposure or exhaustion.

One fraud, "C.L. Clark," convinced the gullible media that he was the *Richmond's* sole survivor, telling a detailed and emotional tale. His story was discredited and he disappeared, but not before his tale was printed by the press.

The body of Captain George W. Stoddard, found floating off Silver Creek about eight miles east of Dunkirk, and the body of Walter Goodyear, the First Mate, washed ashore, carried watches which were frozen at the same time: 12:20. Presumably that was the time (12:20 A.M.) the men took to the water.

The 1,083-gross-ton *Dean Richmond*, named after the president of the New York Central Railroad, was a wooden arch-type, twin-propeller-driven freighter designed to carry both cargo and passengers. She was the largest package freighter on the Great Lakes when she was built in 1864 by Quayle & Martin of Cleveland, Ohio. Given official number 6102, she measured 238' in length, 35' in beam, and 13' 5" in draft. Steel arches and new boilers enhanced the aging ship in 1887, when she continued to run freight between Lake Superior and Lake Erie ports. By 1890, she plied only Lake Erie routes.

The *Dean Richmond* had been quite accident prone. On June 28, 1865, she collided with the steamer, *Illinois,* which sank at Point Pelee on Lake Erie. She ran ashore at Grand Traverse on Lake Michigan in July, 1868, suffering $700 worth of damage. She experienced an engine breakdown on Lake Huron in April, 1870, costing $3,500 to repair. Her grounding in the St. Clair River in March, 1871, was a $300 loss in damages. She burned and sank in Mud Lake, a portion of the St. Mary's River near Sault Ste. Marie, on October 29, 1871, with the loss of one life. The ship was raised and towed to Buffalo, where repairs and rebuilding cost an incredible $135,000! She ran ashore on North Manitou Island in October, 1876, freed herself, and arrived in Chicago with so much water in her holds that she immediately went into drydock for repairs. Collisions with schooners in 1878 and 1880 resulted in minor damage claims assessed against the *Dean Richmond*. She ended up frozen fast in the ice on Lake Michigan in late January, 1887, and mid-February, 1888, sustaining damage.

The DEAN RICHMOND *at Buffalo, NY, in 1870.* THE GREAT LAKES MARINE COLLECTION OF THE MILWAUKEE PUBLIC LIBRARY/WISCONSIN MARINE HISTORICAL SOCIETY.

The mystery of the *Dean Richmond* increased with time, as did the purported value of her cargo. One 1961 magazine article stated that "...her cargo nominates her as the most valuable known wreck in Lake Erie. Her finder will be richer, to the tune of close to a half million dollars, and perhaps more!...."

The *Dean Richmond* was one of the most hunted (and most elusive) shipwrecks in the Great Lakes. Gary Kozak, living and working in Derby, New Hampshire, but born and raised in Windsor, Ontario, spent eight summers systematically sidescanning segments of Lake Erie in his quest for the *Dean Richmond*. He amassed a fleet of 31 shipwrecks before he finally found the *Richmond* in 1984. Some salvage work was done, causing controversy.

A diver descending to the wreck of the *Dean Richmond* will reach the hull at about 100'; the photogenic wreck sits in about 120' completely inverted and dynamited open at one point. The huge debris field supposedly contains zinc ingots. The wreck is penetrable, but only by divers specially trained and prepared for this sort of diving. The interior silts up all too easily and reduces visibility to zero. The *Dean Richmond* is usually buoyed during the scuba diving season.

Tonawanda

(#15 on the map on p. 63)

VESSEL NAME:	TONAWANDA
RIG:	wooden propeller (steamer)
DIMENSIONS:	202' 3" x 32' 3" x 13' 3"
LAUNCHED:	Monday, April 28, 1856; Buffalo, New York
DATE LOST:	Tuesday, October 18, 1870
CAUSE OF LOSS:	foundered
CARGO:	corn, flour, lead
LIVES LOST:	none (from 11 on board)
GENERAL LOCATION:	2.5 miles off Windmill Point, Ontario
DEPTH:	40' - 50'
ACCESS:	boat
DIVING SKILL LEVEL:	intermediate
DIVING HAZARDS:	silting, disorientation, fish nets, current
CO-ORDINATES:	Lat/Lon: 42.50.31 / 78.58.18
	Loran:

The wooden steamer, *Tonawanda*, heavily loaded with 19,000 bushels of corn, 1,500 barrels of flour, and 750 pigs of lead from Chicago to Buffalo, broached in a gale off Point Abino, Ontario, about 15 miles west of Buffalo, on Tuesday, October 18, 1870. Her rudder jammed and the ship became uncontrollable, so an anchor was released to hold the vessel in place. Unfortunately, the chain parted and the *Tonawanda* drifted helplessly before the wind.

The crew labored hard to increase the steam and to hoist the fore-staysail (early steamships carried masts and sails in case of an emergency), and these actions would likely have saved their ship. However, waves had destroyed the two forward and midship gangways, and Lake Erie water rushing into the hull soon extinguished the boiler fires.

The *Tonawanda* flew her flag upside down (a common distress signal), but before tugboats could arrive at the scene, most of the crew abandoned ship. Her two engineers, two firemen, the second mate, the steward, two deckhands, and the captain's daughter filled and lowered the lifeboat, while the captain and the first mate remained with the endangered vessel. The people in the lifeboat spent five terrifying hours bobbing around in the immense threatening seas before finally reaching the safety of the Canadian shore.

The captain and the first mate remained with the Tonawanda and, before long, their distress signals were answered. The tugboats, *F.L. Danforth* and *J.C. Harrison* suddenly appeared on the crests of the rolling seas, secured lines to the Tonawanda, and started towing her into port.

But the *Tonawanda* suddenly listed and sank. There was barely enough time to cut the towlines and rescue the two men on board. the large steamer, however, was now definitely at the bottom of Lake Erie. The ship was valued at $35,000, and her cargo at $40,000. Fortunately there had been no loss of life.

Nine months later, in the summer of 1871, the tug, *Rescue,* commenced salvage operations, which were still in progress as of September 8th. They apparently proved unsuccessful except for removing much of the cargo. The wreck of the steamer, *Tonawanda,* has become a popular scuba dive site in Canadian waters of Lake Erie.

Built by Buell B. Jones at Buffalo, New York, and launched on Monday, April 28, 1856, the 882-gross-ton package freight steamer, *Tonawanda,* measured 202' 3" in length, 32' 3' in beam, and 13' 3' in draft. Her official number was 24110. Her direct-acting engine and boiler came from the Shepard Iron Works in Buffalo.

The *Tonawanda* had her share of accidents during her 14 years afloat. She ran ashore near Mackinac in July of 1856, during her first season, and had to be lightered (unloaded and towed) off. On July 6, 1857, she was seriously damaged by fire off Presque Isle, Michigan, on Lake Huron. She burned at Chicago and arrived at Buffalo for a rebuilding on June 22, 1866. On May 18, 1869, she sustained considerable damage in a collision with the steamer, *Equinox,* at Clay Banks, Wisconsin.

Today, the wreck of the *Tonawanda* sits in 50' of water, with portions of the wreck towering 10' off the bottom. The wooden hull is holding up relatively well considering the shallow water conditions. Do not drag your anchor along the lake's sandy bottom in an attempt to find or set into this shipwreck; that could damage the remains. At the stern the rudder, the four-bladed propeller, and a bearing at the propeller shaft are of interest to visiting divers. The best view of the wreck is on her starboard side, at the stern and midship areas. The port side has an average rise of about five feet, reaching seven feet at midship. The bow is fairly collapsed and shows little profile. A slight current sometimes runs in a northerly direction. Canadian law prohibits the removal of anything from shipwrecks. Unfortunately, zebra mussels now cover much of the *Tonawanda,* but there is enough of her to see and identify to make this an interesting exploration.

Two Fannies   (#16 on the map on p. 63)

VESSEL NAME:	TWO FANNIES
RIG:	three-masted bark (barque)
DIMENSIONS:	152' x 33' x 12'
LAUNCHED:	1862; Peshtigo, Wisconsin
DATE LOST:	Sunday, August 10, 1890
CAUSE OF LOSS:	foundered
CARGO:	iron ore
LIVES LOST:	none (from 8 on board)
GENERAL LOCATION:	4.8 miles north of Bay Village, Ohio
DEPTH:	52' - 61'
ACCESS:	boat
DIVING SKILL LEVEL:	intermediate
DIVING HAZARDS:	depth, silting, disorientation, hypothermia
CO-ORDINATES:	Lat/Lon: 41.33.850 / 81.55.280
	Loran: 43773.1 / 57385.2

The 492-gross-ton, three-masted bark (sometimes called a schooner), *Two Fannies,* left Escanaba, Michigan, for Cleveland, loaded with 800 tons of iron ore. Built in 1862 by George Spear at Peshtigo, Wisconsin, and given official number 24144, she was 28 years old, but her crew still had faith in her stout timbers. She measured 153' x 33' x 12'. Captain Alfred Miller of Kenosha, Wisconsin, and others owned her. The *Two Fannies* entered the choppy waters of Lake Erie late in the evening of Saturday, August 9, 1890. At 10:30, the lookout saw water rising in the hold. A seam had opened! The crew manned the pumps frantically, but by 1:30 A.M., the holds held four feet of water.

"The water came in faster and faster," recounted Captain Miller, "and although we kept her headed for Cleveland, we made little progress. Finally, the boat refused to obey her rudder and I knew she was going to the bottom very shortly. I called all hands and we launched the yawl with some difficulty, Mate Losie getting his foot badly hurt. We got in just in time to get away from the schooner before she made the final plunge, and then set off on our perilous trip for Cleveland twenty miles away. We hardly expected to be able to reach shore in safety, and were further discouraged by the fact that although we sighted several tugs, we were unable to attract their attention."

The crew rowed hard for several hours. When the sun rose, the passing steamer, *City of Detroit,* spotted them. However, the rescue almost became a tragedy, as the yawl narrowly escaped being pounded to pieces against the large ship. The exhausted crew in the yawl broke several oars in attempting to fend off the huge steamer. Only two men from the yawl were removed by means of ropes, it having been such a risky business that the others preferred to wait in hopes that the waves would subside. The steamer whistled for assistance, and shortly the tug, *James Amadeus,* came out to meet them. The remaining six crewmembers were safely removed aboard the tugboat and taken to Cleveland.

"I had no idea that little yawl could have carried eight people 15 miles through such a sea as was running last night," Mrs. Alice Stowell, Captain Miller's niece who was working as the ship's cook, remarked once safely ashore. "Eight people and a cat." The cat, a gift from her little girl, had been restless all evening, likely aware that the ship was doomed. Mrs. Stowell, when ordered into the yawl, grabbed an extra dress and her purse, and tucked the cat inside her bosom. Even so, she later claimed, "I lost all hope of reaching the shore alive."

The *Two Fannies* sits upright in about 61' of water. Her large rudder and rudder post are of interest to underwater explorers, even though her stern has collapsed. Beam supports and the centerboard box are easy to see, since the decking has fallen off. Two capstans, one at the bow and another at midship, plus a windlass and chain at the bow, some deadeyes, and a winch at midship, make up quite an impressive collection of nauticalia on this shipwreck.

The bark, Two Fannies, *valued at $11,000, carried no insurance. However, her cargo of iron ore was insured.*   The Great Lakes Marine Collection of the Milwaukee Public Library/Wisconsin Marine Historical Society.

Willis

VESSEL NAME:	WILLIS
RIG:	three-masted schooner
DIMENSIONS:	131' 7" x 27' 9" x 9'
LAUNCHED:	spring, 1872; Manitowoc, Wisconsin
DATE LOST:	Monday, November 11, 1872
CAUSE OF LOSS:	collision with bark, ELIZABETH JONES
CARGO:	barley
LIVES LOST:	none
GENERAL LOCATION:	off Wheatley and Pt. Pelee, Ontario
DEPTH:	60' - 73'
ACCESS:	boat
DIVING SKILL LEVEL:	intermediate-advanced
DIVING HAZARDS:	depth, silting, fish nets, hypothermia
CO-ORDINATES:	Lat/Lon: 41.55.88 / 82.09.67
	Loran: 43897.6 / 57349.8

The three-masted schooner, *Willis,* sank within ten minutes after a collision with the bark, *Elizabeth Jones,* at about 1:45 A.M. on Monday, November 11, 1872 about 15 miles off the Canadian shore east of Point Pelee, Ontario. Measuring 131' 7" in length, 27' 9" in beam, and 9' in draft, and built at Manitowoc, Wisconsin by Peter Larson in early 1872, the single-season schooner was owned by James R. Slauson and Captain William R. Pugh of Racine, Wisconsin.

The schooner, *Willis,* had sailed into the night downbound with 17,250 bushels of barley from Chicago to Buffalo. The bark, *Elizabeth Jones,* was heading from Buffalo to Chicago fully loaded with coal. The two ships saw each other's lights while still a fair distance away, yet last minute misjudgements caused the bow of the *Jones* to slice into the *Willis'* port side. The *Jones* received mere scratches by comparison to the *Willis,* which started to settle within two minutes and sank in about ten. The *Willis'* crew launched their lifeboat and rowed to the safety of the *Elizabeth Jones,* which conveyed them to Detroit. Once there, both captains denounced the accuracy of the other's lights and sailing directions. The ensuing court case lasted 13 years before being resolved in favor of the *Willis.*

Within two days of her sinking, a steamer crashed into the *Willis'* mizzenmast, breaking it off. Her other two masts came down shortly thereafter.

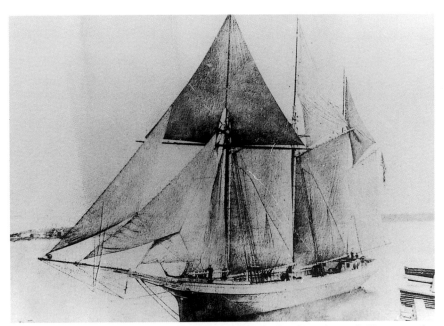

No photograph of the short-lived schooner, WILLIS, has been located. However, the three-masted schooner, ROUSE SIMMONS, measuring 130' x 28' 8" x 8', resembled the WILLIS. *Besides having similar measurements and tonnage, they were both built in Wisconsin at about the same time.* THE GREAT LAKES MARINE COLLECTION OF THE MILWAUKEE PUBLIC LIBRARY/WISCONSIN MARINE HISTORICAL SOCIETY.

The wreck of the *Willis* was originally located in the 1960's by Michael Schoger, a hardhat diver, now retired, who spent much of his life working on the submerged gas wells in western Lake Erie. Definite identification resulted when a Cleveland scuba diver found the *Willis'* tonnage numbers carved into the rear hatch combing.

The steering gear at the stern of the *Willis* is impressive to behold, even though the ship's wheel itself was removed. Several deadeyes and blocks remain, even though a scuba diver seems to have gone on a wreck-stripping rampage in the summer of 1989. Two teardrop-shaped brass portholes are also missing from the ship's otherwise handsome transom. A capstan, bilge pump, and long portion of the bowsprit help make this an exciting dive. The smallest of the spars straddling the starboard rail could possibly be the bowsprit of the bark, *Elizabeth Jones,* left there after the collision (even though the collision occurred on the port side of the *Willis,* the *Elizabeth Jones'* bowsprit could conceivably have come to rest on the other side.)

The schooner, *Willis,* considered by many to be the best, most intact shipwreck in the Point Pelee area, will not disappoint visiting underwater explorers with her fine lines, history, and mostly intact features.

ABOVE: *This artist's rendition of the* WILLIS *shows how she rests in 73' of Lake Erie water.* ARTWORK BY PETER RINDLISBACHER, COURTESY OF THE OWNER, ROY PICKERING. BELOW: *Blocks, deadeyes, and other items of standing rigging lying on the deck of the schooner,* WILLIS, *make exploring this shipwreck unique.* PHOTO BY CRIS KOHL.

3 Lake Huron Shipwrecks

econd largest of the five Great Lakes (only Superior is larger), Huron is
also considered to be the second "least settled" (again, Lake Superior has
the "wildest," or least built up, shoreline of all the Great Lakes, although
it can claim cities larger than any of those on Lake Huron).

Lake Huron, named by the French after their Indian allies, has the
distinction of being the first of the Great Lakes to be seen by Europeans. French
explorer Étienne Brûlé first ventured into this enormous body of water via the
Ottawa and Mattawa Rivers in 1609 or 1610, followed shortly thereafter by
Samuel de Champlain. By 1638, a Jesuit mission had been established among
the Huron Indians near present-day Midland, Ontario, in the southeastern corner
of Georgian Bay, but was destroyed eleven years later by warring Iroquois. After
that, the center of French activity in the Great Lakes shifted to Sault Ste. Marie
on the St. Mary's River and St. Ignace on the Straits of Mackinac.

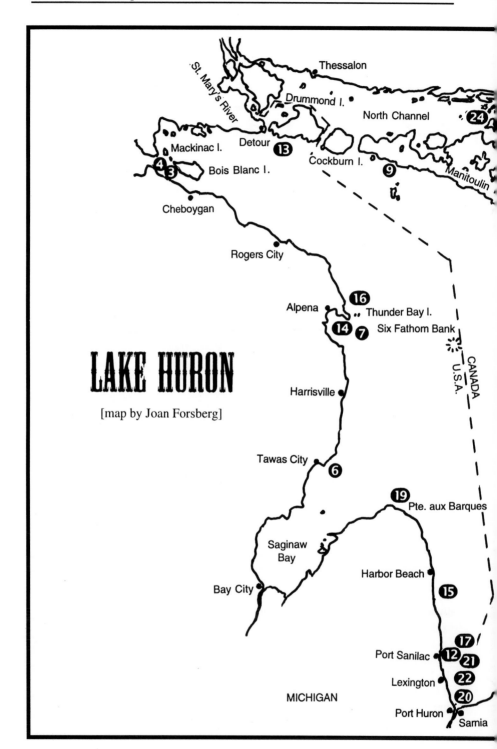

LAKE HURON

[map by Joan Forsberg]

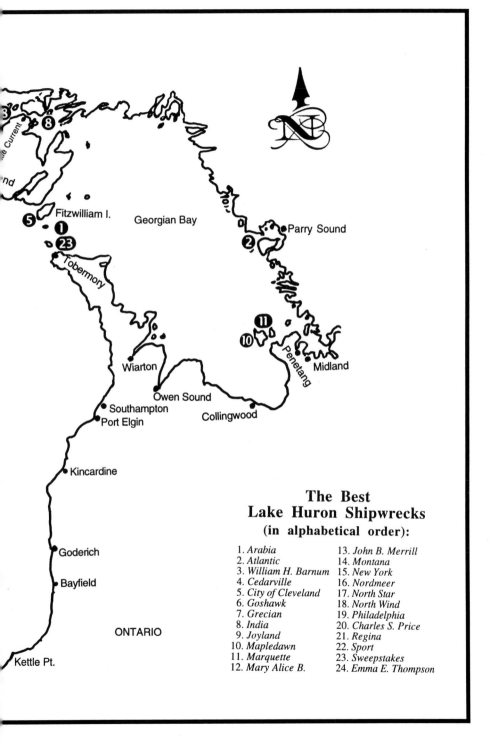

The Best
Lake Huron Shipwrecks
(in alphabetical order):

1. *Arabia*
2. *Atlantic*
3. *William H. Barnum*
4. *Cedarville*
5. *City of Cleveland*
6. *Goshawk*
7. *Grecian*
8. *India*
9. *Joyland*
10. *Mapledawn*
11. *Marquette*
12. *Mary Alice B.*
13. *John B. Merrill*
14. *Montana*
15. *New York*
16. *Nordmeer*
17. *North Star*
18. *North Wind*
19. *Philadelphia*
20. *Charles S. Price*
21. *Regina*
22. *Sport*
23. *Sweepstakes*
24. *Emma E. Thompson*

After the defeat of the French in the Seven Years' War (1756-1763), British penetration of the lower Great Lakes developed strongly. The current boundary between Canada and the United States, first drawn at the end of the American Revolution (1775-1783), was firmly in place by the end of the War of 1812.

Georgian Bay, a part of Lake Huron, is immense. Early explorers considered it to be a "Great Lake" unto itself --- indeed, the 7,000 square miles in Georgian Bay/North Channel cover almost the same surface area as all of Lake Ontario! The largest group of islands in any of the five Great Lakes are in Georgian Bay/North Channel, making this by many accounts the best region in the lakes for boating and water sports.

Here are some quick facts about the lake:

- Lake Huron is bordered on the north and east by the province of Ontario in Canada, and on the west by the state of Michigan in the United States. The international boundary line cuts angles up the middle of the lake's main body for a total distance of 261 miles.

- Lake Huron is about 206 miles long and 101 miles wide at its broadest point.

- The deepest point in Lake Huron is 750 feet, or 125 fathoms, at a point 26.5 miles SSW from Cove Island Light near Tobermory, Ontario, and 58 miles ESE from Thunder Bay Island Light near Alpena, Michigan. The average, or mean, depth is 195 feet.

- The surface area of Lake Huron is 23,000 square miles, 13,900 of them in Canada and the other 9,100 in the United States.

- Lake Huron's chief water inflow is from Lake Michigan through the Straits of Mackinac, and from Lake Superior by means of the St. Mary's River. Lake Huron sits 579 feet above sea level, the same elevation as Lake Michigan. These are the only two Great Lakes that share the same surface height. Lake Huron discharges at its southern end into Lake Erie by way of the St. Clair River, Lake St. Clair, and the Detroit River.

- A shoal spot where the depth is only about 36 feet (six fathoms) exists in the middle of Lake Huron halfway between Michigan's thumb at Pointe aux Barques, and the tip of Ontario's Bruce Peninsula at Tobermory. This remote area is likely rife with shipwrecks just waiting to be discovered!

- The first ship on the upper Great Lakes, that is, above Niagara Falls, was also that area's first shipwreck, and I believe it wrecked in Lake Huron. The story of LaSalle's ship, the *Griffon,* also spelled *Griffin,* has been told often in the last three centuries: how it was constructed along the Niagara River in early 1679, how it then crossed Lake Erie, ventured through the Detroit River-Lake St. Clair-St. Clair River system, cruised up Lake Huron and into the Green Bay area of Lake Michigan to pick up a load of furs before it sailed into mystery and history on the return journey. The *Griffon* simply disappeared with all five hands. At least a dozen places have claimed to be the final resting spot of the fabled *Griffon.* Irrefutable evidence has not surfaced, but the strongest claim comes from the western end of Manitoulin Island at Mississagi Straits, where the shorebound remains of a lead-caulked ship were found. Unfortunately, what there was left of this shipwreck disappeared in a 1942 storm, but not before locals recovered some of the timbers, caulking, and fastenings, now on display in nearby museums. The Mississagi Straits claim is thus far the strongest.

- There are over 30,000 islands in eastern Georgian Bay's "30,000 Islands" archipelago. In 1981, an old-time sailor told me that "If you haven't run aground here yet, you're doing something wrong." These islands are one reason that Lake Huron has the highest number of shipwrecks of any of the Great Lakes (about 1,320).

- The largest cities on Lake Huron are Sarnia, Ontario, with about 80,000 inhabitants, and Bay City, Michigan, with about 70,000. Other notable port communities include Port Huron, Michigan (50,000), Alpena, Michigan (14,000), and Goderich, Ontario (11,000). Lake Huron's shoreline is the least populated of all the Great Lakes. Even remote and wilderness-wrapped Lake Superior has larger cities on it than does Lake Huron!

- Manitoulin Island is the largest freshwater island in the world (1,073 square miles). This Ontario landmass separates the North Channel from the rest of Lake Huron.

- The worst marine disasters on Lake Huron include the loss of the steamer, *Pewabic,* in a collision with her sister ship, the *Meteor,* off Alpena, Michigan, on August 9, 1865; about 100 people died, and a valuable cargo of copper ingots went to the bottom in 163 feet of water; and the sinking of the steamship, *Asia,* on storm-tossed Georgian Bay waters on September 14, 1882, with the loss of 123 people. Two survived. The *Asia* remains undiscovered.

- Lake Huron contains the wreck of the *Minnedosa,* the largest sailing vessel ever constructed on the Canadian side of the Great Lakes. That ship sank off Michigan's thumb on October 20, 1905, with the loss of all nine hands. David Trotter located this shipwreck in 1991 in about 220 feet of water.

- The worst Great Lakes storm in recorded history did its most damage on Lake Huron on November 8-11, 1913. Eight steel freighters and their entire crews were lost; three remain unlocated.

- The first underwater park or preserve in the Great Lakes was created in 1972 at Tobermory, Ontario, in a relatively small area with a high concentration of shipwrecks, a total of twenty-one wrecks, none of which is further than five miles from the small fishing and tourist community of Tobermory. Note: annual diver registration at the park registration office is mandatory before scuba diving in this underwater park, formally called Fathom Five National Marine Park. There is an registration fee of a few dollars, good for diving the whole calendar year at Tobermory. Certification cards are required to register.

- The only ship so far in Lake Huron which was purposely scuttled for the creation of a scuba dive site was the old Atlantic schooner named the *Caroline Rose,* sunk in 55 feet of water just outside Tobermory's underwater park boundaries in August, 1990.

- Michigan has four Lake Huron underwater preserves established at Alpena (with seventeen shipwrecks plus five more, mostly ones deeper than recommended sport diving limits just outside the preserve boundary), Mackinac (containing ten shipwrecks, five of which are on the Lake Huron side of this underwater preserve), the thumb area (with fifteen located shipwrecks, several of which are beyond recommended sport diving limits), and Sanilac County (which has nine located shipwrecks).

- In Lake Huron proper (excluding Lake St. Clair, the St. Clair River, and the St. Mary's River), there are about 1,200 shipwrecks, most of which have not yet been located, or will never be located because they were smashed into thousands of pieces of potential firewood when storm-tossed waves pounded them onto rocky shores.

Arabia

(#1 on the map on pp. 130-131)

VESSEL NAME:	ARABIA
RIG:	bark (barque)
DIMENSIONS:	131' x 26' x 12'
LAUNCHED:	Tuesday, April 26, 1853; Kingston, Ontario
DATE LOST:	Sunday, October 5, 1884
CAUSE OF LOSS:	foundered
CARGO:	corn
LIVES LOST:	none
GENERAL LOCATION:	off Echo Island, north of Tobermory, ON
DEPTH:	102' - 117'
ACCESS:	boat
DIVING SKILL LEVEL:	advanced
DIVING HAZARDS:	depth, darkness, silting, hypothermia
CO-ORDINATES:	Lat/Lon: 45.18.71 / 81.40.44
	Loran: 30202.9 / 48669.8

The wreck of the bark, *Arabia,* is the most intact shipwreck in the Tobermory area, which is itself famous as the place where the first underwater park in the Great Lakes was created back in 1972.

The 309-ton bark, *Arabia,* departed Chicago on her final voyage on Wednesday, October 1, 1884, heading to Midland, Ontario, at the southern end of Georgian Bay, with 20,000 bushels of corn. Captain Henry Douville sailed his ship up Lake Michigan, through the Straits of Mackinac, and towards Tobermory across Lake Huron. On Saturday, October 4, 1884, while still about 70 miles west of Tobermory, violent storm conditions developed. Waves battered the *Arabia* repeatedly with savage intensity. Before long, the ship began leaking badly. After several hours of strenuous pumping, the weary crew realized the hopelessness of their situation. After they passed the Cove Island Lighthouse, their vessel began to sink. At about 3:00 A.M., Sunday, October 5, 1884, Captain Douville gave the order to launch the yawl boat and abandon ship. The bark sank in deep, icy water off Echo Island just after the last man scrambled onto the yawl boat.

The *Arabia's* crew bobbed around in these tempestuous conditions until just after sunrise, when a passing tugboat rescued them and transported them to Wiarton, Ontario.

The three-masted *Arabia,* built by George Thurston at Kingston, Ontario, and launched on Tuesday, April 26, 1853, measured 131' in length, 26' in beam, and 12' in draft. Thurston was an experienced shipbuilder who built 24 vessels between 1842 and 1869.

The *Arabia* spent her first year sailing Lake Ontario routes, but in 1854, made the big crossing from the Great Lakes to Glasgow in the British Isles, loaded with 14,000 bushels of wheat and 500 barrels of flour. The canals in the St. Lawrence River had been improved by 1848, the beginning of large cargo movements between Canada and Britain. The *Arabia* returned to the Great Lakes the following year, carrying a cargo from Britain all the way to Chicago. For the remaining 30 years of her life, the *Arabia* carried general bulk cargoes between the eastern Great Lakes and Lake Michigan.

The *Arabia* was not without her little mishaps in life. The Kingston, Ontario newspaper of Saturday, October 19, 1867, reported that "the barque, *Arabia,* while in tow of a tug, and passing through the harbor with a cargo of grain, ran aground on Thursday at the shoal near Point Frederick, on which there is at present a low depth of water. She remained in that position until yesterday morning, when her cargo being lighted, she floated off."

For almost 90 years, the final resting place of the *Arabia* somewhere off Echo Island north of Tobermory, Ontario, remained a mystery. Commercial fishermen in the area knew the wreck was nearby, because they were bringing in catches of corn-stuffed fish. Finally, late in 1971, Tobermory Captain Albert Smith pinpointed the wreck. Stan McClellan, of the Ontario Ministry of Natural Resources (and a Past President of the Ontario Underwater Council), directed the first investigation, which resulted in the identification of the *Arabia.*

The *Arabia's* hull, lying north-to-south, is split fore and aft along the keel, with the sides intact, but leaning. A rudder 16' 7" long lies flat near the ship's wheel and steering gear. some deadeyes still appear along the railing, particularly the port one. There is a cooking stove near the stern, plus a door, a table, and a centerboard winch. The afterdeck, separated from the hull, rests against the starboard quarter. The three masts have all collapsed and are located alongside the wreck. A capstan hangs under the decking next to the centerboard box, or well. At the bow are the magnificent bowsprit, originally 35' long, now somewhat broken off, but still impressively complete, aimed slightly upwards as if yearning for the surface, resplendent in its hanging chains. Catheads and ship's wooden-stock anchors on both port and starboard sides, a large windlass with a pawl bitt, a samson post and a pump complete the list of interesting items at the bow. The *Arabia* is in such excellent shape because she sits in freezing, dark water 102' to 117' deep, an icewater showpiece, and one of Canada's most famous shipwrecks.

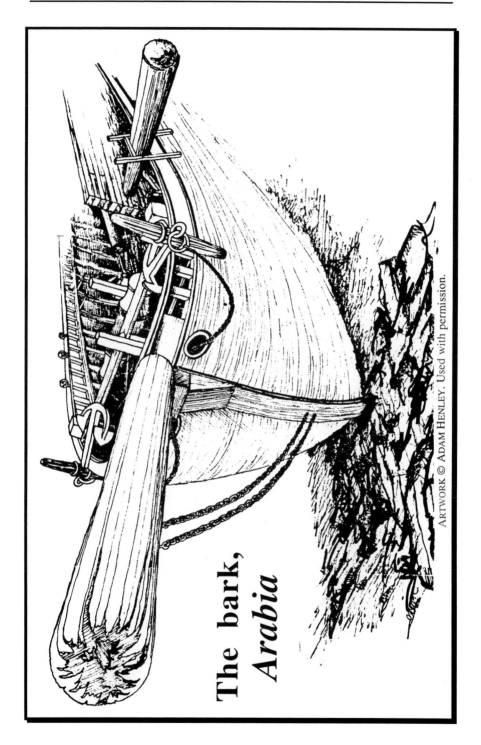

The bark,
Arabia

ARTWORK © ADAM HENLEY. Used with permission.

There are usually two mooring buoys attached to 500-pound concrete blocks, one positioned near the bow and the other one off the stern, both along the starboard side of the shipwreck. Thin lines usually run from the concrete block to the *Arabia* in case of diminished visibility.

Numerous artifacts from the bark, *Arabia,* are on display at the Fathom Five National Marine Park diver registration office: some corn from her cargo, a carpenter's auger bit and a "long arm" horsing iron (a caulking tool), the brass ship's bell with an iron clapper, a stoneware jug (from a Brantford company, circa 1867-1873), an ironstone china bowl from England (1862-1880), and ironstone dish from the British Wedgwood & Company (circa 1880), a lantern burner and a lantern chimney.

Lastly, the *Arabia* is a deep dive, suitable only for advanced divers who have much experience. Because she seems to sing a sort of siren's song that lures inexperienced visitors to her site, at least seven scuba divers have died there over the years. This is cold, deep, dark water, and every precaution must be utilized. Unfortunately, novice or intermediate divers have been tempted to reach this wreck; some succeeded, some didn't. Know your own limitations.

Diver Roy Pickering explores the deadeyes and blocks on the bark, ARABIA'S, *port rail. This site is for very experienced divers only.* PHOTO BY CRIS KOHL.

Atlantic

(#2 on the map on pp. 130-131)

VESSEL NAME:	ATLANTIC, launched as the MANITOULIN
RIG:	passenger steamer
DIMENSIONS:	147' x 30' x 11'
LAUNCHED:	1880; Owen Sound, Ontario
DATE LOST:	Tuesday, November 10, 1903
CAUSE OF LOSS:	burned
CARGO:	general (hay, coal oil, etc.)
LIVES LOST:	none (from 27; 24 crew, 3 passengers)
GENERAL LOCATION:	west of Parry Sound, ON, in Georgian Bay
DEPTH:	6' - 50'
ACCESS:	boat
DIVING SKILL LEVEL:	novice-intermediate
DIVING HAZARDS:	silting, adverse weather, hypothermia
CO-ORDINATES:	Lat/Lon: 45.20.02 / 80.15.39 (old system)
	Loran: 29661.88 / 48743.12

Flames fanned by the fierce gale of Tuesday, November 10, 1903, destroyed, for the second and last time, the combination passenger/package freight steamer, *Atlantic,* on the eastern edge of Georgian Bay, that body of water sometimes referred to as "the sixth Great Lake." No lives were lost, although in her first incineration on May 18, 1882, when she was named the *Manitoulin,* about 20-30 people perished. This tragedy took place off Shoal Point, Manitowaning Bay, Manitoulin Island, in northern Lake Huron. Her relatively new hull at that time was deemed salvageable and the vessel was rebuilt at Owen Sound, Ontario, and renamed the *Atlantic.* [This steamship *Atlantic* is not to be confused with the controversial steamer, *Atlantic,* which lies off Long Point, Ontario, in 163' of Lake Erie water. That's an entirely different story.]

For 20 years, the *Atlantic* served the northern Georgian Bay communities well, flying the flag of the Northern Navigation Company.

In her final demise on Tuesday, November 10, 1903, the *Atlantic,* enroute from Collingwood, Ontario, to Byng Inlet in the northern part of Georgian Bay, was struggling to stay afloat in a powerful storm, her hull leaking badly, slowly steaming her way into the lee of the Pancake Islands in an attempt to reach the safe harbor of Parry Sound, Ontario. The engineers left the engine room and headed for the lifeboats, a sure sign that something was amiss. The ship might have succeeded in reaching her haven if fire had not broken out in the hay

ABOVE: *Cheerful crowds of turn-of-the-century passengers posed on the foredeck of the steamer,* ATLANTIC, *in the late 1890's before the ship carried them to the scenic wonders of Georgian Bay.* ARCHIVES OF ONTARIO.   BELOW: *The* ATLANTIC *burned twice in her lifetime, once with heavy loss of life in 1882 when she was named the* MANITOULIN, *and finally in 1903 after she had been rebuilt and renamed the* ATLANTIC. INSTITUTE FOR GREAT LAKES RESEARCH, BOWLING GREEN STATE UNIVERSITY, OHIO.

The steamer, *Atlantic*

ARTWORK © ADAM HENLEY. Used with permission.

stored in the forward hold. The furious autumn winds whipped the flames along the entire length of the steamship in mere minutes. Miraculously, the passengers and crew all escaped safely into the lifeboats and rowed away from the conflagration. A passing tug picked them up.

Built originally by John Simpson at Owen Sound, Ontario, for the Great Northern Transit Company in 1880, the 706-ton wooden propeller measured 147' in length, 30' in beam, and 11' in draft.

Easily located are the *Atlantic's* propeller and the huge rudder lying in less than 10' of water on the western edge of the Spruce Rocks, south of Spruce Island, several miles west of Parry Sound, Ontario. The superstructure totally burned off or caved in on the hull, and, lying there on a steep slope with the stern in the shallows and the bow in deeper water, the seascape of tangled debris that includes chain, capstan, gears, boiler, engine, and other machinery proves irresistible to visiting scuba divers. A snowmobile sits on the lake bottom right off the bow of the *Atlantic*. Launching an inflatable boat from nearby Killbear Provincial Park has worked well for many scuba divers visiting the *Atlantic*.

Be careful when boating into these island-, islet-, rock-, and reef-strewn waters. They're not called the "30,000 Islands" for nothing! A west wind can prove challenging at this open site which begins in only a few feet of water and drops down to about 50'.

A stainless steel identification marker was placed several years ago on the historic wreck of the ATLANTIC *near Parry Sound, Ontario. The remains of this 147-foot-long steamer descend a steep slope from 6' to about 50'.*   PHOTO BY CRIS KOHL.

Barnum, William H.

(#3 on the map on pp. 130-131)

VESSEL NAME:	WILLIAM H. BARNUM
RIG:	wooden, propeller-driven steamer
DIMENSIONS:	218' 6" x 34' 8" x 21' 4"
LAUNCHED:	Saturday, April 5, 1873; Detroit, Michigan
DATE LOST:	Tuesday, April 3, 1894
CAUSE OF LOSS:	foundered
CARGO:	corn
LIVES LOST:	none
GENERAL LOCATION:	5.5 miles SE of Old Mackinac Point, MI
DEPTH:	58' - 75'
ACCESS:	boat
DIVING SKILL LEVEL:	intermediate-advanced
DIVING HAZARDS:	depth, penetration, hypothermia, silting
CO-ORDINATES:	Lat/Lon: 45.44.42 / 84.37.53
	Loran: 31205.5 / 48153.3

In the history of the Great Lakes, some captains or ship owners pushed their abilities, their ships, and their luck to the limit by squeezing as many cargo-hauling trips into a single seven-month sailing season as possible. They started out before the ice had melted, and stayed out until threatened with freeze-up. Often ships and their masters, restless after five dormant months in winter lay-up, would run through the lakes with large winter remnants still visible.

The aging steamer, the *William H. Barnum,* sank early in the shipping season on Tuesday, April 3, 1894, when ice cut through her hull and she foundered in the Straits of Mackinac, half a mile offshore and about five miles southeast of Mackinac City, Michigan. The ship was bound from Chicago, where she had wintered, to Port Huron, Michigan, with 55,000 bushels of corn.

Ironically, the *Barnum* was too much in need of repairs, "unseaworthy," to use formal wording, for any underwriter to insure her; by some miracle of rhetoric, her owners arranged with one insurance company to cover their ship to the tune of $22,000 for one trip only, this first one of the shipping season from Chicago to Port Huron. The condition was that the *William H. Barnum* be repaired at Port Huron once the vessel arrived there. So the steamer, under a 29-year-old master taking command for the first time, Captain William Smith of Marine City, Michigan, headed north up Lake Michigan from Chicago with 18 other ships at noon on April 1, 1894, the time given by the underwriters as the official opening of the 1894 shipping season.

The underwriters lost their high-risk gamble. The *Barnum* sank before reaching Port Huron and before repairs could be made.

Captain Smith had noticed the wind picking up as he entered the Straits of Mackinac, but his inexperience painted him into the corner of an icepack. The battering ice, driving wind, and pounding waves proved too much for the *Barnum's* old, wooden hull, and the seams opened. More and more holes allowed the freezing water to pour in, and the pumps could no longer keep up. The *Barnum* desperately blasted a distress call on her steam whistle, and a nearby tug, the *Crusader,* raced to her assistance. Unable to tow the *Barnum* into the shallows due to the pack ice, the *Crusader* ended up removing all hands from the sinking steamer. They watched their ship sink at 6:00 A.M., April 3, 1894.

Drawing of the steamer, WILLIAM H. BARNUM, *in 1873, by Samuel Ward Stanton, 1895.*

Norm McCready of Indianapolis and his team of divers located the wreck of the *William H. Barnum* in 1963. The rudder was recovered and put on display in St. Ignace in the summer of 1969. The *Barnum,* one of the Straits Underwater Preserve's most popular dive sites, sits upright and quite intact in 75' of water. Nauticalia found on the wreck include a windlass, the engine, and the boiler. Part of the main deck is collapsing, and the stern was destroyed when the rudder was dynamited out, but the double-decking allows for penetration by trained, experienced divers. Fish abound at this site in the summertime.

Cedarville

(#4 on the map on pp. 130-131)

VESSEL NAME:	CEDARVILLE; launched as the A.F. HARVEY
RIG:	steel propeller
DIMENSIONS:	588' 3" x 60' 2" x 30'8"
LAUNCHED:	Sat., April 9, 1927; River Rouge, Michigan
DATE LOST:	Friday, May 7, 1965
CAUSE OF LOSS:	collision with the TOPDALSFJORD
CARGO:	limestone
LIVES LOST:	10 (from 35 on board)
GENERAL LOCATION:	2.75 miles E of Old Mackinac Point, MI
DEPTH:	40' - 106'
ACCESS:	boat
DIVING SKILL LEVEL:	intermediate
DIVING HAZARDS:	depth, penetration, silting, hypothermia
CO-ORDINATES:	Lat/Lon: 45.47.13 / 84.40.13
	Loran: 31210.7 / 48130.6

The tragic loss of ten lives in the 1965 sinking of the huge, steel freighter, *Cedarville,* near the Straits of Mackinac left many families feeling deep, personal losses, particularly in the town of Rogers City, Michigan, which nine of the ten lost crewmembers had called home.

The 38-year-old triple expansion engine of the *Cedarville* propelled her smoothly at full speed, slicing through the dark, fog-shrouded waters approaching the Straits of Mackinac. The ship had departed Calcite, Michigan, near Rogers City, at five o'clock that morning, Friday, May 7, 1965, with over 14,000 tons of limestone for Gary, Indiana. Three miles east of the Mackinac Bridge, the *Cedarville* established VHF radio communication with an eastbound German ship, the *Weissenberg.* The fog had thickened, third mate Charles Cook diligently manned the radar unit, and wheelsman Leonard Gabrysiak maintained his heading. But Captain Martin Joppich gave no orders for the *Cedarville* to slow down. The *Weissenberg* sailed under the Bridge at 9:38 A.M. and informed the *Cedarville's* radio operator that there was actually another vessel ahead of the *Weissenberg* in the narrow strait!

Captain Joppich desperately attempted to radio this mystery ship, but received no answer. These were frantic minutes. Somewhere out there in the thick fog, steaming in his general direction, was a ship with which he could not establish communication!

The 588' CEDARVILLE *sank in a collision with the Norwegian freighter,* TOP-
DALSFJORD, *on May 7, 1965. Ten lives were lost.* GREAT LAKES MARINE COLLECTION OF
THE MILWAUKEE PUBLIC LIBRARY/WISCONSIN MARINE HISTORICAL SOCIETY.

Captain Joppich ordered the *Cedarville's* speed reduced and commanded a
slight turn to starboard. On his radar, Cook suddenly, and seemingly out of
nowhere, picked up the mystery ship. It was dead ahead! A lookout at the bow
yelled, "There she is," and the wheelsman stared wide-eyed at the unstoppable
point of a steel bow emerging from the fog about 100 feet off the *Cedarville's*
port bow. Captain Joppich fired orders in rapid succession: "Hard to starboard!"
"Full speed ahead." The bows of the ships missed each other, but now Joppich
had to get the rest of the *Cedarville* out of the collision course. With a "Hard to
port" command, he tried to swing the stern clear, but it was too late. The ships
were too close to each other and traveling too fast to avoid a collision.

The mystery ship plowed into the *Cedarville's* port side near midship,
chiseling deeply into her steel hull between the seventh and the eighth hatches.
Then the motion and the noise of grinding steel stopped, and all was quiet. The
mystery vessel pulled out and the two ships lost sight of each other in the dense
fog. Joppich's next orders were more serious: "Stop engines!" "Drop the
anchor!" "Sound a general alarm!" "Radio a Mayday!" "Activate the collision tar-
paulin!" This latter command was useless, as the collision gap was far too large
to be covered by the emergency tarp. Joppich radioed the *Weissenberg*, angrily
demanding to know the name of the ship which had just collided with his.

"The *Topdalsfjord*," came the reply. This was a Norwegian vessel.

Joppich ordered the anchor raised at 10:10 A.M. and attempted to beach

The steamer, *Cedarville*

ARTWORK © CHUCK AND JERI FELTNER. Used with permission.

his ship at Mackinaw City. He warned the *Weissenberg* to stay clear, all the while broadcasting a Mayday distress message. At 10:25, the *Cedarville,* almost full of water, tipped over to starboard and plummeted through 106' of water. She had traveled a little over two miles from the point of collision, but was still two miles from shore. Ironically, the collision had occurred only two miles offshore. The captain had ordered his stricken ship to sail in the wrong direction!

All of the *Cedarville's* men ended up in the water, but the *Weissenberg* had followed her course on radar and quickly launched lifeboats. They picked up 27 men, one of whom was dead; another died shortly after being rescued.

Five of the eight missing crewmembers were found within days of the sinking. Another body was located 200' off the wreck in 1966 by shipwreck hunter John Steele. Another body was reportedly found near the wreck in 1976. One body is still missing.

The job of salvaging the *Cedarville* was judged unfeasible. On August 24, 1965, Captain Joppich pleaded guilty to four charges of faulty seamanship; his master's license was suspended. In 1967, the *Cedarville's* owner, U.S. Steel Corporation, was ordered to pay damages to survivors and the families of the lost; in 1969, $2.4 million was awarded. Appeal followed appeal over many years before claimants received any money.

Launched as the *A.F. Harvey*, official number 226492, at River Rouge, Michigan, on Saturday, April 9, 1927, the ship was renamed *Cedarville* in 1957. This 8,575-gross-ton behemoth measured 588' 3" in length, 60' 2" in beam, and 27' 8" in draft. She was reboiled and restacked at Rogers City in 1961.

One of the best known and most popular shipwreck dive sites in the Straits Underwater Preserve, the *Cedarville* lies on her starboard side in 106' of water, rising to within 40' of the surface. Penetrate only if trained/experienced, and don't even think about seeing all of this enormous shipwreck in one dive!

Sharon Troxell explores the CEDARVILLE'S *tilted pilothouse.*   PHOTO BY CRIS KOHL.

Cleveland, City of

(#5 on the map on pp. 130-131)

VESSEL NAME:	CITY OF CLEVELAND
RIG:	wooden propeller (steambarge)
DIMENSIONS:	255' 7" x 39' 5" x 18' 4"
LAUNCHED:	Saturday, June 17, 1882; Cleveland, Ohio
DATE LOST:	Sunday, September 15, 1901
CAUSE OF LOSS:	stranded
CARGO:	ore
LIVES LOST:	none
GENERAL LOCATION:	between Tobermory and Manitoulin I., ON
DEPTH:	10' - 30'
ACCESS:	boat
DIVING SKILL LEVEL:	novice-intermediate
DIVING HAZARDS:	remote location, silting, winds from w. or n.
CO-ORDINATES:	Lat/Lon: 45.28.22 / 81.50.72
	Loran: 30256.2 / 48587.4

Winter came quite early at the end of 1901 when, at 4:00 A.M. on Sunday, September 15, a blinding snowstorm and southwest gale forced the large, twin-decked, four-masted, wooden steamer, *City of Cleveland*, off course and onto the rocks of Little Perseverance Island (a very small island just north of Perseverance Island), about 18 miles north of Tobermory, Ontario.

When the ship first struck the shoal, Captain Merwin Stone Thompson found that his damaged vessel was taking on water. The crew barely had time to launch the lifeboat, which they hastily released and quickly reached the safety of shore, where two tarpaulins became a tent and a fire was started. The *City of Cleveland,* loaded with 2,300 tons of iron ore from Michipicoten, Lake Superior, had been headed for the blast furnaces at Midland, Ontario, when she sank.

Four days later, the entire crew was still on the island and their food provisions were diminishing quickly. Their ration was a single piece of bread a day per man. Their ship was overdue, but no one knew what had happened to the vessel or to the crew. Exposed to the bad weather, the men were in great distress.

At that point, the passing steamer, *H.R. Dixon,* sighted the wreck of the *City of Cleveland.* Captain Baxter noticed that the seas had carried away the ship's cabin and a portion of the main deck, and that only the railing at the bow was visible above water. Captain Baxter, presuming that the crew had reached the island, lowered a boat to go in search of survivors. It did not get far when the *City of Cleveland's* crew appeared in their lifeboat, rowing like fiends to reach the *Dixon.* The steamer carried them to South Bay on Manitoulin Island, where the crew hired a tug to return to their wrecked ship in an attempt to recover some of their private property. as many of the men had lost everything except the clothes they wore. The vessel was completely underwater now, so they were not very successful. Returning to Killarney, the crew caught a steamer which took them to Sault Ste. Marie; from there, they headed to their respective homes.

Subsequent salvage efforts failed, but the ship was stripped of some of her large nautical components, and she was declared a total loss, with her final enrollment being surrendered at Cleveland on March 31, 1902.

The DETROIT FREE PRESS of August 6, 1902, reported that wrecking master Harris W. Baker was planning to undertake a salvage of the sunken steamer, *City of Cleveland,* which was lost in Georgian Bay the previous September, but by then, after a winter on the rocks, the ship was unsalvageable.

Built at Cleveland, Ohio, by Thomas Quayle and Sons and launched on June 17, 1882, the 1,609-gross-ton *City of Cleveland,* official number 126033, measured an impressive 255' 7" in length, 39' 5" in beam, and 18' 4" in draft.

The four-masted steamer, CITY OF CLEVELAND, *was miraculously salvaged after this June, 1889 sinking along Lake Superior's treacherous North Shore. The ship was not as lucky on Sunday morning, September 15, 1901, when she ended her career in a similar position, badly hogged, twisted, broken, and in deeper water, at Georgian Bay north of Tobermory, Ontario.* AUTHOR'S COLLECTION.

The 255-foot *City of Cleveland* started life as a four-masted schooner-barge, but was built along the lines of a steamer. She was one of the largest craft on the lakes (the famous, five-masted *David Dows,* the largest schooner in the world when she was launched at Toledo in 1881, was only ten feet longer than the *City of Cleveland* when she was built in 1882!). Two years after her launching, a steam engine and all its accompanying hardware were added to the *City of Cleveland,* converting her from a schooner-barge to a steambarge. The ship maintained her four masts and sails, and continued to sail for the Bradleys of Cleveland, who owned her until her demise in 1901.

The *City of Cleveland* is not only the largest shipwreck in the Tobermory area, but also the most impressive of all the shallow-water wrecks there. Tobermory is the scene of the creation of the first underwater park in the Great Lakes, set up in 1972 and now called the Fathom Five National Marine Park. With the *City of Cleveland's* bow in only ten feet of water, and her stern in 30', her decks and sides have been flattened by natural elements. The steam engine, massive boilers, rudder, and enormous propeller are quite interesting and photogenic. Occasionally charter boats out of Tobermory will run this far north to take scuba divers to the *City of Cleveland;* when they do, it's a full-day trip due to the distance, but it's well worth it. Try to pick a day when the wind conditions are right, ideally out of the east or south, or no wind at all. The prevailing western winds often stir up this open site. It's an easy dive, but be careful here; medical assistance is far away from this remote area.

The CITY OF CLEVELAND'S *enormous engineworks provide incredible exploration and underwater photography. The wreck sits in 10' to 30' of water.* PHOTO BY CRIS KOHL.

Goshawk

(#6 on the map on pp. 130-131)

VESSEL NAME:	GOSHAWK
RIG:	schooner-barge
DIMENSIONS:	180' x 32' 4" x 11' 5"
LAUNCHED:	1866; Cleveland, Ohio
DATE LOST:	Wednesday, June 16, 1920
CAUSE OF LOSS:	foundered
CARGO:	salt
LIVES LOST:	none
GENERAL LOCATION:	3 miles NE of Tawas Point, Michigan
DEPTH:	40' - 50'
ACCESS:	boat
DIVING SKILL LEVEL:	intermediate
DIVING HAZARDS:	disorientation, silting
CO-ORDINATES:	Lat/Lon: 44.14.95 / 83.24.96
	Loran: 31049.3 / 49055.5

No one knows why this schooner was named after a bird (a goshawk, or goose hawk, a member of the falcon family similar to a sparrow hawk), other than because these birds are fast and can maneuver skillfully. Perhaps the ship's owner hoped that his craft would be endowed with similar characteristics.

The *Goshawk* didn't maneuver very well at all when the ship, with a crew of eight, lost a man overboard on Tuesday, April 6, 1880, out of Chicago bound for Buffalo with grain on her first trip of the season. Sailor Frederick Cook, of Port Colborne, Ontario, fell off the boom of the mizzenmast just as night was descending upon the lakes and a late snowstorm began. He was tossed a plank to hold onto, but by the time the *Goshawk* had stopped and a lifeboat was launched, the victim had disappeared. Cook probably survived only a few minutes in Lake Michigan in early April before succumbing to hypothermia. The lifeboat with four crew in it then got lost looking for the victim. Before long, the three men left on board the *Goshawk* (the captain, second mate, and cook) gave up on the rescuers! They waited out the night. The next morning, with nary a soul in sight, they attempted to sail the *Goshawk* back to Chicago, but found that the three of them could not raise the anchor! Distress signals soon brought a tug to fetch them. How embarrassing to lose five of your eight crew on the first trip of the season only a few miles out of port! Captain Edward Morton was very much relieved when the four rescuers boarded the *Goshawk* the

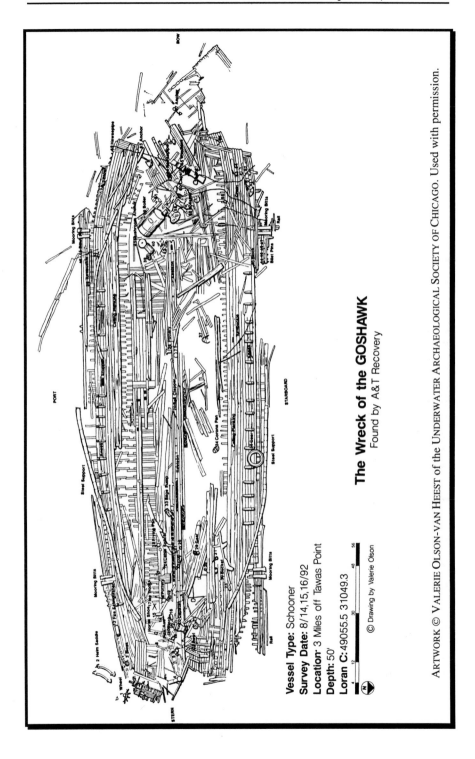

The Wreck of the GOSHAWK
Found by A&T Recovery

Vessel Type: Schooner
Survey Date: 8/14,15,16/92
Location: 3 Miles off Tawas Point
Depth: 50'
Loran C: 49055.5 31049.3

© Drawing by Valerie Olson

next evening; they had landed their lifeboat south of Chicago and flagged down a passing train to bring them back. Frederick Cook, however, was lost.

Birds such as goshawks usually have control of their movements in the wind. Not so the schooner *Goshawk!* Early on November 12, 1880, while a tug was towing the *Goshawk* into Buffalo harbor, the wind caught the schooner and forcefully pushed her into the docked schooner, *William Shupe.* Both schooners lost their bowsprits and jibbooms, while the *Shupe* also broke her rudder when she was forced against the pier. The *Goshawk* did not have a very good 1880.

However, the *Goshawk's* longevity far overshadowed her 1880 record. Built by Ira Lafrinier at Cleveland, Ohio, in 1866, the ship finally foundered in Lake Huron in 1920. Wooden ships averaged almost 20 years before they became unseaworthy, but the staunch *Goshawk* worked on the Great Lakes for 54 years!

The aging *Goshawk,* loaded with salt and towed by the tug, *P.J. Ralph* on a trip from Port Huron, Michigan, to Duluth, became waterlogged and sank on June 16, 1920, three miles northeast of Tawas Point, Michigan, the crew escaping in a lifeboat. This 501-gross-ton ship measured 180' x 32' 4" x 11' 5". The *Goshawk* was the oldest working vessel on the Great Lakes when she sank.

The schooner, GOSHAWK, *became a barge in 1902.*   GREAT LAKES MARINE COLLECTION OF THE MILWAUKEE PUBLIC LIBRARY/WISCONSIN MARINE HISTORICAL SOCIETY.

Located in 1990 by A&T Recovery of Chicago, the *Goshawk* was surveyed by an international team of amateur archaeologists, including the author, in August, 1992. Badly broken up in a broad area about 180' by 80', the *Goshawk* sits in 50' of water; only the rudder post sticks up taller than the average rise of 5'. The many artifacts include a windlass, capstan, bilge pump, donkey boiler, ship's wheel, and four anchors! The site is not usually buoyed.

ABOVE: *An international team of amateur, but dedicated, scuba divers and researchers surveyed the* GOSHAWK *site in August, 1992. The site, so full of artifacts, so broadly broken up, took nine divers several days to photograph/videotape/sketch. Here, a tape measure runs across a collapsed capstan.* BELOW: *The* GOSHAWK'S *wheel, one of the easily identified items, sits off the port quarter.* PHOTOS BY CRIS KOHL.

Grecian

(#7 on the map on pp. 130-131)

VESSEL NAME:	GRECIAN
RIG:	steel steamer
DIMENSIONS:	296' 2" x 40' 4" x 21' 1"
LAUNCHED:	Thursday, Feb. 26, 1891; Cleveland, Ohio
DATE LOST:	Friday, June 15, 1906
CAUSE OF LOSS:	foundered
CARGO:	none
LIVES LOST:	none (from 20 on board)
GENERAL LOCATION:	off Alpena, Michigan
DEPTH:	70' - 105'
ACCESS:	boat
DIVING SKILL LEVEL:	intermediate-advanced
DIVING HAZARDS:	depth, penetration, silting, hypothermia
CO-ORDINATES:	Lat/Lon: 44.58.04 / 83.12.01
	Loran: 30832.7 / 48713.2

The *Grecian* was tough --- she sank twice before she finally stayed put!

The steel freighter, *Grecian,* loaded with coal and sailing through thick fog, struck a rock and sank near DeTour, Michigan, in northern Lake Huron on June 7, 1906. Refloated and towed to DeTour, where her cargo was emptied, the ship received a temporary patch to keep her afloat until she reached the Detroit drydocks, where permanent repairs would be made. While slowly en route to Detroit, once again through thick fog, in tow of the steamer, *Sir Henry Bessemer,* at 9:00 P.M., Friday, June 15, 1906, the *Grecian* started to fill fast from water gushing into the hold. The ship sounded distress signals and sank "in 18 fathoms of water" off Alpena, MI. The temporary patch hadn't held. The *Bessemer* removed the *Grecian's* crew, who lost most of their personal property.

The lost ship, which belonged to the Pittsburgh Steamship Company, measured 296' 2" in length, 40' 4" in beam, and 21' 1" in draft. Launched at Cleveland, on Thursday, February 26, 1891 as hull #40 and official #86136, the 2,348-gross-ton *Grecian* was a duplicate of the *Saxon, German, Briton, Roman,* and *Norman,* the latter of which had also sunk near Alpena, on May 30, 1895. The TOLEDO BLADE of June 18, 1906, reported: "[The *Grecian*] will never be recovered as divers cannot work on her at the depth to which she is sunk...."

This popular site, usually buoyed, offers many on-deck sights at 70': tools, railing, bitts, machinery. The propeller sits in 105'. Below deck (there are three levels at the stern), deeper, for trained and experienced divers only, are the engine and boilers. The *Grecian* is broken in two, with the bow collapsed.

ABOVE: *The steel freighter,* GRECIAN, *underway on Lake Huron.* GREAT LAKES MARINE COLLECTION OF THE MILWAUKEE PUBLIC LIBRARY/WISCONSIN MARINE HISTORICAL SOCIETY. BELOW: *A diver dives straight down into the hatch of the* GRECIAN *in Michigan's Thunder Bay Underwater Preserve.* PHOTO BY CRIS KOHL.

India

(#8 on the map on pp. 130-131)

VESSEL NAME:	INDIA
RIG:	wooden steam barge
DIMENSIONS:	215' 9" x 36' 4" x 15'
LAUNCHED:	Tuesday, July 25, 1899; Garden Island, ON
DATE LOST:	Tuesday, September 4, 1928
CAUSE OF LOSS:	burned
CARGO:	none
LIVES LOST:	none
GENERAL LOCATION:	N side W. Mary I., E of Little Current, ON
DEPTH:	15' - 30'
ACCESS:	boat
DIVING SKILL LEVEL:	novice-intermediate
DIVING HAZARDS:	minimal: silting, remoteness
CO-ORDINATES:	Lat/Lon: 45.58.15 / 81.45.55 (old system)
	Loran: wreck location is marked on chart

The 29-year-old, oak-hulled steamer, *India,* caught on fire and burned to a total loss in the eastern end of the North Channel on Sept. 4, 1928. The ship, enroute from Lake Michigan to Dunkirk, New York, on Lake Erie, had lost her loading boom and began to take on water. The captain headed the *India* to Manitoulin Island for a replacement boom. The ship was anchored off West Mary Island when the second engineer discovered a fire under the boilers at 5:30 P.M., but it could not be controlled or extinguished. To this day, speculation is rife as to whether the fire was accidental or intentional. The 976-gross-ton ship, official #107735, measured 215' 9" in length, 36' 4" in beam, and 15' in draft.

The *India,* fourth steambarge in a series belonging to the Calvin fleet, was built at famous Garden Island off Kingston, Ontario, in 1899, and launched on Tuesday, July 25, 1899. In 1922, the *India* sank in the Welland Canal and was abandoned to Sarnia's famous Reid Wrecking Company, which salvaged the ship and sold her to Crawford & Company of Montreal. The Ramsey Brothers of Sault Ste. Marie, Ontario, purchased the *India* in 1926 and operated the ship until her demise in 1928. In 1929, a yacht ran afoul of this wreck and two lives were lost, while another yacht was damaged there in 1930.

Located just to the east of the northernmost point of land on small West Mary Island, about eight miles east of the town of Little Current, Ontario, the *India* rests in about 30' of water, rising to within about 15' of the surface, from which this huge wreck can usually be spotted from a boat such as an inflatable. This site can also be accessed by boat from the town of Killarney, Ontario. West Mary Island is about three miles northeast of Strawberry Light, North Channel. The triple expansion engine, twin boilers, and four-bladed propeller are the highlights of this shipwreck site. The huge, wooden hull lies bow west, stern east. Much wreckage lies off the main site.

ABOVE: *The steamer,* INDIA, *ablaze about eight miles east of Little Current, Ontario on September 4, 1928. She sank in 30 feet of water.*   GREAT LAKES MARINE COLLECTION OF THE MILWAUKEE PUBLIC LIBRARY/WISCONSIN MARINE HISTORICAL SOCIETY. BELOW: *The shallow* INDIA *wreck offers worthwhile sights.*   PHOTO BY CRIS KOHL.

Joyland

(#9 on the map on pp. 130-131)

VESSEL NAME:	JOYLAND; ex-WILLIAM A. HASKELL
RIG:	wooden propeller
DIMENSIONS:	250' 5" x 37' x 14' 3"
LAUNCHED:	Thursday, April 10, 1884; Detroit, Michigan
DATE LOST:	autumn, 1930
CAUSE OF LOSS:	burned, abandoned
CARGO:	sand
LIVES LOST:	none
GENERAL LOCATION:	Burnt Island, Manitoulin Island, Ontario
DEPTH:	1' - 16'
ACCESS:	shore
DIVING SKILL LEVEL:	basic
DIVING HAZARDS:	none; just practice safe diving; have fun!
CO-ORDINATES:	Lat/Lon: wreck is visible from shore
	Loran: wreck is visible from shore

Manitoulin Island in Canada's northern Lake Huron exudes humility and an old-fashioned pioneer spirit that belies the fact that it is the world's largest freshwater island. Considering the global fascination with extremes, this location has somehow remained a well-kept secret, in spite of its highway connection with mainland Ontario near Sudbury, and three-hour ferry connection with Tobermory at the tip of the Bruce Peninsula.

On Manitoulin Island, friendly, family-operated restaurants occupying turn-of-the-century buildings have not yet been replaced by the bright lights and neon indifference of shiny-new fast food eateries. Forests and farm fields roll for hours as one drives across this sparsely-populated outpost in Canada's most populous province. At the extreme southwest corner, the last commercial fishing community on the island still operates at Burnt Island; this is the location of the steamer, *Joyland,* a surprisingly interesting shallow water shipwreck.

Burnt Island is actually a peninsula now, and the gravel road from the main highway to the fishing community is well-maintained during the spring, summer, and early fall. However, there is a virtually overgrown, camouflaged road (or wide trail) that cuts off on the right (north) side of the road, running about one-quarter of a mile to the water's edge at Burnt Island Harbor. Driving a car there will require caution, but in a truck, this short jaunt shouldn't be a problem, making the *Joyland* a convenient, drive-to divesite. Walk in from the gravel road and check out the conditions before you venture in with a vehicle. This compact, rough roadway through the bush ends about 30' from the entry point to the shipwreck! One of the *Joyland's* two boilers sits rusting a bit further up along the shore.

The WILLIAM A. HASKELL, *later renamed the* JOYLAND, *was a large, wooden steamer with twin boilers and twin smokestacks.* GREAT LAKES MARINE COLLECTION OF THE MILWAUKEE PUBLIC LIBRARY/WISCONSIN MARINE HISTORICAL SOCIETY.

Built as the wooden steamer, *William A. Haskell,* at Detroit, Michigan, by the Detroit Dry Dock Company in 1884, with twin boilers and twin smokestacks, she carried package freight from Ogdensburg on the St. Lawrence River to the Great Lakes ports of Milwaukee and Chicago for most of her life (an inexplicable quirk of marine tradition requires the use of the feminine pronoun "she" for a vessel named after a man!). Measuring 250' in length, with 1,530 gross tons, this ship was conscientiously constructed with the enlarged Welland Canal in mind. Reconstructed between 1875 and 1887, this new canal allowed vessels up to 262' in length to bypass Niagara Falls between Lake Erie and Lake Ontario.

Canadian interests, namely the Montreal Transportation Company, purchased the *William A. Haskell* on March 12, 1916, and renamed her *Joyland;*

as such, she carried mostly wheat or barley cargoes to Montreal. On April 27, 1922, weighed down by a full load of corn, she ran aground on Little Round Island in the St. Lawrence River near Clayton, New York, after snapping her transmission line between the wheel and the rudder. The underwriters gloomily declared the *Joyland* a total loss, but she was released and rebuilt at Port Dalhousie, Ontario, where she was converted to a sandsucker in 1924, close to the end of her long career.

The *Joyland's* ultimate demise is neither dramatic nor particularly historic. The tired, old steamer simply ran aground at Manitoulin Island in 1926, and, although the Fox Island Sand & Gravel Company purchased the vessel from the salvage underwriters in hopes of restoring her to service, she remained aground. In the autumn of 1930, her huge, wooden superstructure caught fire and everything of wood above the waterline was destroyed, putting an end to salvage hopes. The *Joyland* was over 40 years of age when she stopped operating — certainly a respectable age for a wooden steamer.

There is an unconfirmed story that a man suffered a head injury on the *Joyland,* and that he died on Burnt Island as a result, but it is not known if this took place before or after the vessel was abandoned there.

Between 1926 and 1930, tourists visited the grounded JOYLAND *at Burnt Island for some adventurous exploring. The ship never returned to service, burning to the water line on site in late 1930.* GREAT LAKES MARINE COLLECTION OF THE MILWAUKEE PUBLIC LIBRARY/WISCONSIN MARINE HISTORICAL SOCIETY.

ABOVE: *Thanks to darkroom technology, a blow-up of the* JOYLAND'S *aft end when she was abandoned at Burnt Island in 1926 reveals two sandsucking scoops leaning over the stern railing.* GREAT LAKES MARINE COLLECTION OF THE MILWAUKEE PUBLIC LIBRARY/WISCONSIN MARINE HISTORICAL SOCIETY. BELOW: *These large scoops from the sandsucker,* JOYLAND, *can be examined at close range in about 15' of water by visiting scuba divers today.* PHOTO BY CRIS KOHL.

Huge gears and other machinery from the JOYLAND, *half buried in the Lake Huron sands, offer underwater exploration opportunities galore.*   PHOTO BY CRIS KOHL.

"My father removed one of the *Joyland's* boilers in 1934. It's rusting away on the shore now," revealed George Purvis (in a 1994 interview), the head of the commercial fishing family which first set up its operations at Burnt Island in the 1880's. That boiler acts as an above-water guide to this site today.

Numerous items of interest await visiting scuba divers at a maximum of 16' under the surface of Lake Huron's cool, blue waters. Lying about 100' offshore and perpendicular to it, with the bow pointing towards the shore, the *Joyland's* sights include an enormous, upright, four-bladed propeller, the second boiler which is still on the shipwreck, a massive, wooden hull, a multitude of spikes and bolts, as well as a prop shaft and related equipment. Large sandsucking scoops that trailed off the stern of the ship in her latter years of service as a sandsucker remain conspicuous at the site.

This wreck site was nicknamed "the honeymoon wreck" a number of years ago when a friend of mine, who first told me about it, explored Manitoulin Island on her honeymoon. She and her husband, an experienced scuba diver, went diving on the *Joyland* together.

When you arrive there and take a casual stroll around the area, you too will feel that there is something romantic about the place.

Mapledawn   (#10 on the map on pp. 130-131)

VESSEL NAME:	MAPLEDAWN; launched as MANOLA
RIG:	steel propeller
DIMENSIONS:	349' 1" x 40' 2" x 21' 3"
LAUNCHED:	Tuesday, January 21, 1890; Cleveland, Ohio
DATE LOST:	Sunday, November 30, 1924
CAUSE OF LOSS:	stranded
CARGO:	barley
LIVES LOST:	none
GENERAL LOCATION:	W side, Christian Island, Georgian Bay, ON
DEPTH:	10' - 30'
ACCESS:	boat
DIVING SKILL LEVEL:	novice
DIVING HAZARDS:	minimal; some jagged steel
CO-ORDINATES:	Lat/Lon: 44.51.52 / 80.14.50 (old system)
	Loran: 29655.3 / 48931.5

In shallow water on the northwest side of Christian Island in lower Georgian Bay, near the town of Penetanguishene, Ontario, lie the remains of one of the largest, and most photogenic and interesting, shipwrecks in the area.

The *Mapledawn* began life as the steel freighter named the *Manola* when she was launched on January 21, 1890, by the Globe Shipbuilding Company at Cleveland, Ohio. The Minnesota Steamship Company owned the ship from 1890 until 1901, when the Pittsburgh Steamship Company bought her. Purchased by the United States Shipping Board, Washington, D.C., for use in overseas waters in World War I, the steel *Manola* had to be cut in half in order to get the ship through the old Welland Canal in late 1918. The plan was to tow the two halves through the Welland, across Lake Ontario, and down the St. Lawrence River to Montreal, where the portions would be reunited and the ship could then sail to Europe. As cruel fate and harsh irony would have it, two things happened after the *Manola* was cut in two: the bow half sank in a storm with the loss of all 11 lives on board while being towed across Lake Ontario (see pp. 19-22), and World War I ended.

The orphaned tail end of the *Manola* sat at Montreal for several months before Davie Shipbuilding Ltd., of Lauzon, Quebec, constructed a new bow. The 2,404-gross-ton *Manola*, which then measured 249' 7" in length, 40' 2" in beam, and 21' 3" in draft, was purchased by the Canada Steamship Lines in 1920 and renamed *Mapledawn*. After a collision which sank the schooner-barge, *Brookdale,* at Montreal on June 1, 1923, the *Mapledawn* was rebuilt at Collingwood, Ontario. The 3,100-gross-ton vessel's new, impressive, and final, dimensions were 349' 1" in length, 40' 2" in beam, and 21' 3" in draft; 100' of length had simply been added to the ship.

On Nov. 30, 1924, a blinding snowstorm and the gales of November stranded the *Mapledawn,* loaded with barley for Port McNichol, on Christian Island. Two weeks of salvage recovered 75,000 bushels of barley, but the ship was declared a total loss. Some machinery was removed at that time, but considerably more of this shipwreck was salvaged in 1942 during the metal shortage in World War II. Ultimately, indirectly, this ship served in a World War.

A photograph taken in the 1960's depicts about half a dozen suited-up scuba divers taking a break sitting on the steel hull of the *Mapledawn* which emerges on a *Titanic*-like angle about 20' above the water. Less than 20 years later, Mother Nature had flattened or submerged the entire hull so that today, nothing of the *Mapledawn* can be viewed above water. The main sections of the twisted wreckage, which lie in 15' to 30', include the winch and chains, engine, and gigantic boilers. The propeller lies in 30' about 50' off the stern.

When you explore the remains of the *Mapledawn's* stern area, remember that the original bow half of what you are looking at is a couple of hundred miles away in Lake Ontario, and that those shipwreck remains, too, are one of the 100 best Great Lakes shipwrecks!

The wreck of the steel freighter, MAPLEDAWN, *is one of the most popular scuba dive sites in lower Georgian Bay. Named the* MANOLA *when launched in 1890, the original bow half of this shipwreck is one of the "100 best" in Lake Ontario (see pp. 19-22 for that unusual story!)* GREAT LAKES MARINE COLLECTION OF THE MILWAUKEE PUBLIC LIBRARY/WISCONSIN MARINE HISTORICAL SOCIETY.

Hundreds of scuba divers, often aboard charter boats from nearby Penetanguishene, Ontario, visit and explore the dramatic, twisted, steel remains of the wreck of the steamer, MAPLEDAWN, *in Georgian Bay every year.*   PHOTO BY CRIS KOHL.

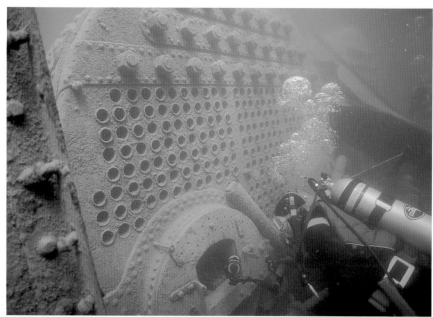

ABOVE: *The huge boiler from the* MAPLEDAWN *attracts visiting divers because of its overpowering size and photogenic qualities.* BELOW: *A diver glides past large gears lying in the shallows. The enormous amount of broken up metal at this site is spread over a large area, all of it offering interesting items to explore.* PHOTOS BY CRIS KOHL.

The steamer, *Mapledawn*

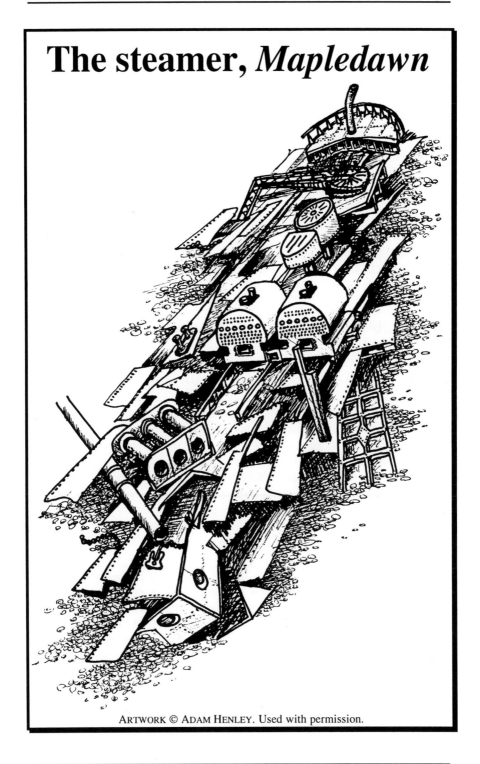

ARTWORK © ADAM HENLEY. Used with permission.

Marquette

(#11 on the map on pp. 130-131)

VESSEL NAME:	MARQUETTE
RIG:	bark (or barque)
DIMENSIONS:	139' 3" length
LAUNCHED:	1856; Newport (Marine City), Michigan
DATE LOST:	Thursday, November 28, 1867
CAUSE OF LOSS:	foundered
CARGO:	corn
LIVES LOST:	none
GENERAL LOCATION:	NE side, Hope Island, Georgian Bay, Ontario
DEPTH:	29' - 45'
ACCESS:	boat
DIVING SKILL LEVEL:	novice-intermediate
DIVING HAZARDS:	minimal; silting
CO-ORDINATES:	Lat/Lon:
	Loran: 29620.0 / 48917.0

On September 13, 1975, Gerry Lowden of Toronto discovered a completely intact sailing vessel of relatively early vintage off Hope Island in lower Georgian Bay. Situated in only 45' of clear, fresh water, this unidentified shipwreck was the talk of the diving community, with word of this unique discovery spreading like wildfire. Charter boats took divers to the site. Many private powerboats also arrived at the scene. Within a year, many of the irreplaceable artifacts had been stolen by people who apparently had to prove to the world what great scuba divers they were. They seemed to need "tokens of accomplishment" (to quote David Trotter) to prove themselves to their peers and to awestruck non-divers.

I have long talked about our limited, non-renewable shipwrecks in the Great Lakes, and our dependence upon their intactness to attract scuba divers to our specific underwater parks or preserves, to our waterfront communities, and to our Great Lakes scuba dive shops and charter boat services. As Rick Jackson, the first President and one of the founders of the marine conservation group named Save Ontario Shipwrecks (S.O.S.) put it in 1986, "...up until a few years ago, every known shipwreck in Ontario was being vandalized by divers....[Great Lakes] Sport diving, it seemed, was pre-occupied with its own self-destruction." Fortunately, divers today are better educated and more considerate.

This wreck was referred to for almost ten years as "the Hope Island Wreck." Research in 1985 by Ottawa's Ken McLeod, members of the Ontario

Marine Heritage Committee, and the late Dr. Richard Wright of the Institute for Great Lakes Research (now the Center for Archival Collections), Bowling Green State University, Ohio, proved this wreck to be that of the bark, *Marquette.*

No photograph of the MARQUETTE *has surfaced, but the* EMERALD, *pictured here, was similar to her. The 394-ton* EMERALD *measured 145' in length, compared to the 331-ton (426 tons old measure)* MARQUETTE'S *139' 3" length.*   AUTHOR'S COLLECTION.

The press reported on Wednesday, November 27, 1867: "BARQUE MARQUETTE ASHORE. The barque *Marquette,* bound from Chicago to Collingwood with a cargo of corn, is ashore at Hope Island, in Georgian Bay. Advices to this effect have been received by the insurance agents in Chicago. No particulars are given as to the condition of the vessel and her cargo."

The next day, November 28, 1867, an updated report read: "BARQUE MARQUETTE. It seems that this vessel sprung a leak during heavy weather on Lake Huron, and was run ashore on Hope Island, where she now lies full of water. She was bound for Collingwood with a cargo of corn from Chicago. It is feared that she will prove a total loss, as the lateness of the season must retard wrecking operations. The *Marquette* was built at Newport, Michigan, in 1856 and measures 426 tons burthen. She received large repairs in 1861, rated B1 [a medium condition insurance rating], and is worth about $15,000. She is owned in Chicago." Built by J. Bushnell, the ship, official #16396, was 139' 3" long.

Two wooden-stock bow anchors, with chains still connecting them to the windlass, attract immediate attention at this fascinating site. Other attractions include a samson post, double framing, centerboard box and winch, main mast step, a capstan inside the hull, hatch coaming, planksheers, transom and rudder.

The staunch, oak hull of the schooner, MARQUETTE, *is almost completely intact. These chains, bolted to the lower bow stem, drop and disappear into the sandy bottom of Georgian Bay in Lake Huron. Originally they angled upwards tautly to the ship's bowsprit, which is missing, likely broken off by the storm which sank this vessel. The site still contains anchors, chains, the windlass, the centerboard box, and centerboard winch, among many other items.* PHOTO BY CRIS KOHL.

The schooner, *Marquette*

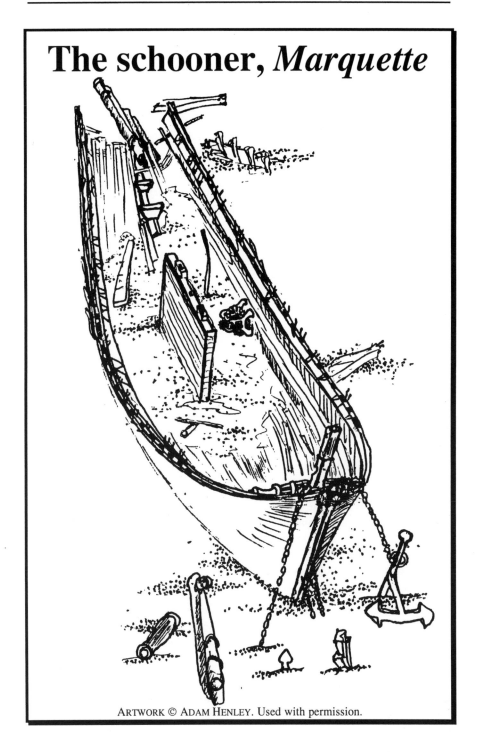

ARTWORK © ADAM HENLEY. Used with permission.

Mary Alice B.

(#12 on the map on pp. 130-131)

VESSEL NAME:	MARY ALICE B.; launched as QUINTUS
RIG:	steel-hulled tug
DIMENSIONS:	62' 1" x 17' x 6' 3"
LAUNCHED:	1931; Duluth, Minnesota
DATE LOST:	Friday, September 5, 1975
CAUSE OF LOSS:	foundered
CARGO:	none
LIVES LOST:	none
GENERAL LOCATION:	about six miles SE of Port Sanilac, MI
DEPTH:	82' - 98'
ACCESS:	boat
DIVING SKILL LEVEL:	intermediate-advanced
DIVING HAZARDS:	depth, silting, penetration, hypothermia
CO-ORDINATES:	Lat/Lon: 43.22.34 / 82.26.31
	Loran: 30790.8 / 49520.5

The tugboat, *Mary Alice B.,* is one of Lake Huron's newest, or youngest, shipwrecks, but this interesting vessel has become, in a very short period of time, one of the lake's favorite destinations for scuba divers.

The *Mary Alice B.* sank on Friday, September 5, 1975, but it took scuba divers years to locate this diminutive shipwreck. In 1986, Michigan divers Wayne Brusate and Gary Biniecki decided to embark upon the supposedly simple task of searching for and locating this tug, but instead, found a much bigger prize: the steel freighter, *Regina,* which had vanished with all hands in the worst storm in recorded Great Lakes history, the Great Storm of November, 1913 (read about the *Regina* later in this chapter).

A year later, Wayne again went looking for the *Mary Alice B.,* but instead found the historic tug named *Sport,* one of the first vessels built utilizing steel construction, and the victim of a fierce storm in December, 1920 (read about the *Sport* later in this chapter).

The shy and evasive *Mary Alice B.* was launched in 1931 as the *Quintus* in Duluth Minnesota, where the 65-foot steel tug was constructed by the Marine Iron and Ship Building Company for the U.S. Army Corps of

Engineers. First assigned in Buffalo, New York, on Lake Erie, the ship was stationed in Detroit by 1951.

After 31 years of employment with the U.S. Army corps of Engineers, the *Quintus* was sold in 1962 to private enterprise, Detroit's Fuller Towing Company, which renamed her the *Bonanka,* after the owner's three daughters, <u>Bo</u>nnie, <u>Nan</u>cy, and <u>Ka</u>thy. The vessel was remeasured from her original dimensions of 65' 6" x 18' 4" x 7' 8" to 62' 1" x 17' x 6' 3". *Bonanka's* 235 horsepower engine could easily move her 46 gross (31 net) tons up and down the Detroit River working mostly at towing jobs.

The steel tugboat, MARY ALICE B., *when she was still the* BONANKA *(1962 to 1975). She was launched as the* QUINTUS *in 1931.*   PHOTO COURTESY BILL HOEY.

In the mid-1960's, the *Bonanka* changed owners again, transferring to Malcolm Marine of Marine City, Michigan, for use mainly in lower Lake Huron and the St. Clair River. Two highlights of the tug's career at this stage was the salvage of the cargo from the grounded freighter, *Nordmeer,* in Lake Huron in 1967 (read about the *Nordmeer* later in this chapter), and the installation of the Detroit water intake in the same lake.

Then, in 1972, the aging *Bonanka* again transferred ownership, this time to a private individual in Cleveland, Ohio, on Lake Erie, who promptly renamed the ship *Lomax.* In early 1975, the tug's final owner, Peter Bill and Associates of Detroit, purchased the vessel and renamed her the *Mary Alice B.*

Under her new name and new owner, the *Mary Alice B.* lasted less than one season.

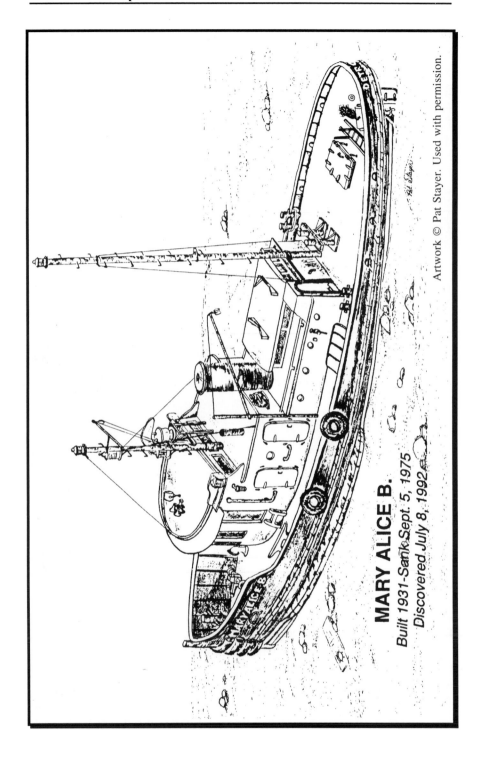

MARY ALICE B.
Built 1931-Sank Sept. 5, 1975
Discovered July 8, 1992

Artwork © Pat Stayer. Used with permission.

ABOVE: *Co-discoverer of the tug,* MARY ALICE B., *Pat Stayer, explores the wheelhouse of this upright, intact shipwreck. The wooden ship's wheel is definitely the focal point of this shipwreck.* BELOW: *Pat Stayer browses past the* MARY ALICE B.*'s name still clear on the port bow.* PHOTOS BY CRIS KOHL.

Returning from another salvage expedition to upper Lake Huron on Friday, September 5, 1975, the *Mary Alice B.,* in tow of the tug, *Dolphin I,* became waterlogged and started sinking in the middle of the night off Port Sanilac, Michigan. The crew of the *Dolphin I* manned two pumps in an effort to control the rising water in the *Mary Alice B.,* but when water poured through the gunwales, they jumped back onto their tug and cut their doomed partner loose. She sank stern first, air pressure blowing out all of her pilothouse windows as she disappeared from view.

The elusive resting place of the *Mary Alice B.* finally became known when Michigan divers, researchers, and charterboat operators Jim and Pat Stayer, and buddy David Fritz, picked up this shipwreck on their sidescan sonar on July 8, 1992. They surveyed, photographed, sketched, and videotaped this vessel in its entirety, including its story in their book, SHIPWRECKS OF SANILAC.

Since that time, scuba divers from afar have made this site one of their main destinations in lower Lake Huron. The thrilling appeal of an upright, intact shipwreck in a maximum of 98' of clear fresh water cannot be overestimated.

A large, wooden ship's wheel in the easily accessible pilothouse catches divers' attentions immediately, even from outside the wreck, where one can gaze inside through one of the many glassless windows. Access to the ship's galley rewards divers with views of dishes still stacked in their designated places.

The engine room is penetrable by experienced divers only, and even for them, this area tends to silt up quite easily, causing potential disorientation.

The best time to scuba dive the Great Lakes is in May or June --- if you can stand the cold! By May, the winter ice has just melted, and visibility will be at its best, around 40 to 50 feet. Algae blooms of late summer sometimes reduce the visibility to about ten feet, although this lower limit is the exception rather than the rule.

The *Mary Alice B.* rests within the boundaries of Michigan's Sanilac Shores Underwater Preserve, and is marked by a mooring buoy every spring, usually placed there by Jim and Pat Stayer, who, with others, were instrumental in the creation of this preserve several years ago. The Michigan Bottomlands Act and the state's underwater preserve system help ensure that these shipwrecks and their artifacts remain intact on the lake bottom for future visitors to appreciate.

Whether you visit the *Mary Alice B.* in May or in October, the excitement of exploring a shipwreck that actually still resembles a ship will be well worth the effort of getting yourself out there. Scuba charter boats operate regularly out of Lexington and Port Sanilac, Michigan, the wreck lying a couple of miles offshore about halfway between those two Great Lakes seaports.

Merrill, John B.

(#13 on the map on pp. 130-131)

VESSEL NAME:	JOHN B. MERRILL
RIG:	three-masted schooner
DIMENSIONS:	189' x 34' x 13' 3"
LAUNCHED:	1873; Milwaukee, Wisconsin
DATE LOST:	Saturday, October 14, 1893
CAUSE OF LOSS:	foundered
CARGO:	coal
LIVES LOST:	none
GENERAL LOCATION:	south side of Drummond Island, Michigan
DEPTH:	30' - 80'
ACCESS:	boat
DIVING SKILL LEVEL:	intermediate-advanced
DIVING HAZARDS:	depth, silting, entanglement, hypothermia
CO-ORDINATES:	Lat/Lon: 45.54.98 / 83.43.91
	Loran: 30880.28 / 48191.97

As the schooner, *John B. Merrill,* pulled away from the dock in Buffalo, New York, loaded with coal for Marquette, a black cat which Capt. Boyce's wife had befriended made a daring ten-foot leap off the ship onto the dock. Recognizing a sure sign that bad luck lay ahead, the ship sailed anyway.

A few days later, on Saturday, October 14, 1893, a severe storm shook the entire Great Lakes area, sinking 11 ships, one of which was the three-masted schooner, *John B. Merrill.* She was being towed by the steamer, *F.E. Spinner,* both laden with hard coal, when the schooner broke away from the *Spinner* and ran onto the rocks of Holdridge Shoal, off Drummond Island about 12 miles east of Detour, Michigan. All hands, including the captain's wife and their family dog (felines apparently have a big edge over canines when it comes to sensing disaster), were rescued by local commercial fishermen after about a day aground. On November 1, 1893, the PORT HURON DAILY TIMES reported that the ship "had broken up and nothing remains to show where she struck."

The DULUTH NEWS TRIBUNE of October 18, 1893, and other local newspapers, printed lists of losses in this severe storm, with locality and values:

Steamer *Dean Richmond,* foundered off Dunkirk, $110,000 (see pp. 119-121).
Steamer *Wocoken,* foundered Lake Erie, $75,000.
Schooner *James D. Sawyer,* stranded Charlevoix, $34,000.
Schooner *Minnehaha,* stranded Onekama, Mich., $48,000.
Schooner *Hunter,* stranded New Buffalo, Mich., $1,800.

Schooner *Volunteer,* stranded Port Crescent, $2,000.
Tug *Acme,* foundered Lake Huron, $25,000.
Yacht *Enterprise,* stranded Georgian Bay, $1,000.
Schooner *Annie Falconer,* ashore Lake Ontario, $6,000.[Recovered in 1894]
Barge *Knight Templar,* stranded Cheboygan, $4,000.
Schooner *John B. Merrill,* ashore Drummond Id., $20,000.

In addition to these marine losses, which claimed over 50 lives, this storm caused a railway wreck at Wellville, Ohio, in which four people were killed.

The 640-gross-ton *John B. Merrill,* official number 75592 and built by Allan McClelland & Company at Milwaukee, Wisconsin in 1873, lasted 20 years on the Great Lakes. She measured 189' in length, 34' in beam, and 13' 3" in draft. Her first certificate of enrollment was issued to owner J. Porter on August 29, 1873 when the ship was brand new, and her last certificate of enrollment was surrendered at Buffalo, on October 19, 1893, citing the cause of surrender as "Total wreck." The Cornell brothers (owners) had her fully insured.

Discovered in 1992 by John Steele and Sam Mareci, the wreck of the schooner, *John B. Merrill,* is the most popular divesite in this infrequently-visited area. Her anchor lies in about 30', with chain cascading down to 65' where the forward keelson is located. Evidence exists that the ship broke up violently on the rocks above, then slid down to these depths. The hull's starboard side lies with the outside facing up in about 70'; the port side lies with the inside facing up at about 75'. Meanwhile, decking has been turned upside down near the bow area in 80'. Because the ship is broken up, there is no actual penetration opportunity/danger. Beware of loose overhangs near the bow. The debris field is fairly expansive, so go exploring!

Drawing of the three-masted schooner, JOHN B. MERRILL, *lost off Drummond Island, Lake Huron, on October 14, 1893. No lives were lost.*   AUTHOR'S COLLECTION.

Montana

(#14 on the map on pp. 130-131)

VESSEL NAME:	MONTANA
RIG:	wooden steamer
DIMENSIONS:	236' 3" x 36' x 14'
LAUNCHED:	Tuesday, June 18, 1872; Port Huron, MI
DATE LOST:	Monday, September 7, 1914
CAUSE OF LOSS:	burned
CARGO:	none
LIVES LOST:	none (from 14 on board)
GENERAL LOCATION:	off Alpena, Michigan
DEPTH:	33' - 74'
ACCESS:	boat
DIVING SKILL LEVEL:	intermediate
DIVING HAZARDS:	depth, silting, disorientation
CO-ORDINATES:	Lat/Lon: 45.58.97 / 83.15.81
	Loran: 30856.2 / 48699.9

The *Montana's* launch at Port Huron, Michigan, on Tuesday, June 18, 1872, was such an embarrassment that, had the owner been a superstitious sort, he would have sold the ship immediately. It took three days to launch!

Constructed by Alexander Muir, with A/W. Smith serving as master carpenter, the 1,535-gross-ton, wooden steamer, *Montana,* was scheduled to be launched on Saturday (a day on which a large crowd would certainly be present), June 15, 1872. As it turned out, the weather was excellent, the crowd was large and enthusiastic, and the ship was ready to go. When workers removed the stops from under the skids, the *Montana* started to slide slowly down the angled ramp, as planned for this spectacular side-launch on Port Huron's Black River. However, the low water level that June and an enormous mud bank between the ship and the water stopped the steamer dead in her tracks. Three local tugs were hired to pull the new ship into the water. Dredges removed some mud. Pontoons were attached to the steamer. But the *Montana* would not budge. Finally, the powerful wrecking tug, *Prindiville,* was contracted to assist and, with the other tugs, managed to launch the *Montana* at 5:30 P.M., Tuesday, June 18, 1872, three days in the making and considerably over-budget. This was the longest launch in Great Lakes history. The huge crowd had thinned considerably by then.

The *Montana,* however, enjoyed one of the longest, most productive, and least troubled careers on the Great Lakes, first as a combination passenger and freight ship, then as a bulk freighter. She operated for an incredible 42 years!

The steamer, Montana, *operated on the Great Lakes for 42 years before her demise five miles off Alpena, Michigan, in 1914.* Great Lakes Marine Collection of the Milwaukee Public Library/Wisconsin Marine Historical Society.

The *Montana's* wooden hull, decking, housing, and below-deck appointments had dried up considerably over the course of four decades, and finally, on late Sunday evening, September 6, 1914, while the empty, 236-foot-long ship was steaming to John Island, Ontario, for a load of lumber, she caught on fire.

Captain George C. Burns stated, "The fire started in the forward end and gained headway so rapidly we had no time to investigate its origin." The new, metal yawl boat was launched, since the tinder-dry steamer was speedily covered with flames. Captain Burns stood on the rail of his burning ship while the mate ensured that all the crew were in the yawl boat; to make doubly sure, Burns had his chief engineer also count heads. By the time he was satisfied that every man had escaped the doomed ship, Capt. Burns' clothing was ablaze and his face was singed. He jumped, then was taken into the yawl; his injuries were minimal.

By this time, it was around 9:00 P.M. A group of spectators had gathered on the shore near Alpena, watching the blaze at sea, and the Thunder Bay Island lifesaving crew had launched their rescue boat. The *Montana's* crew, rowing furiously against heavy seas towards shore, was rescued by the passing steamer, *Alpena,* and taken to Alpena. The lifesaving crew, unaware that the *Montana's* crew had been rescued, bobbed around the burning ship for five hours, ready to save anyone who might be in need of rescue. The *Montana* sank just before 2:00 A.M., Monday, September 7, 1914. Her crew was well-treated at Alpena, and they caught a train home to Detroit the next day (except for one man, who was given a job as a fireman on the rescuing steamer, *Alpena!)*

Even in her old age, the *Montana* was valued at $12,000; she was partially insured. The press reported that "...There is said to be about 12 fathoms of water where she sank, which would make recovery of the hull and machinery almost too difficult to be undertaken." Twelve fathoms (72') was pretty accurate.

Years later, the *Montana* became one of the most popular scuba dive sites in the Alpena area. Although the ship burned to the waterline, the hull is intact and upright, with items such as windlass, anchor chain, capstan, boiler, rudder, and huge, four-bladed propeller. The highlight is the towering engine.

A scuba diver explores the intricacies of the most conspicuous feature of the MONTANA *shipwreck, namely the upright double steeple compound engine which towers more than 40' above the lake bottom and comes to within about 33' of the surface. The wreck, which burned to a total loss on Sept. 6-7, 1914, lies in Michigan's popular Thunder Bay Underwater Preserve at Alpena.* PHOTO BY CRIS KOHL.

New York   (#15 on the map on pp. 130-131)

VESSEL NAME:	NEW YORK
RIG:	wooden steambarge
DIMENSIONS:	184' 8" x 29' 4" x 11' 8"
LAUNCHED:	September, 1856; Buffalo, New York
DATE LOST:	Saturday, October 14, 1876
CAUSE OF LOSS:	foundered
CARGO:	three barges in tow
LIVES LOST:	1 (from a total of 16 on board)
GENERAL LOCATION:	12.3 miles from Port Sanilac, Michigan
DEPTH:	100' - 118'
ACCESS:	boat
DIVING SKILL LEVEL:	advanced
DIVING HAZARDS:	depth, silting, disorientation, hypothermia
CO-ORDINATES:	Lat/Lon: 43.36.23 / 82.28.24
	Loran: 30761.0 / 49411.9

The scuba divers flipped a coin to see who, from their group, would be the first to descend to this unidentified object rising about 20' from the 118-foot depth marking the bottom of Lake Huron. Pat Stayer and Tim Juhl won. When they reached the 100' depth, the silhouette of an enormous boiler awaited them in the near distance. Pat almost descended into the gaping hole left by a missing smokestack. Further along the deck, they looked up and were startled to see a wooden arch hovering over their heads --- the intact, wooden arch often used as bracing in early Great Lakes steamers.

This was in August, 1988. A month earlier, this group, consisting of Gary Biniecki, Tim Juhl, and Jim and Pat Stayer (collectively known then as the Great Lakes Shipwrecks Exploration Group), had located their first shipwreck, the large schooner-barge, *Checotah,* which was only a few hundred feet away from this new discovery! Accidentally picked up on their depth sounder while searching around the area of the *Checotah,* possibly for the *Cheetah's* missing stern cabin, this find turned out to be a totally different shipwreck!

But 14 months later, they still did not know the identity of their second find. They had finished the research and survey work on the *Checotah,* their first discovery. A steam gauge engraved with "Davis Patent, July 2, 1867" offered the first clue to dating the mystery vessel as having sunk after 1867. Later discoveries (other gauges, a steam whistle, a hand cart, a large dinner platter) offered no clues to the ship's identity. The team focused on the unusual, early engine.

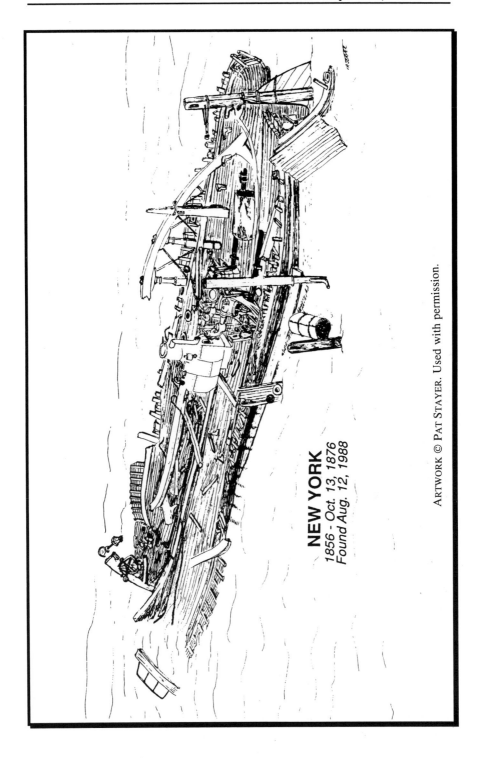

NEW YORK
1856 - Oct. 13, 1876
Found Aug. 12, 1988

ARTWORK © PAT STAYER. Used with permission.

An expert at the Smithsonian Institution in Washington, D.C., offered some assistance, and referred the team to C. Patrick Labadie, the curator of Duluth's Canal Park Marine Museum and a man knowledgeable about early steamers. Pat Labadie located information in his files about the dual oscillating steam engine of the steamer, *New York*, which had steam valves designed by H.O. Perry. The dive team had suspected that the wreck could be that of the *New York,* but they lacked sufficient evidence to prove it. On October 8, 1989, Pat Stayer located a tiny brass plaque on the wreck's engine which read "H.O. Perry Patent -- March 25, 1856." The steamer, *New York,* had been identified!

Built by Bidwell, Banta & Co., and launched in September, 1856, at Buffalo for owner S.D. Caldwell of Dunkirk, the 833-gross-ton steamer, *New York*, measuring 184' 8" in length, 29' 4" in beam, and 11' 8" in draft, ran as a passenger steamer for 18 years. After being damaged in a Lake Erie stranding on Nov. 3, 1874, the *New York* was refitted as a lumber trade steambarge.

The *New York* left Cove Island, Ontario, on Friday, the 13th of Oct., 1876, towing three barges, all four ships lumber-laden. In mountainous seas that night off Point aux Barques, Michigan, the towlines parted and the *New York* began leaking badly. She headed for the shallows, but sank while still in deep water. Capt. Michael Galvin controlled the crowded yawl boat containing the 15 men and one woman from the *New York* for almost six hours before they were rescued by the small schooner, *Nemesis,* and its four crewmembers. During the harrowing, dangerous rescue, William Sharks, a fireman on the *New York,* fell overboard and was drowned. The crowded, little *Nemesis* sailed on to Port Huron. The three vessels that the *New York* had been towing arrived safely there later.

Definitely the highlights of a *New York* dive are the engine and arch.

The wooden steamer, NEW YORK, *as she looked while underway in 1856. No photograph of this early ship has been found to date, but one could be waiting silently inside an old family album.* ARTWORK © ROGER DEAN. *Used with permission.*

Nordmeer (#16 on the map on pp. 130-131)

VESSEL NAME:	NORDMEER
RIG:	steel freighter
DIMENSIONS:	470' 8" x 60' 9" x 28' 2"
LAUNCHED:	1954; Flensburg, West Germany
DATE LOST:	Saturday, November 19, 1966
CAUSE OF LOSS:	stranded
CARGO:	990 coils of heavy steel worth $1 million
LIVES LOST:	none (of 43 on board)
GENERAL LOCATION:	7 miles NNE Thunder Bay Island Light, MI
DEPTH:	0' - 40'
ACCESS:	boat
DIVING SKILL LEVEL:	novice-intermediate
DIVING HAZARDS:	penetration, silting, disorientation
CO-ORDINATES:	Lat/Lon: 45.08.13 / 83.09.33
	Loran: 30790.7 / 48634.7

The German motorship, *Nordmeer* (meaning "North Sea"), was built in 1954 at Flensburg, Germany. On Saturday night, November 19, 1966, the 470-foot-long, steel freighter, *Nordmeer,* ran aground on the Thunder Bay Island shoals in Lake Huron about 20 miles east of Alpena, Michigan. The winds were light and the night was clear; it was clearly human error that allowed the unforgiving shoal to tear holes into the ship's bottom in the course of a few seconds. The 8,683-gross-ton freighter, which had a draft of 26', sank in 22' of water. A later inquiry ruled that the ship's first mate had made a wrong turn.

The modern ore carrier, *Samuel Mather,* picked up 35 of the *Nordmeer's* 43 crew. The captain and seven hand-picked men who had remained on board were quickly removed by the U.S. Coast Guard several days later when a wild storm threatened to kill them. After salvage crews successfully recovered most of the *Nordmeer's* cargo of heavy, coiled steel, the vessel split in two.

Until the early-1990's, part of the wreck of the *Nordmeer* was still above water, visible from several miles away. Mother Nature has seen to it that the ravages of wind, waves, and ice have totally submerged this careless vessel. The engine room, with its photogenic diesel engine, and other parts of the *Nordmeer* are no longer as safe to enter now. Caution, training and experience are vital for safe penetration diving. Examining the outside perimeter of this shipwreck also makes an excellent dive. A wooden salvage barge lies storm-sunk on the *Nordmeer's* port side. The *Nordmeer* makes for fascinating exploration.

The 470-foot German freighter, NORDMEER, *with the mountains of Norway in the background in this company photograph, was owned by the Nordstern Steam Ship Company of Hamburg.* GREAT LAKES MARINE COLLECTION OF THE MILWAUKEE PUBLIC LIBRARY/WISCONSIN MARINE HISTORICAL SOCIETY.

The final crewmembers were removed from the NORDMEER *on Nov. 29, 1966.*

ABOVE: *This 1986 photograph was taken almost 20 years after the* NORDMEER *stranded. Unfortunately, because of the natural ravages of ice, wind, and waves, much of the wreck's superstructure now lies submerged.* BELOW: *Diver Roy Pickering examines the* NORDMEER'S *diesel engine below deck.* PHOTOS BY CRIS KOHL.

North Star

(#17 on the map on pp. 130-131)

VESSEL NAME:	NORTH STAR
RIG:	steel propeller
DIMENSIONS:	299' 5" x 40' 8" x 21' 6"
LAUNCHED:	Tuesday, February 12, 1889; Cleveland, OH
DATE LOST:	Wednesday, November 25, 1908
CAUSE OF LOSS:	collision with the NORTHERN QUEEN
CARGO:	flour, wheat, and shingles
LIVES LOST:	none (from 22 on board)
GENERAL LOCATION:	5.3 miles off Port Sanilac, Michigan
DEPTH:	80' - 103'
ACCESS:	boat
DIVING SKILL LEVEL:	advanced
DIVING HAZARDS:	depth, penetration, silting, nets
CO-ORDINATES:	Lat/Lon: 43.23.97 / 82.26.50
	Loran: 30787.3 / 49508.1

Six steel ships were constructed in 1888-1889 by the Globe Iron Works Company of Cleveland, Ohio, for the Northern Steamship Company, and all six were exactly alike. These 2,476-gross-ton vessels measured 299' 5" in length, 40' 8" in beam, and 21' 6" in draft, and each carried three pole spars and one smokestack. Their names reflected their ownership: *North Wind, North Star, Northern Light, Northern Queen, Northern King,* and *Northern Wave.*

Of these six, the *North Star* met her demise first. Coincidentally, another "100 best" shipwreck is one of her sister ships, the *North Wind* (see pp. 194-195), which happened to be the last of these six to sail the inland seas.

Launched on Tuesday, February 12, 1889, the *North Star* experienced an unfortunate encounter within months of sliding down the ramp. On June 19, 1889, she collided with the 260-foot steamer, *Charles J. Sheffield,* west of Whitefish Point on Lake Superior in heavy fog, sending the *Sheffield* plunging into the depths within eight minutes. The *North Star,* however, had pressed her bow to the *Sheffield's* side after the impact of the collision, giving the latter's crew time to board the *North Star* before their ship sank. In May, 1890, a judge held both ships equally at fault and adjusted the costs of damages accordingly. The Northern Steamship Company, owners of the *North Star,* were not satisfied with the verdict and appealed the case to a higher court. The *North Star-Sheffield* case spent years in litigation, concluding with both ships being equally at fault.

Later that year, in early October, 1889, the *North Star* stranded briefly on Topsail Island shoal, damaging two of her bottom plates and requiring repairs in drydock. Her first year afloat had not passed without major incidents. However, not all of the news was negative. On October 15, 1889, the *North Star* arrived at Duluth from Sault Ste. Marie, having made that 400-mile run in 28 hours and 40 minutes, the fastest time ever made by any ship.

The next 17 years passed without major incidents for the *North Star.* Her ownership changed to the Mutual Transit Company of Buffalo in 1903, and a minor collision with the steamer, *William G. Pollock,* on Lake Superior on September 19, 1908, damaged both ships only slightly.

The steamer, NORTH STAR, *was almost 300' long.* GREAT LAKES MARINE COLLECTION OF THE MILWAUKEE PUBLIC LIBRARY/WISCONSIN MARINE HISTORICAL SOCIETY.

At five o'clock in the morning of Wednesday, November 25, 1908, the *North Star* ran upbound through dense fog while enroute from Duluth to Buffalo with a load of flour, wheat, and shingles. About five miles southeast of Port Sanilac, Michigan, one of her sister ships, the *Northern Queen,* also owned by Mutual Transit and steaming equally fast with similar disregard for visibility conditions, collided with the *North Star*, gouging a gigantic gash into the latter's starboard bow area abreast of the pilot house. The *North Star,* her builder's hull number 23 and official number 130435, sank "in sixteen fathoms" so quickly that Captain D.L. Cartwright and his crew barely had time to launch lifeboats and escape to the sister ship, which transported them to Port Huron. Neither captain discussed the accident, saying only that the fog was so thick that they did not sight each other until it was too late to avoid a collision. The *North Star* and her cargo were valued at $250,000; she carried a total of $120,000 in insurance. Another sister ship, the *Northern Light*, which was also owned by Mutual Transit, carried the crew to Buffalo. A new *North Star* was launched in 1909.

The broken remains of the steel steamer, *North Star,* lie in 80' to 103' of water about 5.3 miles southeast of Michigan's Port Sanilac harbor. The bow faces southwest, and this wreck is usually buoyed at the engine in the stern area. The triple expansion steam engine has remained stalwartly upright, rising almost 30' from the lake bottom, while the rest of the wreck seems to be falling apart around it. The twin boilers lie along the starboard side of the shipwreck not far from the engine. Behind the engine lies the relatively intact stern section, angled to starboard, with a capstan in mid-deck and a four-bladed propeller off the back, with a spare propeller blade lying on the lake bottom along the starboard quarter. Several open hatches in midship offer penetration possibilities for the trained, prepared, and experienced. Winches, pumps, and other machinery are mounted between hatch openings. The intact bow section, almost completely broken off and lying on its own because of the collision point on the starboard bow, yields a capstan, two sets of bits, and an anchor caught under the wreckage on the lake floor. A debris field lies along the starboard side.

The wreck of the *North Star* was located in the 1960's by John Steele of Waukegan, Illinois, a well-known wreck hunter who spent four decades researching, locating, and exploring scores of Great Lakes shipwrecks.

The twisted steel wreckage of the steamer, NORTH STAR, *which sank in a 1908 collision with her sister ship and sits in about 103' of water, offers opportunities for deep exploration and dramatic photography.* PHOTO BY CRIS KOHL.

North Star
Sank November 25, 1908

ARTWORK © PAT STAYER. Used with permission.

North Wind   (#18 on the map on pp. 130-131)

VESSEL NAME:	NORTH WIND
RIG:	steel propeller
DIMENSIONS:	299' 5" x 40' 8" x 21' 6"
LAUNCHED:	Tuesday, July 31, 1888; Cleveland, Ohio
DATE LOST:	Thursday, July 1, 1926
CAUSE OF LOSS:	stranded
CARGO:	grain
LIVES LOST:	none (from more than 20 on board)
GENERAL LOCATION:	Robertson Rock, North Channel, Ontario
DEPTH:	80' - 110'+
ACCESS:	boat
DIVING SKILL LEVEL:	advanced
DIVING HAZARDS:	depth, penetration, silting, hypothermia
CO-ORDINATES:	Lat/Lon: 46.03.45 / 82.12.56
	Loran:

By the summer of 1926, the *North Wind* was the only vessel remaining on the Great Lakes from the fleet of six, mighty, sister ships launched for the Northern Steamship Company in 1888-89. The *North Star* had been the first to disappear from sight, sinking in Lake Huron after a collision with her sister ship, the *Northern Queen,* on November 25, 1908 (see pp. 190-193). The *Northern Queen* was sold for saltwater use in 1917 and was scrapped there in 1925. The *Northern Light* was sold for saltwater use in 1917, sinking off the Florida Keys on November 8, 1930. The *Northern King* and the *Northern Wave* were both sold for saltwater use in 1917, and both were scrapped there in early 1926.

The lonely, aging sister, the *North Wind,* did not have long to wait before joining her siblings. On Thursday, July 1, 1926, she stranded on Robertson Rock, near Clapperton Island in Lake Huron's North Channel, and slid into deep water within two hours. No lives were lost when the crew took to the lifeboats and rowed to the town of Little Current, Ontario, where one of the crewmembers sold his lifeboat to a local resident and then promptly disappeared! The *North Wind* saw six years of service (1917-1923) on the Atlantic Ocean out of Boston. The 299' ship had been cut in half for transit through the Welland Canal's 260' locks in 1917, and again for her return to the Great Lakes in 1923.

The *North Wind's* name is faint on the bow, with two anchors and an anchor winch at the bow. Portholes exist at 80' and 100', and a four-bladed propeller sits on the deck at 110'. The wheelhouse is missing, blown off when the ship sank. The wreck is caving in, so penetration is not recommended.

ABOVE: *The 2,476-gross-ton, 299' steamer,* NORTH WIND, *sank on July 1, 1926.* GREAT LAKES MARINE COLLECTION OF THE MILWAUKEE PUBLIC LIBRARY/WISCONSIN MARINE HISTORICAL SOCIETY. BELOW: *Stanchions and ladders show only part of the intact nature of the* NORTH WIND *shipwreck.* PHOTO BY DAVID OSTIFICHUK.

Philadelphia   (#19 on the map on pp. 130-131)

VESSEL NAME:	PHILADELPHIA
RIG:	iron propeller
DIMENSIONS:	236' x 34' 3" x 14'
LAUNCHED:	1868; Buffalo, New York
DATE LOST:	Tuesday, November 7, 1893
CAUSE OF LOSS:	collision with the steamer, ALBANY
CARGO:	coal and misc. merchandise
LIVES LOST:	16 (from crew of 22)
GENERAL LOCATION:	12 miles off Pte. aux Barques, Michigan
DEPTH:	105' - 125'
ACCESS:	boat
DIVING SKILL LEVEL:	advanced
DIVING HAZARDS:	depth, hypothermia, penetration, silting
CO-ORDINATES:	Lat/Lon:
	Loran: 30786.44 / 49183.96

Two lifeboats were desperately launched in the dark, foggy night on Lake Huron. The first one contained 22 men, while the second held 24. The first one reached shore safely. The second was found offshore the next day, overturned and almost broken in half. As the press reported: "The [lifeboat's] port bow was stove in from the stem back to the second thwart clear to the keel., which shows that it was struck by a rapidly moving object of larger size."

Twelve lifejacketed bodies, one of them terribly mutilated (the body had a crushed skull and a broken leg) and a couple of others with quite noticeable bruises, bobbed nearby. These 12 bodies were the only ones to be found from the 24 who were aboard this lifeboat. The other 12, apparently without lifejackets, sank to the bottom. The sea had been calm that night, so the signs of violence on the lifeboat and bodies were strangely inexplicable.

These lifeboats had contained, in mixed numbers, the entire crews of two, large, iron-hulled ships that should have passed in the night, but didn't.

The Anchor Line package freighter, *Philadelphia,* loaded with coal and general merchandise such as bottles of ketchup, olive oil, and hand lotion, jars of strawberry preserves and apple butter, and iron stoves, was upbound on Lake Huron from Erie, Pennsylvania, to Duluth, Minnesota, on the night of November 6-7, 1893. The Western Transit steamer, *Albany,* was downbound on the same lake at the same time with a cargo of grain from Milwaukee to Buffalo. Thick fog banks hovered in layers along the routes of these two ships. At about two o'clock in the morning of Tuesday, November 7, 1893, the *Philadelphia's* bow sliced about six feet into the *Albany's* steel hull on the port side just forward of the No. 2 gangway. For several moments, both ships stayed stuck together. Then the *Philadelphia* pulled out.

The *Philadelphia's* bow was stove in, but seemed to be holding up well against the pressure of Lake Huron's water. The *Albany,* on the other hand, displaying a wide, gaping wound, was recognizably doomed. A line was attached to the sinking ship's bow, and she was towed for about half an hour before she sank in 149' of water, her crew taking to a yawl boat and transferring to the *Philadelphia* just in time. The *Philadelphia* then continued to race full-steam against time towards shore, but her wound, too, proved fatal, and she sank in 125' of water half an hour after the *Albany* succumbed. The 46 men of the two crews took to the two lifeboats while the Philadelphia's engine was still steaming her towards shore. Analysts later theorized that, had the *Philadelphia* not towed the stricken *Albany* for those 30 minutes, she herself would have made it to shore. As usual, hindsight offers clear vision in tragedies such as this. The collision occurred about eight miles off Michigan's thumb. The two shipwrecks lie about 2.5 miles apart.

The iron-hulled freighter, PHILADELPHIA. GREAT LAKES MARINE COLLECTION OF THE MILWAUKEE PUBLIC LIBRARY/WISCONSIN MARINE HISTORICAL SOCIETY.

Both crews aboard the *Philadelphia* intermingled in the darkness while filling two lifeboats. The first yawl boat contained the two captains, five men from the *Philadelphia,* and 15 men from the *Albany;* the second boat carried 16 men from the *Philadelphia* and eight men from the *Albany.* The two small boats stayed in contact with each for a short period of time by shouting. Although apart, both boats heard the loud sound made by the *Philadelphia* as she sank. Then they drifted even further apart, and heard no more from each other.

Five hours of backbreaking rowing brought the first yawl with 22 men ashore near Pointe aux Barques. But the second lifeboat was missing. The local lifesaving crew found the upside-down, broken lifeboat eight miles offshore. They, with help from the passing steamer, *City of Concord,* recovered 12 bodies. The *City of Concord* took them to Tawas, Michigan, the nearest upbound port.

One theory was that a mystery steamer had collided with the second lifeboat in the night, killing all on board. But no ship's foghorn had been heard, nor lights seen. Captain McDonald of the *Albany* did not think that the lifeboat was run over by a mystery steamer. His explanation for the bodies being bruised was that the men were injured when they abandoned the sinking *Albany;* they were forced to jump or slide down ropes to get to the lifeboat. He thought some of them might have hit the lifeboat when they jumped. Other people conjectured that the badly mutilated body had been drawn into the propeller of the *City of Concord* as she steamed around in the fog recovering bodies.

Some reports stated that there were 23, not 22, men in the first lifeboat. Two revelations clouded the number. One report that a survivor from the second lifeboat was secreted away was purely mythical. Another account, also probably incorrect, was that there had been a stowaway aboard the *Philadelphia.*

The iron-hulled freighter, *Philadelphia,* official number 20142, was built at Buffalo by David Bell in 1868. The 1,463-gross-ton ship measured 236' in length, 34' 3" in beam, and 14' in draft.

Great Lakes shipwreck hunter, John Steele, located the wreck of the *Philadelphia* in the spring of 1973. The wreck sits upright in 105' to 125' of water, with noteworthy sights including the engine, two boilers, rudder, propeller, stern capstan, and, on the port deck, a load of cast-iron stoves, some of which have spilled onto the lake floor or into the cargo holds. The bow damage is evident, and the port bow anchor, on the lake floor, leans against the hull.

The *Philadelphia* is one of the many shipwrecks in Michigan's Thumb Underwater Preserve. It is usually buoyed in the springtime.

ABOVE: *Pat Stayer descends into Lake Huron.* BELOW: *The* PHILADELPHIA'S *rust-covered stern capstan stares eerily at visiting scuba divers.*   PHOTOS BY CRIS KOHL.

Price, Charles S.

(#20 on the map on pp. 130-131)

VESSEL NAME:	CHARLES S. PRICE
RIG:	steel propeller
DIMENSIONS:	504' x 54' x 30'
LAUNCHED:	Saturday, May 14, 1910; Lorain, Ohio
DATE LOST:	Sunday, November 9, 1913
CAUSE OF LOSS:	capsized in storm
CARGO:	soft coal
LIVES LOST:	all hands (28)
GENERAL LOCATION:	11 miles SE of Lexington, Michigan
DEPTH:	40' - 65'
ACCESS:	boat
DIVING SKILL LEVEL:	intermediate-advanced
DIVING HAZARDS:	depth, limited penetration, jagged edges
CO-ORDINATES:	Lat/Lon: 43.09.17 / 82.21.80
	Loran: 30799.6 / 49622.5

The Great Storm of November 9, 1913, the most severe ever recorded on the Great Lakes, terrorized the inland seas for 16 howling hours and resulted in the loss of 19 ships, the stranding of 19 others, and the deaths of about 250 people. The *Charles S. Price* is one of the more famous of these lost vessels.

The 6,322-gross-ton *Charles S. Price* was a 504' steel steamer, with a length of 504', a huge beam of 54' and a draft of 30'. Launched on Saturday, May 14, 1910 at Lorain, Ohio, she carried heavy loads of iron ore downbound and coal upbound during her short, three-year life.

On the first day after the Great Storm, people on shore near the Port Huron lighthouse station saw an enormous, overturned ship floating in Lake Huron. For several days, this unidentified "mystery ship" made headlines all around the Great Lakes. Eight steel freighters had gone missing with all hands in Lake Huron during this storm (alphabetically, they were the ten-year-old, 416' *Argus;* the brand new 550' Canadian ship, the *James Carruthers,* the newest and largest of these losses; the ten-year-old, 416' *Hydrus;* the five-year-old, 432' *John A McGean;* the three-year-old, 504' *Charles S. Price;* the six-year-old, 249' *Regina;* the four-year-old, 504' *Isaac M. Scott;* and the oldest one, the 30-year-old, 250' *Wexford),* and speculation as to which one of those eight this "mystery ship" happened to be ran amuck. Conjecture was that there were still men alive

ABOVE: *The 504' steel steamer,* CHARLES S. PRICE, *was one of eight huge ships which disappeared on Lake Huron in the worst Great Lakes storm in recorded history.* GREAT LAKES HISTORICAL SOCIETY, VERMILION, OHIO. BELOW: *The enormous floating hull of a "mystery ship" made headlines all around the Great Lakes. It turned out to be the* CHARLES S. PRICE. *All 28 of her crew had perished.* GREAT LAKES MARINE COLLECTION OF THE MILWAUKEE PUBLIC LIBRARY/WISCONSIN MARINE HISTORICAL SOCIETY.

inside the overturned hull, and that the stern of this "mystery ship" was stuck not on the lake bottom, but atop another shipwreck, namely another one of the missing freighters. Both imaginative ideas turned out to be wrong.

Early on Saturday morning, November 15, 1913, Detroit hardhat diver, William Baker, from on board Captain Robert Thompson's tug, *Sport* (see pp. 213-218), descended along the slippery steel hull of the "mystery ship" in rough waters in hopes of unlocking the biggest secret of the lakes. Anxious marinemen, insurance underwriters, wives, mothers, sons, daughters, and many more, awaited the news. When he surfaced, Diver Baker and Captain Thompson headed tightlipped right to the office of THE TIMES-HERALD newspaper in Port Huron. There, Baker announced to the eager reporters and to an anxious world that this unidentified ship that had turned turtle was the steamer, *Charles S. Price!*

The "mystery ship" was a mystery no longer.

Baker stated: "We laid near the wreck all night on the tug *Sport* waiting for the dawn of morning and had everything arranged to make the descent at the earliest possible moment. I was ready at 5:30 and at 6:00 o'clock I had started down. The tug was anchored with her bow pointing about north-west, parallel with the wreck, and the stern of the tug was about abreast of the bluff at the steamer's bow. We threw a line to which was attached about 100 pounds of scrap iron, over the wreck to keep the stern as close as possible to the wreck. We were on the starboard side of the wreck.

"As I started down, I felt her sides all the way down for 20 feet. Then I lost [the wreck] again, but I kept on going down expecting to run into it. When I discovered that I was too far down, I started to come up again and found the wreck again coming up. I ran into the pipe rail around her Texas work. I hung on there until I found out where I was at. Then I went down that pipe rail until I ran into the bulwarks of the wreck, the bulwarks were painted white. There was a round railing on the edge of the bulwarks and I went around that railing until I ran across her name.

"There I stopped and took my time. I read her name twice and the letters spelled out for me "CHARLES S. PRICE." Her full name is there. I read the name over twice to be absolutely positive. The name is painted in black letters on white bulwarks....I went on further forward to the stem to see if there were any damaged plates to indicate if there had been a collision or if the boat had been damaged in any way....I was pulling myself along on this rail all the time. I went to the after side of the forward house. I found nothing there that showed any signs of a collision, and at that time the sea was coming up.

"I was under the water in all about an hour and the length of the wreck that I investigated was about 48' of the starboard bow. I did not have a chance to go any further on the wreck and did not get inside of her as the sea began to toss me about and I had to give it up. I had secured her name and also the fact that the ship had not been struck forward, that is at least not on the starboard side.

Front page of the extra edition of THE PORT HURON TIMES-HERALD *newspaper on Saturday, November 15, 1913, the day that hardhat diver William H. Baker of Detroit went over the side of the tug,* SPORT, *and identified the "mystery ship" as the* CHARLES S. PRICE, *the bow of which had been floating in lower Lake Huron since the dreadful Great Storm of Sunday, November 9, 1913.* AUTHOR'S COLLECTION.

"The bow of the *Price* is being buoyed up by the air that was held in her when she went over. There is now two streams of bubbles coming out of the bow and there seems to be no doubt but what the boat will continue to settle down as soon as the air leaks out of her, which it is doing gradually."

Captain Robert Thompson of the *Sport* added to the story: "I got in touch with Diver Baker on Friday afternoon. The weather has been so bad that you had to have somebody that you could depend on. I had to have a diver that could do the work and I got the best one on the lakes, Mr. Baker.

"There has been so much anxiety over the name of the mystery ship that I decided that if it was possible to get it, now was the time. We laid near the wreck all night and had everything in readiness for the attempt to lower the diver at 5:30 o'clock this morning. At six o'clock, Mr. Baker went over the stern of the tug *Sport* in an effort to get the name of the boat.

"With the assistance of Peter Bachus, one of the most expert diver attendants on the lakes, who was on board to take care of Mr. Baker, we lowered Mr. Baker over the stern of the boat. It took some time to get our tug in position to lower the diver as she dragged her anchor several times...."

In conclusion, Thompson added, "I am of the opinion that there are some of the bodies of the crew in the boat, although they may all have had time to take to the lifeboats. Both the diver and myself believe that the members of the crew who worked in the engine room and aft are still in the steel hull."

This drawing of "The position of the ill-fated freighter unidentified" appeared in THE DAILY TIMES *newspaper of Fort William (Ontario) on Friday, November 14, 1913.* AUTHOR'S COLLECTION.

Two days later, on November 17, 1913, the upside-down bow of the *Charles S. Price* disappeared from view under Lake Huron's waters.

THE PORT HURON TIM
PORT HURON, MICHIGAN, MONDAY, NOVEMI

HULL OF STEAMER PRICE NOW · HAS DISAPPEARED FROM VIEW

Seve R

FOR NEARLY WEEK NO ATTEMPT WAS MADE TO RELEASE IT FROM BOTTOM

LIFEBOAT FOUND ON SHORE NEAR GODERICH

Front-page headlines of the last edition of THE PORT HURON TIMES-HERALD, *for Monday, November 17, 1913.* AUTHOR'S COLLECTION.

All 28 men aboard the *Charles S. Price* were dead, and only seven bodies had washed ashore by November 15, 1913. A few more were located after that date, but some very likely remained with the ship, to sail this ghostly freighter forever on the quiet seas of the underwater world. The body of one *Price* sailor which had washed ashore supposedly wearing a Regina lifejacket immediately sparked controversy (see the *Regina* story, pp. 207-212). The *Price* sailor was identified by Milton Smith, former engineer on the *Price,* who, based on his premonition of doom, had left the ship at Cleveland the day before the storm.

For about 60 years, the *Charles S. Price* was the only wreck of the eight lost on Lake Huron on November 9, 1913, whose location was known. Several salvage attempts over the years always ended in failure. Four other losses from the Great Storm of 1913 were located in the 1970's and 1980's (the *Isaac M. Scott,* the *Argus,* the *John A. McGean,* and the *Regina*). Three wrecks remain lost to date: the *James Carruthers,* the *Hydrus,* and the *Wexford.*

The wreck of the *Charles S. Price* lies upside-down on a sand-and-rock bottom in 40' to 65' of water. Several scrap-metal salvage attempts, plus the ravages of time and nature, have left the wreck in a broken, caved-in condition. Although most heavily deteriorating in midship, the rest of the vessel is also getting weaker every year. The huge, impressive, four-bladed propeller is worth seeing, but penetration dives are not recommended on this wreck. A slight current exists at this site. The jagged steel edges of the *Price* are hard on drysuits and wetsuits alike, so watch your buoyancy and maneuverability. Do not attempt to see this entire 504' wreck on a single tank of air unless you happen to be a marathon swimmer. Doing one dive on the bow and another on the stern will offer leisurely moments to explore the hull and both sides of the wreck. Remember that the middle of the shipwreck is considerably collapsed.

The sunken, overturned bow of the freighter, CHARLES S. PRICE, *still resembles, after almost a century underwater, that bow of the floating "mystery ship" which captured the imaginations and pathos of so many people in 1913.*   PHOTO BY CRIS KOHL.

Remember also, as you explore this massive tangle of tortured steel ribbing and plating, the horrible deaths suffered by literally hundreds of Great Lakes sailors who perished in The Great Storm of November 9th, 1913, and the thousands of grieving people (friends, relatives, career colleagues, strangers) left behind to mourn them. The full extent of such a catastrophe can barely be imagined by people today. Explore these shipwreck remains and think about the fact that something big happened here so long ago.

Regina

(#21 on the map on pp. 130-131)

VESSEL NAME:	REGINA
RIG:	steel propeller
DIMENSIONS:	249' 7" x 42' 6" x 20' 5"
LAUNCHED:	1907; Dumbarton, Scotland
DATE LOST:	Sunday, November 9, 1913
CAUSE OF LOSS:	capsized in storm
CARGO:	gas & sewer piping and general cargo
LIVES LOST:	all hands (20)
GENERAL LOCATION:	6.5 miles from Lexington, Michigan
DEPTH:	60' - 83'
ACCESS:	boat
DIVING SKILL LEVEL:	intermediate-advanced
DIVING HAZARDS:	depth, penetration, silting, jagged steel
CO-ORDINATES:	Lat/Lon: 43.20.46 / 82.26.90
	Loran: 30801.7 / 49534.9

Eight enormous freighters sank with all hands on Lake Huron in The Great Storm of November 9, 1913, the most intensely violent and destructive upheaval of weather in the recorded history of the Great Lakes.

Five of those eight ships have been located to date, namely the *Argus,* the *John McGean,* the *Charles S. Price,* the *Regina,* and the *Isaac M. Scott.* They all lie upside-down, attesting to the unimaginable force of nature which flipped 500-foot-long freighters displacing thousands of tons each as if they were mere hamburgers on a grill. It will be interesting to see, in the years to come, if the last three that await discovery, the *James Carruthers,* the *Hydrus,* and the *Wexford,* were also turned topsy-turvy during this incredible aberration of nature.

A very bad-tempered Mother Nature can be blamed for having converted mere mortals' vessels into unsalvageable piles of metal, but who was to blame for the dead, shore-tossed body of John Groundwater, the chief engineer on the steamer, *Charles S. Price,* wearing a lifejacket from the steamer, *Regina?*

The story of the *Price* sailor found along the Canadian side of Lake Huron wearing a *Regina* lifejacket became ingrained in Great Lakes folklore from the very day of its discovery. The lakes' ancient mariners mustered their collective wisdom and told a likely tale of the ships having collided during the storm, with (at least) one of the *Price's* crew clambering onto the *Regina* before the vessels parted, the *Price* mortally wounded. Later, when it became clear that the *Regina* was also doomed to sink, anybody who happened to be on board donned a *Regina* lifejacket.

The steamer, REGINA, *carried a cargo of general merchandise when she was lost with all hands in The Great Storm of Nov. 9, 1913.* GREAT LAKES MARINE COLLECTION OF THE MILWAUKEE PUBLIC LIBRARY/WISCONSIN MARINE HISTORICAL SOCIETY.

Recent attempts at historical analysis conjecture that the reversed lifejacket may have been caused by human scavengers on shore, opportunists who carted away the washed-up cargo of a ship or the contents of a dead man's pockets just as readily as children today skip flat stones off the watertop. The law, however, frowns upon the picking of pockets from either living or dead men, as well as the removal of property that rightfully belongs to others, but which has taken a slight detour from its destination. Theorists feel that human jackals, ransacking whatever washed up on the beach, observed that law enforcement was nearby, and hastily returned their ill-gotten loot indiscriminately to the cadavers strewn among the flotsam. In a situation like this, it could be argued, not all of the almost-pilfered lifejackets ended up on their original wearers.

Poor record-keeping can also been suggested as a cause for this mix-up. Lifejackets, since they were the property of the shipping company, were almost immediately removed from recovered bodies. The people whose grim job it was to collect the corpses and deliver them to a makeshift morgue perhaps couldn't remember precisely anymore which body wore a *Price* or which one a *Regina* lifejacket, so, not wishing to appear incompetent, they wrote down whatever name they found easier to spell.

A 1916 salvage attempt on the *Charles S. Price* raised her from the lake floor and exposed her bottom to the sunlight (before declaring the freighter unsalvageable and dropping her back to the lake floor). One source has indicated that the *Price* did have a 40'-wide hole on the port side near the engine room, possibly caused by a collision with the *Regina*. Time and salvage attempts have perhaps eradicated any evidence of a collision with another steel vessel.

Capt. Edward McConkey of the *Regina* apparently stayed with his ship to the very end, his body washing ashore the following spring. In his pocket was his diary with detailed accounts of family and shipboard life. The final entry was made on Nov. 8, 1913, the day the first winds of The Great Storm blew. Caringly dried by his widow, the diary is now in the museum at Goderich, Ontario.

The REGINA *made front page news in* THE PORT HURON TIMES-HERALD, *Nov. 12, 1913.*

The 1,957-gross-ton steamer, *Regina,* was launched in Dumbarton, Scotland, in 1907. This steel ship, official number 124231, was contructed by the firm of A. MacMillan and Son as hull #419. The vessel, owned by Montreal firms during her six short years afloat, boasted a powerful triple expansion engine, a pair of large, Scotch boilers, a length of 249' 7", a beam of 42' 6", and a draft of 20' 5". The *Regina* was a "canaler," a ship specifically constructed with the maximum lock length of the old Welland Canal in mind.

On July 1, 1987, divers Wayne Brusate and Gary Biniecki, while side-scanning for the wreck of the tug, *Mary Alice B.* (see pp. 174-178), found a much larger target --- the 250' steel steamer, *Regina.* The hull contained major cracks, one set of anchor chains was out, indicating the vessel tried to ride out the storm in a stationary position, the telegraph (or chadburn) in the engine room was on STOP, and all of her lifeboats were gone.

There were no witnesses to the sinking, and dead men tell no tales.

Controversy over salvage rights pitted friends against each other and against the state of Michigan. Paneling below deck was reportedly torn apart by night divers in quest of a mythical treasure in gold and silver coins. Salvaged *Regina* scotch and champagne were surprisingly consumed at the Maine wedding of

The steamer, *Regina*

ARTWORK © PAT STAYER. Used with permission.

a South Carolina scuba diver (and covered by PEOPLE Magazine!) A controversial auction of *Regina* artifacts was held at the Dossin Marine Museum in Detroit in early December, 1987. Among the sales: a sealed flask of scotch sold for $100, an empty beer bottle for $30, and a large lump of coal for $35! Our jaws dropped. This auction was so factious that nothing like it has followed!

The *Regina,* one of the premier dive sites in the Great Lakes, lies almost totally upside-down in 60' to 83' of water. A 55-foot gap in midship on her port side, apparently not so much caused by a collision with a ship as by an encounter with the hard lake bottom, exposes the cargo, some of which has spilled to the lake floor. One need not penetrate this wreck for a good dive. One large anchor remains in its place at the overturned bow. Large brass letters at the bow spell out the name R-E-G-I-N-A (upside-down, of course). The massive rudder and mighty, four-bladed propeller are highlights at the stern. Cargo crates and machinery litter the lake floor. Remember that artifact recovery is illegal, and penetration diving is the realm of the trained, experienced, and prepared.

Incidentally, Canadians pronounce the name of the *Regina* so it rhymes with "angina," as in "Ri-jine-a," whereas U.S. residents say "Ri-jeen-a," the British (but not the Latin) way of pronouncing the Latin word for "queen." The ship was a Canadian vessel, named after a city in western Canada (which Canadians pronounce "Ri-jine-a") by the Canadian company which ordered the ship's construction, so guess who's probably right.

Inside the upside-down steel hull of the REGINA, *in about 80' of water, things can get pretty dark, silty, and tangled. There are interesting sights to be seen, such as this complete brass porthole still in place, but remember that shipwreck penetration diving requires special training, experience, and preparation.* PHOTO BY CRIS KOHL.

It is difficult to say precisely where the mooring lines to the steamer, REGINA, *will lead the underwater explorer (if passing freighters haven't inadvertently taken them all out!) The stern buoy will drop descending divers right onto the huge, four-bladed propeller (remember, this wreck is virtually upside-down).*   PHOTO BY CRIS KOHL.

Sport

(#22 on the map on pp. 130-131)

VESSEL NAME:	SPORT
RIG:	steel tug
DIMENSIONS:	56' 7" x 14' 7" x 9'
LAUNCHED:	1873; Wyandotte, Michigan
DATE LOST:	Monday, December 13, 1920
CAUSE OF LOSS:	foundered in storm
CARGO:	none
LIVES LOST:	none (from 6 on board)
GENERAL LOCATION:	3 miles off Lexington, Michigan
DEPTH:	35' - 50'
ACCESS:	boat
DIVING SKILL LEVEL:	novice-intermediate
DIVING HAZARDS:	silting, hypothermia, boating traffic
CO-ORDINATES:	Lat/Lon: 43.15.98 / 82.27.93
	Loran: 30824.9 / 49569.2

The tug, *Sport,* became the recipient of the state of Michigan's first underwater historical marker on August 4, 1992.

Launched in 1873 at Wyandotte, Michigan, at the yard of Earl Brock Ward's Iron Works, and designed by Ward's superintendent, Frank E. Kirby, who went on to achieve greatness in marine architecture, this small tugboat was one of the first in the world to be constructed of Bessemer steel, a revolutionary product. However, because this steel ship was built at an iron works yard, some historical sources listed her hull material as "iron." The 45-gross-ton *Sport,* official number 115152, measured 56' 7" in length, 14' 7" in beam, and 9' in draft.

For the *Sport's* first two years, she did towing work at Captain E.B. Ward's large sawmill at Ludington, Michigan. Captain Ward died in 1875, but the *Sport* remained in those Lake Michigan waters. According to Polk's and Beeson's guides, the *Sport* was owned in 1879 by James Foley of Ludington; in the 1880's by Robert Caswell of Ludington; from 1890 to 1893 again by James Foley of Ludington; from 1894 to 1896 by Warren A. Cartier of Ludington; from 1906 to 1909 by George R. Cartier of Ludington; and from 1910 to 1912 by the Cartier Lumber Company of Ludington.

On May 7, 1913, Captain Robert P. Thompson of Port Huron, Michigan, purchased the tug, *Sport,* and owned her until her demise in 1920.

Over the next 47 years, the stout *Sport* worked in such remote places as New Orleans, but spent the vast majority of her life in the Great Lakes. Probably her most publicized moment (prior to her sinking) occurred in late 1913, when the *Sport* was instrumental in identifying the mystery ship, an enormous steel hull floating upside-down in lower Lake Huron after the incredibly destructive storm of Sunday, November 9, 1913, the worst storm in Great Lakes recorded history. Detroit hardhat diver, William Baker, made a highly publicized underwater exploration in rough seas on November 15, 1913, from the tug, *Sport,* to identify the unknown vessel as the 504-foot steel steamer, *Charles S. Price* (see pp. 200-206).

Inland Lloyds listed the value of the *Sport* as being $13,000 in 1875, $11,000 in 1879, $10,000 in 1882, $9,000 by 1887, $8,500 in 1889, $8,000 in 1893, $7,000 in 1895, and $6,000 in 1906. Inland Lloyds, in their "remarks" column, identified the *Sport's* construction material as "steel" in every entry. The vessel received new steel topsides in 1880. Throughout the 1880's, the *Sport* continued to tow log rafts on Lake Michigan, steaming farther afield as local supplies of lumber diminished. The tug was reboiled in 1889, and in 1910, for a change of pace, the *Sport* was chartered for fishing out of Kenosha.

The tug, Sport, *one of the first vessels ever constructed of steel, was built in 1873 at Wyandotte, Michigan, spent most of her long career in Lake Michigan, and sank in a severe December storm on Lake Huron in 1920.* Great Lakes Marine Collection of the Milwaukee Public Library/Wisconsin Marine Historical Society.

ABOVE: *The heavy bell from the tug,* SPORT, *was one of the most interesting visual attractions at the site, but it was stolen in June, 1989. A $500 reward for information leading to the discovery of the diver who stole the bell was offered by the Sanilac Shores Underwater Preserve Committee. This amount was later increased to $1,000. Contact that group for more information.* BELOW: *Diver Joan Forsberg closely examines the* SPORT'S *wheel in 47' of water.* PHOTOS BY CRIS KOHL.

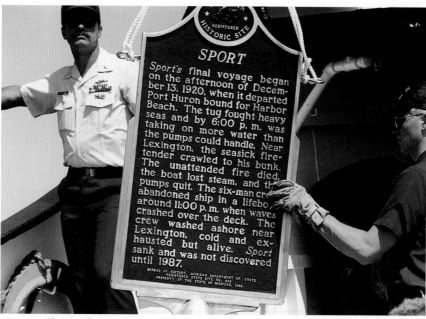

ABOVE: *The tug,* SPORT, *became the first shipwreck in Michigan waters honored with its own historical marker. The Michigan Department of State and the state's Bureau of History requested some unusual assistance from the U.S. Coast Guard cutter,* BRAMBLE, *stationed at Port Huron, Michigan, to assist with the task. Many state dignitaries and guests were on board.* BELOW: *The historical marker in place just off the* SPORT'S *port side is read with enthusiasm by visiting diver, Joan Forsberg.* PHOTOS BY CRIS KOHL.

The tug, *Sport*

ARTWORK © PAT STAYER. Used with permission.

The *Sport* steamed up Lake Huron following the Michigan shoreline on the afternoon of Monday, December 13, 1920. The wind increased all afternoon, and by 6:00 P.M., a fierce, 60-mile-an-hour gale from the southeast buffeted the small vessel. She was taking on water from the large pounding waves that crashed onto her topsides, and at 6:30 P.M., Captain Thompson, the tug's owner, realized that the pumps could not keep up with the water. The tug's new fireman, still without his sealegs, became seasick and left his post for his bunk without informing anyone. The boiler cooled and the pressure dropped. The pumps stopped working. Captain Thompson decided to turn around and try to make it back to Port Huron, ordering kerosene and oil to be used in the firebox in a desperate effort to get the boiler's pressure back up quickly. But the below-deck waters were rising, and when they finally doused the firebox at about 11:00 P.M., Thompson ordered his five men to don lifejackets and launch the lifeboat. Before they left the sinking *Sport,* they secured a buoy to the uninsured tug.

For almost four hours, the sailors rowed hard into the wind before finally hearing breakers on a shore at 2:30 A.M. The crew landed about one mile north of Lexington, Michigan, and found welcome refuge at the Carter home.

After the storm, Captain Thompson searched for his tugboat or for the buoy which he had attached before leaving his ship. He found neither. The violent waves had torn the floating marker from the sunken tug. The *Sport* remained lost for the next 67 years.

In July, 1986, diver Wayne Brusate, of Marysville, MI, with friends, went out looking for the tug, *Mary Alice B.* (see pp. 174-178) which had been lost only 11 years earlier. Instead, the team accidentally found the wreck of the long-lost large, steel freighter, *Regina* (see pp. 207-212). Undaunted, Brusate, with diver Colette Witherspoon, went out in June, 1987 to locate the tug, *Mary Alice B.,* but instead found the almost-as-long-lost-as-the-*Regina* tug, *Sport.* By this time, Brusate became daunted and stopped looking for the long-sought *Mary Alice B.,* a wreck which the Stayers and their team discovered on July 8, 1992.

The tug, *Sport,* sitting in 50' of water about three miles east of Lexington, MI, is upright, intact, and on a strong starboard list; the port rail rises to 35'. Inside the hull are the high-pressure, non-condensing steam engine and a single Scotch boiler. The tug's bow sits dramatically angled in the lake bottom. The ship's wheel and the steam whistle are dismounted and lie on the lake floor on the starboard side of the *Sport's* hull. The rudder is dismounted, and the four-bladed propeller snapped off at the shaft, one blade broken, and now lies flat in the sand and silt on the *Sport's* stern. Penetration is not recommended, as it would take a very skinny diver to get through the tight area, and it would raise so much silt that nobody could see anything for days. Besides, getting stuck under the engine, boiler, or deck are very real hazards. Unfortunately, the ship's bell and an anchor were stolen by greedy divers, but the many items of interest remaining at this site have induced wits to call the *Sport* "a *Sport* diver's delight."

Sweepstakes (#23 on the map on pp. 130-131)

VESSEL NAME:	SWEEPSTAKES
RIG:	schooner
DIMENSIONS:	119' x 22' 8" x 10' 1"
LAUNCHED:	1867; Burlington, Ontario
DATE LOST:	Sunday, August 23, 1885
CAUSE OF LOSS:	stranded, abandoned
CARGO:	coal
LIVES LOST:	none
GENERAL LOCATION:	at end of Big Tub Harbor, Tobermory, ON
DEPTH:	5' - 20'
ACCESS:	shore or boat
DIVING SKILL LEVEL:	novice
DIVING HAZARDS:	boating traffic, limited access times
CO-ORDINATES:	Lat/Lon: not necessary; buoyed
	Loran: easily visible from the surface!

The 218-ton, twin-masted schooner, *Sweepstakes,* (not to be confused with the larger, 369-gross-ton schooner of the same name launched at Chicago in 1856) built at what was called Wellington Square, but is now named Burlington, Ontario, by John and Melancthon Simpson in 1867, launched on September 24, 1867 (when Canada as a country was almost three months old!), measured 119' in length, 22' 8" in beam, and 10' 1" in draft. The *Sweepstakes* was stranded and seriously damaged at Cove Island, north of Tobermory, on August 23, 1885, but was pulled off and towed by the tug, *Jessie,* to Big Tub Harbor at Tobermory on September 3, 1885. The schooner sank, possibly with a snapped keel, before repairs could be made, and she has rested in that spot for well over 100 years now. Her coal cargo, plus some rigging and fittings, such as anchors, chains, and masts, were salvaged before the rest of the schooner was abandoned.

The *Sweepstakes* was a stout, little workhorse, carrying a variety of loads such as 24,000 bushels of wheat, 356 tons of coal, or, on one trip, 1,000 telegraph poles. By late 1883, George Stewart of Moore Township (south of Sarnia, Ontario) in Lambton County became her sole (and final) owner.

The *Sweepstakes*, one of the best preserved 1800's Great Lakes schooners to be found, is the most popular divesite in Fathom Five National Marine Park, the first underwater park in the Great Lakes, and the first in all of Canada, for that matter! Below-deck access has been limited by the park because divers' bubbles were corroding the deck. Ice and waves have tried to flatten the *Sweepstakes* for years, but scuba divers won't let her collapse. In the early 1970's, the first set of steel rod bracings were attached to the wreck's sides. More bracing was added in more recent years. Of great diver interest are the bow's starboard railing, the windlass, the Roman numeral draft markings, the mast holes, and the centerboard box below deck. The *Sweepstakes* is the most visited shipwreck in all of the Great Lakes due to its intactness and accessibility.

The twin-masted schooner, AZOV, *at 202 gross tons and with measurements of 116' x 24' x 10', very closely resembled the (possibly-never-photographed)* SWEEPSTAKES. *The* AZOV, *which was also built by John Simpson at Wellington Square (Burlington) Ontario, but one year before he constructed the* SWEEPSTAKES, *foundered on October 25, 1911, off Pointe aux Barques, Michigan. The wreck of the* AZOV, *however, drifted across the lake and stranded near Goderich, Ontario.* AUTHOR'S COLLECTION.

ABOVE: *Joan Forsberg studies the schooner,* SWEEPSTAKE'S, *windlass. Members of various Ontario scuba clubs and the Ontario Underwater Council first fortified the* SWEEPSTAKE'S *oak hull with steel rod bracings in the early 1970's. A bright red, plastic plaque which was mounted on the wreck in 1971 stated,* "Schooner SWEEPSTAKES, built 1867, sunk 1896 [sic]. The restoration of this vessel by the Ontario Underwater Council is for you and those who follow. Look and enjoy. Please do not destroy." BELOW: *The intact port railing on the* SWEEPSTAKES *always impresses visitors, divers and glassbottom boat tourists alike.* PHOTOS BY CRIS KOHL.

Thompson, Emma E.

(#24 on map on pp. 130-131)

VESSEL NAME:	EMMA E. THOMPSON
RIG:	wooden steambarge
DIMENSIONS:	125' 9" x 27' 6" x 12' 8"
LAUNCHED:	1875; Saginaw, Michigan
DATE LOST:	Thursday, May 28, 1914
CAUSE OF LOSS:	burned
CARGO:	none
LIVES LOST:	none
GENERAL LOCATION:	E side, Innes Island, North Channel, Ontario
DEPTH:	20' - 30'
ACCESS:	boat
DIVING SKILL LEVEL:	novice
DIVING HAZARDS:	silting, remoteness
CO-ORDINATES:	Lat/Lon:
	Loran:

The waves reached five feet in height while the strong west wind was still picking up, and we had no luck locating the makeshift marker buoy as we bounced along like a cork in a tempest in our inflatable boat. Local divers had warned us that the plastic jug marking the deep wreck of the *North Wind* in the North Channel of Lake Huron occasionally disappeared, by nature or by stealth.

We were not equipped to locate the wreck ourselves in these worsening weather conditions, so we jumped at the chance to flee to the lee of Innes Island and try to locate the recently-discovered remains of the steamer, *Emma E. Thompson,* in shallower, protected water.

The east side of uninhabited Innes Island features a rarity in this rocky part of the Great Lakes: a sandy beach. Our battered inflatable took a breather on this welcomed shore, away from the churning open waters and out of the strong wind. Here, we reorganized our expedition and took stock of the situation.

Innes Island can be reached by boat from one of the marinas on the south shore of the mainland just off the Trans-Canada Highway in northern Ontario. An alternative access is to drive to Manitoulin Island, the largest freshwater island in the world, and boat north from the small town of Kagawong. Both routes cover about the same distance and run through beautiful, undisturbed scenery past hundreds of remote, tree-studded islands in what has been called the most popular boat cruising area of the entire Great Lakes.

About a quarter of a mile off this sandy beach on the northeast side of Innes Island just below Hesson Point, in about 30' of clear, fresh water, the shipwreck named the *Emma E. Thompson* has rested for over 80 years.

Named by a Michigan lumber businessman after his mother, Emma Ellen Thompson (1809-1891), this 126-foot, wooden steamer, built by Ralph Edwards, slid down the launch ramp at Saginaw, Michigan, in 1875. Her high-pressure, non-condensing steam engine could produce 380 horsepower to move her cargoes of lumber and coal at a respectable speed.

The *Emma E. Thompson* changed ownership numerous times, moving to Chicago by 1882 until 1893, then to an owner in Milwaukee before relocating to Traverse City, Michigan, in 1906. In the final two years of her life, 1913 and 1914, James B. Maddock of Detroit owned her.

The *Emma E. Thompson's* value also fluctuated: worth $16,000 in 1882, the vessel lost little by 1885, when she was appraised at $15,000. However, by 1897, her worth had diminished to $6,000. A "large rebuild" in 1898 raised her value to $9,000, which she struggled to maintain for a number of years. At her demise in 1914, she was worth $7,000.

The steamer, EMMA E. THOMPSON, *worked on the Great Lakes for 39 years before succumbing to flames off Manitoulin Island.* GREAT LAKES MARINE COLLECTION OF THE MILWAUKEE PUBLIC LIBRARY/WISCONSIN MARINE HISTORICAL SOCIETY.

In the spring of 1914, dark clouds on the horizon threatened a world still at peace for a few more weeks before the outbreak of World War I. Meanwhile, dark clouds literally forced the *Emma E. Thompson,* en route from French River, Ontario, to Manistee, Michigan, to seek shelter from a storm behind Innes Island (that island has a knack for coming in handy!).

Unfortunately, while the steamer lay at peaceful anchor, she caught fire and burned to the water's edge on Thursday, May 28, 1914. Shortly after four o'clock that morning, one of the crew discovered flames raging near the boiler house. By the time the remainder of the crew were roused to fight the fire, that section of the amidships was ablaze. Those people sleeping in the vessel's stern were just barely able to reach the lifeboat in the forward part of the steamer, so quickly did the flames gain headway.

Captain James Maddock (also the ship's owner) saw to it that no lives were lost among the 11 people on board at the time, but he knew that it had been a close call, and he considered the seven people who had been in the *Thompson's* stern extremely fortunate to escape with their lives. Minus most of their clothes and personal belongings which they were forced to abandon in their haste, the *Thompson's* crew and passengers, many still in their nightclothes, tumbled into the single yawl boat and pulled away just as the entire ship burst into "a mass of flames from bow to stern."

Evidence of the EMMA E. THOMPSON'S *fiery demise lies in the hull, along with numerous items of machinery and tools, in about 25' of water.* PHOTO BY CRIS KOHL.

The author was overwhelmed by the EMMA E. THOMPSON *wreck, a site where a dozen dives would be too few to do it justice. The dramatic scene which will stay forever in his memory is the bow area, with three sets of large-link anchor chains sweeping in smooth, flowing lines from the bow to the lake bottom.* PHOTO BY CRIS KOHL.

In that early morning hour, the captain of the passing passenger steamer, *Germanic,* of the Northern Navigation Company, noticed the lurid glare of smoke in the sky. He changed course and pumped his ship's speed to the limit. The *Thompson's* people, although shivering in the cold of the early morning spring air as they rested on their oars and watched their ship burn, were all safe when the *Germanic* picked them up. Spare clothing was located on board the *Germanic* for the people still in their nightclothes as the rescue ship proceeded to Owen Sound, Ontario. From there, the wreck victims departed for their respective homes.

By 1914, the Great Lakes media had few kind words for aging wooden vessels. The newspaper nearest to the scene of the *Thompson's* sinking, the MANITOULIN EXPOSITOR at Little Current, Ontario, commented that " The boat was an old one and appeared crippled when passing here on Wednesday...."

The steamer, *Emma E. Thompson,* was located by commercial diver, Richard Hammond, of Little Current, Ontario, in 1992. Considering that the ship burned, her remains are impressive, recognizable, and surprisingly complete. The engine, for example, shows very little fire damage, while the boiler displays hinged doors of more detail and intricate construction than are usually seen on a vessel.

This shipwreck, upright and, in large measure, intact, sits embedded in the soft clay and sand bottom. Over half of the large, wooden rudder, for example, is sunk into the lake bottom.

Visiting divers can appreciate many sights: following the hull along the ship's perimeter, exploring inside the hull and viewing the engine, boiler, tools, rope, chains, pumps, and other items, before heading to the impressive bow, with its three sets of anchor chains, one of which leads to an anchor mostly buried in the bottom not too far from the hull.

A boat is absolutely necessary to reach this site, but it need not be a large vessel; our inflatable boat served us very well in this area, even in the rough weather we encountered that first time we visited this site. However you get to the site of the *Emma E. Thompson,* it will be well worth it.

APPENDIX A

Vessel Types

[The artwork for, and the descriptions of, the sailing ships (#1-8) in this appendix originally appeared in the *1885 List of Merchant Vessels of the United States*, while the steamships (#9-16) appeared in *American Steam Vessels* by Samuel Ward Stanton, 1895.]

1. SCHOONER (TWO MASTS). A name applied to vessels of fore-and-aft rig [having sails in front of, as well as behind, the masts, but no yards, or horizontal cross-masts] of various sizes. Schooners have two or more long lower masts without tops, and are sometimes fitted with light square topsails, especially at the fore....The schooner used to be the rig chiefly for small vessels, but some of the more modern schooners measure 800 and 1,000 tons and carry three or four masts.

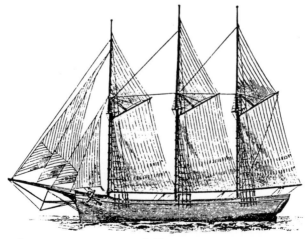

2. SCHOONER (FORE-AND-AFT, THREE MASTS). These were very common on the Great Lakes.

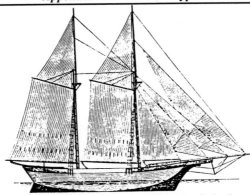

3. SCOW. The scow is a vessel used in the shoal waters of nearly all the States, but principally on the lakes. Scows are built with flat bottoms and square bilges, but some of them have the ordinary schooner bow. Scow-schooners are fitted with two or three masts. Some of them carry bowsprits.... The distinctive line between the scow and the regular-built schooner is, in the case of some large vessels, quite obscure, but would seem to be determined by the shape of the bilge, the scow having in all cases the angular bilge instead of the curve bilge of the ordinary vessel.

4. BARK (OR BARQUE). The bark has only fore-and-aft sails (no yards) on the mizzen [or shortest] mast. Barks are commonly smaller than ships, although some vessels of 1,000 and 1,500 tons are so rigged for sake of economy. They generally carry double topsails.

5. BARKENTINE. The barkentine is rigged with three masts, square-rigged with yards on the foremast only, and fore and aft sails on the main and mizzen masts. Barkentines are generally constructed with great length in proportion to their breadth, and on the lakes are built to suit the peculiar navigation of those narrow waters.

6. BRIG. A two-mast square-rigged vessel. The full-rigged brig has fore and main lower masts, topmasts, and topgallant masts, and yards on each with or without a square mainsail, and carrying also a trysail.

7. HERMAPHRODITE BRIG. The hermaphrodite, or half, brig is a vessel with a brig's foremast and a schooner's mainmast, square-rigged forward and fore-and-aft rigged aft.

8. BRIGANTINE. Its resemblance to the word "brigand" suggests a piratical vessel. The brigantine rig (or brig-schooner) is similar to the hermaphrodite, excepting that brigantines carry a light topsail on the mainmast above the large fore-and-aft mainsail.... The brigantine rig is becoming quite rare in American waters.

9. EARLY STEAMER. The 135' *Walk-in-the-Water,* the first steamboat constructed for use on the upper Great Lakes (1818), carried double midship sidewheels and two tall masts, for emergency sail power, fitted with a square-rigged foresail. The tall smokestack rose between the masts, and she carried a small signal cannon on her bow (steam whistles were not invented until 1843). All accommodations were below deck. This ship stranded and broke up along Lake Erie in 1821.

10. PASSENGER AND FREIGHT SIDEWHEEL STEAMER. The early steamer, the 274' *North Star* (built at Cleveland in 1854 and burned there in 1862) carried her engine, walking beam, boilers, and smokestacks midship, with the pilothouse forward. Arches at midship gave support to the pair of paddlewheels. She was beautiful, splendidly furnished, and fast (17 knots).

11. WOODEN, PROPELLER-DRIVEN, STEAM-POWERED FREIGHTER. The *Badger State,* built at Buffalo in 1862 and lost to flames on the St. Clair River in 1909, carried twin hog arches for structural support, an old style initially retained when steamship design changed from paddlewheel power to propeller power. Engine, boiler, and smokestack were located aft, with a decorative pilothouse, wooden eagle perched atop, forward.

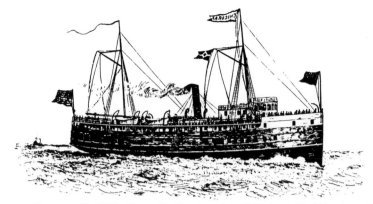

12. PASSENGER STEAMER. The 198' *Chicora* (built at Detroit in 1892, lost with all hands on Lake Michigan in 1895) was a wooden, propeller-driven, steamship powered by a triple expansion engine and two Scotch boilers. The 56 staterooms were beautifully furnished. She carried her pilothouse forward and her single smokestack midship.

13. WOODEN, PROPELLER-DRIVEN, STEAM-POWERED FREIGHTER. The 305' *Thomas Cranage,* the largest wooden steamer afloat in 1893 when launched at West Bay City, Michigan, stranded and broke up on Georgian Bay in 1911. Between the forward pilothouse and the aft propulsion system (engine, boiler, smokestack, propeller, etc.) stood three masts as emergency power.

14. STEEL, PROPELLER-DRIVEN, STEAM-POWERED FREIGHTER. Experiments in hull construction included an iron-hulled freighter, the 299' *Onoko,* built in 1882, and the 301', steel-hulled *Western Reserve* (above) from 1891, both ships built at Cleveland. By 1903, wood as a material for commercial freighters had become obsolete.

15. WHALEBACK. Of the 40 ships built on the Great Lakes between 1888 and 1897 using this novel design, all were bulk freighters except for the one pictured above. The passenger whaleback, *Chistopher Columbus,* was constructed for the 1893 World's Fair in Chicago, and scrapped in 1936. Nicknamed "pigboats," these ungainly, semi-submarine, strong freighters displayed a distinctive snout crowned with triple towrings and on-deck turrets for hull access.

16. TUG. These powerful workhorses with limited, spartan accommodations, and ranging in length from about 40' to 120', worked primarily towing larger ships in and out of harbors and up rivers. Steel later replaced wood construction.

17. DREDGE. These flat-bottomed, rectangular boats, usually towed by a tug but sometimes self-propelled, used steam-powered clambuckets to deepen rivers, harbors, and approaches. A large, box-shaped cabin on deck served to house the crew. These vessels were quite unstable in bad weather. (Drawing from the DULUTH HERALD, April 29, 1909.)

APPENDIX B

Vessel Parts

The following very selective list consists of 57 vessel parts referred to in *The 100 Best Great Lakes Shipwrecks, Volumes I and II.* Anyone exploring a shipwreck should learn to recognize these items for a greater appreciation of their underwater experience. These are all items which are actually found on Great Lakes shipwrecks, so forget about sextants, steerageway, or wigwags.

The line drawings in this section appeared in *Beeson's,* 1894 and 1895.

anchor --- a weighted device used to hold a vessel in place on water. An anchor is lowered to the bottom of the water by means of a line or a chain, until one or both points of the anchor catch onto the bottom. An anchor usually has a long shank (or trunk) and at least two extended flukes (the flat, pointed end of each anchor arm), and, often in the Great Lakes, a wooden stock at its top. These are relatively common sights on shipwrecks in the inland seas.

beam --- 1. the width, or breadth, of a ship at its widest point. 2. a part of a ship's framing which supported the deck.

belaying pins --- Foot-long wooden or metal rods, thicker at one end than the other, used as bracing devices for securing ropes controlling sails or masts. Often found along ship's railings in pin rails, or in round mast rails in the center of the ship. Readily removed, and thus often missing from wrecks.

bell --- a loud, metal, sound-making device used to signal a variety of concerns, such as distress, fog, fire, time, or meals on board a ship. An iron clapper is struck suddenly against the brass or steel sides of the bell, producing a sharp, loud sound. Sometimes marine bells were engraved with the ship's name, making them desirable collectors' items today. Rarely seen on shipwrecks.

bilge pump --- a metal, mechanical device (electric on modern ships), usually mounted on deck, which flushes the water out of the bilge, or the very bottom of the ship, where waste water such as rain or water rushing into a damaged hull collects. Vintage two-man pumps created a vacuum in a long tube which sucked the water out of the ship and deposited it over the side. Bilge pumps are quite common sights on Great Lakes shipwrecks, usually with the removable wooden, seesaw handle missing.

binnacle --- a protective stand or pedestal, often made of wood and brass, harboring the ship's compass, and usually bolted to the deck in a position easily seen by the helmsman at the wheel. This is a rare shipwreck item.

bitt --- a thick vertical post, usually found in pairs, made of iron and capped with an overhanging lip to prevent slippage, bolted to the deck of a ship for securing mooring and other lines. When these units do the same job on a dock, they are called "bollards"; "bitt" and "bollard" are often incorrectly interchanged.

block --- a hardwood (e.g. oak), later metal, round or oval casing for one or more rollers, or sheaves, guiding ropes to a change in direction or for mechanical advantage in lifting heavy loads. Often there is a ring at one end and a hook on the other. Blocks were more common than deadeyes on Great Lakes ships, but, like deadeyes, they were easily removed by divers craving "tokens of accomplishment" in the early days.

boiler --- on a steamship usually, a large, cylindrical heated iron tank used for converting water into steam, producing power to operate an engine. The most common type of boiler on Great Lakes vessels was the Scotch boiler, usually 10' by 14' in size, containing wood or coal burning furnaces below the water and heating tubes, all constructed within a single unit.

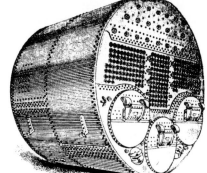

A Scotch boiler is pictured here.

bow --- the front, or forward part of a vessel, sometimes referred to as "the pointy end." Opposite of "stern."

bowsprit --- a long, wooden spar attached to a sailing vessel's bow, extending forward like a unicorn's horn. This often added 30' or more to a ship's length, but it allowed the use of small, efficient triangular headsails ahead of the forward mast. Sometimes incorrectly called a "bowsprint."

bucket --- a nickname for a propeller blade, e.g. "We lost a bucket," meaning we lost or broke a propeller blade. Spare "buckets," or propeller blades, were often carried on board, e.g. the *Myron* in Lake Superior still has one on site.

capstan --- a vertical, rotating, mechanical, metal ratchet device shaped like an hourglassed, cylindrical barrel, used to haul up an anchor or to tighten docking lines in port, similar in function to a windlass, only vertical instead of horizontal. The top of the capstan had six to eight openings, called pigeon holes, along its circular edge, into which sailors inserted wooden capstan bars and worked as a team pushing these bars while walking in a circle and winding the line or chain around the capstan body until the desired tautness was achieved. A more expensive ship often had brass capstan covers, resembling rounded lids, with the ship's name engraved on them, to protect the mechanical components of the barrel from the elements.

cathead --- a thick, wooden, deck-level beam projecting at right angles off the bows (one on the port side, one on the starboard side) used to support the ship's anchors and anchor tackle when not in use (an anchor fluke would also be lashed to the outside of the hull to hold the anchor in place when underway).

centerboard --- a portable keel, housed inside a long, narrow, wooden box below deck, it could be lowered or raised, depending upon the navigation conditions; lowered, the centerboard provided lateral stability against wind, while raised, it allowed ships to traverse shallow waters. On the Great Lakes, it was more common on sailing vessels than on steamers.

chain --- a length of connected, forged or fused, metal links, far stronger than rope and most often attached to the anchor. It was not uncommon for Great Lakes ships to carry 200' of chain for each anchor.

compass --- a round navigation instrument, often in a brass and glass housing gimbaled in a binnacle or stowed in a box, used to indicate the direction, or the heading, of a vessel. Its free-spinning, magnetized needle automatically points to magnetic north, which, by a fortunate coincidence, is pretty close to true north. Great Lakes mariners could work without a sextant due to the relatively short times when they were out of sight of land, but every ship carried a compass.

crosstree --- a wooden or metal horizontal brace used to support a lookout's platform on a mast.

davit --- a curved, metal hoisting arm used to lift a lifeboat from the deck to the water. Davits are used in pairs.

deadeye --- a round, flat block of hardwood (usually oak in the Great Lakes) with three holes drilled into it (giving it the appearance of a skull, and hence the name "deadeye") through which ropes used to trim a ship's standing rigging would be passed. These ropes could be loosened or tightened, depending upon the desired angle of the masts. Deadeyes also worked in pairs, a rope-supported-upper and a hull-attached lower, and it was not uncommon for a three-masted schooner to be rigged with at least 36 deadeyes. Deadeyes on today's Great Lakes shipwrecks usually have the ropes rotted out of them. Often looted by divers in the past.

donkey boiler --- a small boiler which provided steam power for winches and other auxiliary machinery. These could be found on steamships as well as on sailing vessels and barges.

draft, or draught --- the depth of water in which a vessel can float without striking bottom. Draft marks, often in Roman rather than Arabic numerals, grace the stemposts and sternposts of many Great Lakes shipwrecks. These numbers indicated the draft and the trim of a loaded ship.

engine --- the mechanical machinery which converted steam into power for the propulsion of, in this case, a vessel. The two main types of steam engines on the Great Lakes were the steeple compound engine (a two-piston, two-cylinder engine) and the triple expansion engine (a triple-piston, triple-cylinder engine). Early mariners considered each piston to be an "engine," so shipwreck accounts

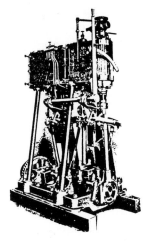

often relate the failure of a ship's "engines" (plural) even though there was only a single propulsion unit on board. Often these massive, upright engines rise impressively 30' above the shipwreck, as in the case of the *Montana* in Lake Huron. A walking beam engine was used in early paddlewheelers, with the very noticeable metal, diamond-shaped, above-deck walking beam moving the piston rod and crankshaft alternately up and down like a seesaw. Two types of steam engines are pictured here.

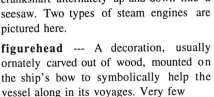

6 in. x 8 in. HIGH PRESSURE.

figurehead --- A decoration, usually ornately carved out of wood, mounted on the ship's bow to symbolically help the vessel along in its voyages. Very few Great Lakes ships carried figureheads: the *Hamilton* and the *Scourge* in Lake Ontario; the *Dunderberg*, the *City of Milwaukee*, and the *James R. Bentley* in Lake Huron; and the *Sandusky* and the *Northerner* in Lake Michigan

frame --- in ship construction, the curved uprights emanating from, and at right angles to, either side of the keel. Many shallow shipwrecks in the Great Lakes consist only of keel and some frames due to destructive ice and wave action. Also called "rib," "futtock," and "timber."

gauge --- a mechanical device tracking one of the different operational aspects of an engine, e.g. a steam pressure gauge, water level gauge, etc. These gauges were made of brass or steel, with indicator faces and needles covered by glass.

hanging knee --- a right-angled (L-shaped), solid piece of wood used as bracing mainly between the inside of the hull and the underside of the deck.

hatch --- a horizontal doorway in the deck of a ship leading to the below-deck area.

hawsepipe --- a short, angled, metal tube running through the hull at deck level, acting as a protective guide for thick ropes ("hawsers") or anchor chains.

head --- 1. the front, or bow, part of a vessel. 2. a shipboard toilet, named after the very front part of the ship's bow where early sailors often relieved themselves over the side. Since the wind usually blew from the stern of a sailing vessel in order to fill the sails, the "head" or bow part of the ship, with the wind at the seamen's backs, became the decidedly favored location for such necessary activity.

hull --- the body, or shell, of a ship, usually made of wood, iron, steel, or composite construction. Planking was secured tightly on the frames which emanated from the keel in order to make the ship watertight. Decking, which covered the top of the hull, was secured to it below deck by means of hanging knees.

keel --- in ship construction, the main structural member, or the backbone, of a ship, extending from bow to stern along the center line at the bottom of the hull. The "laying of the keel" was the first step in a ship's material construction.

lightbulb cage --- a protective wire or metal strap frame around a lightbulb on a ship. Common on newer Great Lakes shipwrecks two types are pictured here.

mast --- a tall, vertical, wooden pole, similar to a telegraph or telephone pole on land, stepped to mid-deck or to the keel of a vessel, supporting sails, spars, and rigging. Early steamships carried short masts for emergency propulsion.

mast hole --- a circular opening in a vessel's deck to allow a mast to be stepped to the keel at the very bottom of a ship. Masts were often dislodged in Great Lakes shipwrecks, leaving only gaping holes.

pilothouse --- the enclosed housing attached to a ship's deck and containing the helm and navigation equipment. Also called a "wheel house."

port --- 1. the left side of a ship when facing forward. Opposite of starboard. 2. a place where a vessel can take refuge. 3. a door in a ship's side.

porthole --- a window on board a ship. Usually round, with thick glass in a metal (brass or steel) frame, and able to be opened from the inside of the ship to let in fresh air, or closed to keep out water in bad weather.

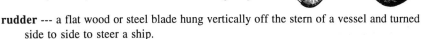

propeller --- two to five blades, usually steel, attached to a hub which rotates and propels a ship forward. Also called a "screw" or a "wheel," and sometimes spelled "propellor." See "bucket." Propeller pictured on right.

rigging --- all the ropes, wires, blocks, deadeyes, sails, booms, and tackle used on a sailing ship.

rudder --- a flat wood or steel blade hung vertically off the stern of a vessel and turned side to side to steer a ship.

rudder post --- the vertical wooden pole used to support the rudder. Also referred to as the sternpost, this often stands upright at a shipwreck site while much of the hull and decking have collapsed around it.

running lights --- lanterns were used in early days to indicate the vessel's moving position at night: a green lantern on the starboard side and a red lantern on the port side.

samson post --- a bitt positioned in the centerline of a ship, often used for towing or for being towed.

smokestack --- a wide, vertical, metal pipe eliminating smoke and fumes from the ship's propulsion center, the engine room, below deck. A chimney on a vessel. Also called simply a "stack" or a "funnel."

starboard --- the right side of the ship when facing forward. Opposite of port.

steam whistle --- a long, hollow, cylindrical device, usually made of brass, used for signaling other ships or people at docks for a number of different reasons: warning, distress, arrival, departure, passing, etc. Often arranged on a smokestack in pairs or triplets for different sound ranges.

steering quadrant --- a pie-wedge-shaped metal framework attached to the top of the rudder stock, with chain or rope running along the arc to the ship's wheel.

stempost --- in ship construction, the curved, almost vertical upward extension of the keel at the bow. The stempost often has draft markings painted on or carved into it.

stern --- the after end, or back part, of a ship, also called the aft. Opposite of "bow."

sternpost --- in ship construction, the vertical extension of the keel which supports the rudder at the aft, or stern, end of a vessel. The sternpost often has draft markings carved into it, like the stempost. The sternpost is also called the "rudder post."

telegraph --- a gonged, mechanical apparatus, usually encased in brass and mounted near the helm, used in pairs for tandem communication between the pilot house and the engine room on steamships. Speed instructions, such as FULL, HALF, SLOW, STOP, and REVERSE appeared under glass with brass indicators. Also called a "chadburn." Usually seen only on virgin shipwrecks.

transom --- the flat, back end of a vessel, located at the extreme stern, and often marked with the ship's name and home port in painted or metal letters.

wheel --- 1. the round wooden or metal steering wheel mounted on deck used to maneuver the rudder. 2. a huge, multi-spoked circle of paddles which propelled the older-style paddlewheel steamer. 3. an old sailor's term for a propeller.

winch --- a mechanical device of several variations with a revolving drum around which is coiled rope, chain, or cable for hoisting or hauling cargo. A centerboard winch was used to raise and lower the centerboard. Later winches were steam-powered. Pictured on right.

windlass --- a horizontal, mechanical, ratchet winch used in the raising of the ship's anchor, and hence, always located at the bow of a ship. Frequently seen on Great Lakes wrecks of older sailing craft.

yawl boat --- 1. on board a ship, a yawl was a small rowboat used as a lifeboat in emergencies. A fine example of one sits on starboard midship of the *Vienna* in Lake Superior. 2. a yawl is also a two-masted sailing vessel, with the mizzenmast (the shorter mast) aft of the vessel's helm, or steering post.

APPENDIX C

100 Deep
Great Lakes Shipwrecks
for Technical Diving

WARNING and DISCLAIMER

These 100 Great Lakes shipwrecks rest at depths beyond the 130 feet recommended by training agencies as the sport diving limit. They are presented here first of all for the historical record, and secondly with the awareness that an ever-growing scuba diving minority is being trained in deep diving skills required for exploring these shipwrecks. The author does not condone diving deeper than the suggested sport diving limit unless the divers have been specially trained in technical diving, are fully prepared to undertake such a diving experience, and possess a large degree of experience, skill, preparedness, and confidence. Such divers bear all responsibility and liability themselves for their actions. The author and publisher accept no responsibility for any loss, injury, death, or inconvenience sustained by any person using information in this book.

You're on your own.

Other Great Lakes states have laws similar to Michigan's: "No person shall recover, alter, or destroy abandoned property which is in, on, under, or over the bottomlands of the Great Lakes, unless the person has a permit issued jointly by the Secretary of State and the DNR (Department of Natural Resources)."

<u>NOTE</u>: The following deep shipwrecks are arranged alphabetically according to each of the Great Lakes.

Deep Lake Ontario Shipwrecks

CORMORANT --- This 18-ton tug foundered three miles north of Oswego, NY, on October 17, 1958 in 135' of water, sitting upright and intact, with the ship's wheel still inside the wheelhouse, a spotlight still in place, and a penetrable engine room. Located in the mid-1980's and kept a secret, this shipwreck looks "just as though she went down last week." Not usually buoyed.

DAVIS, LYMAN M. --- This schooner was one of the last working sailing vessels on the Great Lakes, but she was a remnant of a bygone era, so she was sacrificed for the mindless entertainment of the bored masses in a flaming spectacle off Toronto's Sunnyside Park on June 29, 1934. Her hull lies half buried in the lake's soft bottom in 148' of water. LAT/LON: 43.36.16 / 79.24.97

HAMILTON --- This vintage schooner, built in 1809, foundered on August 8, 1813, in 275' to 289' of water with considerable loss of life in the same squall which capsized the *Scourge* (see below) during the War of 1812 off the Niagara River near present-day St. Catharines, Ontario. These U.S. ships of war rest in Canadian waters, and the U.S. government gave ownership of them to the province of Ontario, which, in turn, gave them to the city of Hamilton, Ontario, for that city's proposed raising of the wrecks as a tourist attraction. Besides requesting the return of any human remains for interment at Arlington National Cemetery, the U.S. government relinquished ownership of these military wrecks on condition that something be done with them by Canadian authorities. Nothing is apparently being done, so technical divers are pounding on the doors of the *Hamilton* and the *Scourge*, seeking loopholes for legal access to these historic, figureheaded shipwrecks laden with cannons, swords, and human remains.

OCEAN WAVE --- This 174' steamer, built at Montreal in 1852, burned and sank with great loss of life on April 30, 1853, in 153' of water off Point Traverse, Ontario, west of Kingston. The wreck lies upside-down with the engine standing upright 0.4 mile from the hull site. Usually poor visibility.

SCOURGE --- This historic, War of 1812, 110-ton schooner, built in 1811, foundered off the Niagara River near present-day St. Catharines, ON, on August 8, 1813, in 275' to 289', along with the *Hamilton* (see above for details).

Deep Lake Erie Shipwrecks

ATLANTIC --- This famous shipwreck, a 267-foot passenger steamer, lies in about 163' of water. This palatial vessel sank with the loss of about 150 lives after a collision with the steamer, *Ogdensburg,* on August 20, 1852. The very photogenic, giant paddlewheels rise to within 135' of the surface. This wreck lies to the southwest of the tip of Long Point. Unfortunately, at press time, this shipwreck was still off limits to scuba/sport divers pending the outcome of the court case which has pitted a California salvage company claiming to have found this so-called "treasure wreck" in 1990 against the

Ontario government and Michael Fletcher, the Port Dover, Ontario diver who located the shipwreck in 1984 and fully documented his find. Reportedly as of June, 1998, a group from Port Dover, Ontario, put a marker buoy on the *Atlantic,* and boats have been visiting the site with scuba divers. Another report states that Canadian authorities are planning to restart their satellite surveillance of this site to keep divers off. Until some things are ascertained, the co-ordinates cannot be published.

ONEIDA --- Nineteen people lost their lives when the steamer, *Oneida,* capsized off Barcelona, New York, on November 11, 1852. The ship sank in 165' of water. LAT/LON: 42.28.88 / 79.51.88

PERSIAN --- This shipwrecks rests in 197' of deep, dark, Lake Erie water, which comes pretty close to the deepest point in the lake at 210'! This four-masted freight steamer burned to a total loss on August 23, 1875 and sank about five miles east of Long Point, Ontario. LAT/LON: 42.33.805 / 79.54.688, LORAN: 44581.7 / 58661.4

SMITH --- This large tugboat, 120' in length, was being towed to Sarnia for a refit at the time of loss in a storm on October 24, 1930. This impressive wreck is upright and intact at a depth of 160' to the southeast off the tip of Long Point, Ontario. LORAN: 44530.0 / 58607.4

UNIDENTIFIED SHIPWRECK --- Known only as the "mast hoop wreck," this schooner, 120' in length, sits in 158' of water. immediately due north of the tip of Long Point. Intact portions of this shipwreck include the bowsprit, deadeyes, and mast hoops.

UNIDENTIFIED SHIPWRECK --- Nicknamed "schooner X," this two-masted ship sits in 163' with its masts rising to 81'. The ship's anchors are in place, complete with bow chains, deadeyes, rigging, and a figurehead. This magnificent shipwreck has been described as "one of the Great Lakes most impressive wrecks." "Schooner X" lies just to the south of the tip of Long Point.

UNIDENTIFIED SHIPWRECK --- Nicknamed the "arch wreck" because of its supporting arches in midship which strengthened the cargo section where most of the weight was located, this steamer (either 178' or 190' in length, depending on who did the measuring) sits upright in 156' of water. The arches rise to within 127'. The ship's engine and the anchors are also still in place, and it reportedly has unusual "square propeller blades." This may be the 583-ton, 1847-built steamer, *Ohio,* which exploded on November 6, 1859 off Long Point, with the loss of two of the 17 people on board. Some say it could be the wreck of the *Idaho,* a 220-foot steamer built in 1863 and lost off Long Point on November 5, 1897. LORAN: 44516.3 / 58587.0. LAT/LON: 42.27.469 / 80.00.987

UNIDENTIFIED SHIPWRECK --- Nicknamed the "Tiller Wreck," because it was steered by a tiller rather than a ship's wheel, this vessel seems to be one of the oldest wrecks in the Long Point area. It is the remains of a sailing vessel 110' in length resting in 162' of water. This shipwreck is upright and intact, displaying yardarms from a mast, plus deadeyes, anchor, and windlass. It lies immediately due east of Long Point's tip.

Deep Lake Huron Shipwrecks

ALBANY --- Launched at Detroit in 1846, this 210', grain-loaded steamer sank in 142' of water off Grindstone City, Michigan, after a collision with the 236' steamer *Philadelphia* on November 7, 1893. Eight lives were lost from this ship. LORAN: 30775.5 / 49174.2, LAT/LON: 44.05.34 / 82.42.03

ARCTIC --- The 193' steamer *Arctic,* built in 1864 at Cleveland, sprang a leak and foundered in thick, smoky weather off Harbor Beach, MI, on September 5, 1893. No lives were lost. The *Arctic* was located in 136' of water by Dave Trotter and his resolute group of divers in 1987. LORAN: 30748.4 / 49371.4, LAT/LON: 43.41.530 / 82.28.637

ARGUS --- This 436' steel steamer, located by divers in 1972, lies upside-down in 220' of water off Michigan's thumb. The ship sank with all hands (25) in the terrible storm of November 9, 1913. LORAN: 30790.6 / 49068.2

BARGE NO. 9 ---The remains of this vessel lie in 150' of water off Port Sanilac, MI. LORAN: 30710.1 / 49478.9, LAT/LON: 43.27.88 / 82.18.22

BARNEY, F.T. --- This two-masted, coal-carrying, 130' schooner, which sank in a collision with the schooner *Tracy J. Bronson* on October 23, 1868, sits in 160' of water off Rogers City, MI. The one intact mast even boasts an intact crowsnest! This ship, built at Vermilion, Ohio, in 1856, was positively identified by Stan Stock in 1989. LORAN: 30984.1 / 48390.7, LAT/LON: 45.29.26 / 83.50.50

BECKER, G.F. --- This undamaged 40' tug, which sank under mysterious circumstances on September 9, 1931 off Michigan's thumb, was found by Dave Trotter and his deep-diving team in 190' of water in 1995.

BENTLEY, JAMES R. --- Discovered by John Steele in 1984 (and afterwards often rediscovered by wanna-be's), this 178' three-masted schooner, built in 1867 at Fairport, Ohio, foundered on November 12, 1878 in 165' of water off Forty Mile Point, MI. The mizzenmast is still upright, but the other masts have toppled. Much silt and low visibility. The unique dragon figurehead is now safe in the Manitowoc, WI, marine museum. LORAN: 31057.7 / 48251.1,   LAT/LON: 45.41.44 / 84.09.11

BRANDY 4 --- The remains of this mysteriously-named vessel sit in 200' of water off Presque Isle, Michigan. LORAN: 30984.0 / 48692.8

CLEMENT, NORMAN P. --- On October 23, 1968, this 44-year-old, British-built, 261' steel tanker was scuttled in 350' of Georgian Bay waters off Christian Island, Ontario. The ship had exploded at Collingwood during welding a week earlier, injuring 11 men. Her cargoes were usually sulfuric acid.

CURRAN, JAMES W. --- The 103' auto ferry, which ran between the two Sault Ste. Marie's, sank in 200' of water 18 miles north of Pointe aux Barques, MI, on May 9, 1964 with the *John A. McPhail* while both vessels were being towed to Kingston, ON. No lives were lost. Found by Stan Stock in the 1980's.

DETROIT --- This sidewheel steamer sank in 200' of water after a collision with the bark, *Nucleus,* in dense fog on May 25, 1854, off Grindstone City, Michigan. The site highlight, a ship's bell, is inscribed "New York, 1844" (the ship was built at Newport, now Marine City, Michigan, in 1846). This wreck was found by Dave Trotter and his determined divers on June 5, 1994. LORAN: 30776.46 / 49105.91, LAT/LON: 44.13.625 / 82.45.341

DORR, E.P. --- This 120' steam tug sank off Grindstone City on Michigan's thumb after a collision in 1856. She sits upright and intact in 178' of water. LORAN: 30779.8 / 49145.5, LAT/LON: 44.08.62 / 82.43.82

DUFFERIN, LADY --- In October, 1886, this 135' schooner-barge stranded on the rocks just outside the present-day boundaries of Fathom Five National Marine Park near Tobermory, Ontario. The wreckage tumbled down a steep incline, 40' to 200'+ deep. Two circles spray-painted onto a cliff mark the site.

Joyce Hayward examines the DUNDERBERG'S *unique figurehead.* PHOTO BY CRIS KOHL.

DUNDERBERG --- This three-masted, 187' schooner sits upright and intact in 155' of water about four miles off Harbor Beach, MI. The one-year-old ship, laden with corn, sank in a collision with the steamer, *Empire State,* on August 13, 1868, with the loss of one life. The highlight of this site rests at a depth of 135': the ornately-carved figurehead (of an alligator, jaw-dropped, tongue protruding, eye still glinting with a dab of red paint) with grapes, birds, and curling vines and branches carved in the trim boards curving back from the bowsprit. The *Dunderberg* was located by Kent Bellrichard in 1971. LORAN: 30740.7 / 49257.0, LAT/LON: 43.45.48 / 82.33.24

EDDY, NEWELL A. --- This three-year-old, 242' schooner-barge foundered in 149' to 167' of water just east of Mackinac on April 20, 1893 with the loss of her grain cargo and all seven people on board. The wreck was discovered on July 25, 1992 by a University of Michigan research team on board the 80' ship, *Laurentian.* LAT/LON: 45.46.90 / 84.13.66

FLORIDA --- This 270' steamer, built at Buffalo, New York, in 1889, sank in about 235' of water between Middle Island and Presque Isle, Michigan, after she was struck by the steamer, *George W. Roby,* on May 20, 1897. The *Florida* was reportedly first located in 1994 by Darryl Ertel, Matt Turchi, Ed Ellison, and Scott Short.

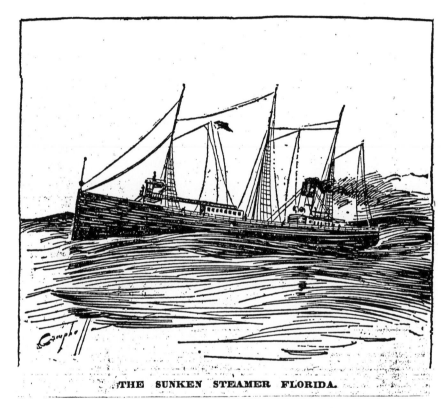

THE SUNKEN STEAMER FLORIDA.

This drawing of "The Sunken Steamer FLORIDA*" appeared in the* DETROIT FREE PRESS *May 22, 1897.*

FOREST CITY --- Stranded and wrecked in fog at Bear's Rump Island off Tobermory, Ontario, on June 5, 1904, this 214' wooden steamer slopes from 60' to 157' of water. The stern at the deep end is particularly scenic. LORAN: 30158.0 / 48675.1, LAT/LON: 45.19.04 / 81.33.52

HANNA, D.R. --- This 532' steel freighter sank after a collision with the steamer, *Quincy A. Shaw* off Alpena, Michigan, on May 16, 1919. The crew was rescued. The wreck lies upside-down in 90' to 140' of water. LORAN: 30771.3 / 48666.4, LAT/LON: 45.05.00 / 83.05.02

GILBERT, W.H. --- This 328' steamer, located in 1983 in 255' of water off Thunder Bay Island, Alpena, Michigan, sank in a collision with the 500' steamer, *Caldera,* on the foggy night of May 22, 1914. LORAN: 30765.8 / 48795.0

IRON CHIEF --- This 212' wooden bulk freight steamer foundered several miles off Grindstone City, Michigan, in 135' of water on October 4, 1904. LORAN: 30779.0 / 49172.0, LAT/LON: 44.05.58 / 82.42.58

JOHNSON, HENRY J. --- The 273' wooden steamer, *Henry J. Johnson,* collided in fog with the steamer, *Fred Pabst,* off Spectacle Reef about nine miles east of Bois Blanc Island on July 24, 1902. The wreck sits in 160' of water off Hammond Bay. LORAN: 31050.0 / 48285.3

LEE, FRED --- Also referred to as the *Frederick A. Lee,* this tug foundered in about 200' of water off Point aux Barques, Michigan, with the loss of all five hands on Friday, November 13, 1936. Dave Trotter's obstinate crew found this wreck in 1996. LORAN: 30780.83 / 49115.23, LAT/LON: 44.12.422 / 82.45.556

MCGEAN, JOHN --- A victim of the Great Storm of November 9, 1913, this 452' steel steamer sank with the loss of all hands in 198' of water. The wreck lies upside-down off Michigan's thumb. The *McGean* was found by Dave Trotter and his crew of fellow enthusiasts in 1986. LORAN: 30723.8 / 49245.9

MCPHAIL, JOHN A. --- This is one of the two car ferries which sank north of Pointe aux Barques, Michigan, while being towed to Kingston, Ontario, on May 9, 1964, and lies in 200' of water. These ships were located by Stan Stock in the 1980's. See also *Curran, James W.* (above).

MILWAUKEE, CITY OF --- This 139' schooner foundered on Friday night, November 5, 1875, in 172' of water off Port Sanilac, Michigan. All hands were saved. The wreck was located by Dave Trotter and his team on July 7, 1990. The bow sports an elegant dragon-shaped figurehead.

MINNEDOSA --- This 245', four-masted schooner was the largest sailing vessel ever built on the Canadian side of the Great Lakes. She sank with all eight hands in a storm on October 20, 1905 off Harbor Beach, Michigan. The wreck, sitting in about 205' of water, was located in 1991 after a long search by Dave Trotter and his group of intrepid searchers/divers.

MONROVIA --- The 430' steel, ocean freighter, *Monrovia,* sank off Alpena, Michigan, in 90' to 150' of water after a collision with the freighter, *Royalton,* on June 25, 1959. The crew was rescued. Most of the steel cargo was salvaged. LORAN: 30724.1 / 48729.1, LAT/LON: 44.58.93 / 82.55.26

MORRELL, DANIEL J. (bow) --- This 60-year-old, 587' steel freighter broke in half during a storm on November 29, 1966 off Michigan's thumb. From her crew of 29, there was only one survivor, Dennis Hale, who floated on a liferaft for 36 hours before being rescued. The stern half powered on into the darkness of night and sank five miles from the bow. The bow rests in 213' of water. LORAN: 30761.4 / 49068.4, LAT/LON: 44.18.320 / 82.45.161

ABOVE: *The 587' steel freighter,* DANIEL J. MORRELL, *carried a short mast on her bow with the letter "C" (for the Cambria Steel Company) on top, being examined here by Joan Forsberg and her burbot buddies. This is in 100' of water.* BELOW: *Diver Joan Forsberg about to enter the* MORRELL'S *pilot house at 142'.*   PHOTOS BY CRIS KOHL.

MORRELL, DANIEL J. (stern) --- The stern half of this enormous steel freighter sits in 225' of water. See above for the story of this sinking. Out of the Blue Productions of Lexington, Michigan, sells an excellent 96-minute videotape entitled *"S.S. Daniel J. Morrell* Remembered." LORAN: 30803.7 / 49086.3, LAT/LON: 44.15.33 / 82.49.90

Dennis Hale, the sole survivor of the tragic 1966 sinking of the freighter, DANIEL J. MORRELL, *gazes emotionally 30 years later across the abandoned shipbuilding yard in Bay City, MI, where the* MORRELL *was launched in 1906.* PHOTO BY CRIS KOHL.

NEW ORLEANS --- The 231', wooden steamer, *New Orleans,* sank in a collision with the huge, 420' steel freighter, *William R. Linn,* on June 30, 1906. No lives were lost. The *New Orleans* sits in about 150' of water off Alpena, Michigan. LORAN: 30808.0 / 48613.7, LAT/LON: 45.10.06 / 83.12.85

NIELSEN, EMMA L. --- This small (98'), 28-year-old schooner sank in a collision with the 346' steel freighter, *Wyandotte,* on June 26, 1911, about 11 miles off Pointe aux Barques, Michigan. The wreck, located by Dave Trotter and his team in April, 1980, sits in 195' of water. LORAN: 30763.9 / 49129.9

NORMAN --- The 296' steel steamer, *Norman,* sank after a collision with the 178' wooden steamer, *Jack,* off Alpena, Michigan, on May 30, 1895. Three lives were lost. The *Norman,* which sits with a 45 degree list in 210' of water, was located by John Steele in May, 1986, on the exact same morning that his colleague, Paul Ehorn, located the nearby *Cornelia B. Windiate* (see below) LORAN: 30809.2 / 48537.3

PERSIAN --- All ten men aboard this schooner lost their lives when the ship sank after a collision with the schooner, *E.B. Allen,* off 40 Mile Point, Michigan, on September, 1868. The *Persian* sits in 159' to 172' of water. LORAN: 31055.0 / 48246.0

PEWABIC --- This 200', wooden, passenger and freight steamer sank in a collision with her sister ship, the *Meteor,* on August 9, 1865 off Alpena, Michigan, with the loss of about 100 lives, one of the worst disasters in the history of the Great Lakes. The *Pewabic* lies in 148' to 168' of water. Out of the Blue Productions of Lexington, Michigan, recounts the story of the *Pewabic* and exploring her remains in their videotape, *"Pewabic,* The Death Ship of Lake Huron." LORAN: 30795.6 / 48723.3, LAT/LON: 44.57.82 / 83.05.96

SAVIDGE, HUNTER --- The 117' schooner, *Hunter Savidge,* sank in about 175' of water off Michigan's thumb when she was hit by a sudden white squall on August 20, 1899. Five lives were lost. This shipwreck was located by Dave Trotter and his team on August 13, 1988. LORAN: 30742.3 / 49175.8

SCOTT, ISAAC M. --- Another victim of the Big Storm of November 9, 1913, this 504' steel steamer lies upside-down in 180' of water off Alpena, MI. All 28 of her crew perished. This shipwreck was located by Kent Bellrichard and his team of Wisconsin divers in September, 1975, while searching for the *Viator* (see below). LORAN: 30758.3 / 48686.8, LAT/LON: 45.02.98 / 83.02.20

SCOTT, THOMAS --- This 136' wooden steamer, which foundered in Georgian Bay off Cabot Head, Ontario, on September 2, 1914, lies in 400' of water. The wreck was located accidentally in the summer of 1994 by a Canadian government vessel surveying the bay bottom. Contact the Canadian government for the co-ordinates.

SMITH, GOVERNOR --- Lying in 184' of water off Grindstone City, Michigan, the 17-year-old, 240' wooden steamer, *Governor Smith,* sank in a collision with the considerably larger steel steamer, *Uranus,* on August 19, 1906. About 28 years later, in a case of delayed retribution, the *Uranus* (by then renamed the *W.C. Franz),* sank in a collision with another ship off Alpena. No lives were lost when the *Governor Smith* sank. The wreck sits upright, but broken. LORAN: 30763.8 / 49141.3, LAT/LON: 44.09.33 / 82.41.90

TYPO --- This 137' schooner, built at Milwaukee, Wisconsin, in 1873, sank in 155' of water near Alpena, Michigan, after a collision with the wooden steamer, *V.H. Ketchum,* on October 14, 1899. Several people perished in this mishap. The wreck sits upright and intact. LORAN: 30825.7 / 48543.4

UNIDENTIFIED BARGE sits in 180' of water off Grindstone City, Michigan. LORAN: 30808.1 / 49123.5, LAT/LON: 44.10.85 / 82.48.67

VIATOR --- Built in Norway in 1904, the 241' steel steamer, *Viator,* was far from home when she sank in a fog-induced collision with the steel freighter, *Ormidale.* No lives were lost, but her cargo of iced fish products accompanied the ship to the bottom in 150' of water off Alpena, Michigan. This shipwreck was located by Kent Bellrichard and his team of Wisconsin divers in 1975. LORAN: 30766.4 / 48715.6, LAT/LON: 44.59.43 / 83.02.07

WINDIATE, CORNELIA B. --- This 138', 18-month-old schooner left Milwaukee with wheat for Buffalo on November 27, 1875. Ship and crew disappeared completely. The *Cornelia B. Windiate* was discovered by Paul Ehorn in May, 1986, on the exact same morning that his colleague, John Steele, located the nearby steamer, *Norman* (see above). The *Windiate* sits in 180' of water off Alpena, Michigan. LORAN: 30824.6 / 48525.3

Deep Lake Michigan Shipwrecks

ALLEN, WALTER B. --- This twin-masted, 137' schooner, built at Ogdensburg, New York, in 1866, foundered in a severe storm off Sheboygan, Wisconsin, on April 16, 1880. No lives were lost. The shipwreck, which sits in 90' to 165' of water, was located by Kent Bellrichard in May, 1975. LORAN: 32637.3 / 48748.0, LAT/LON: 43.53.08 / 87.41.01

BELL, JENNY --- Referred to as the *Jane Bell* by some researchers, this 110', twin-masted schooner capsized and sank in 150' of Green Bay water, a little over a mile southwest of Chambers Island, on October 10, 1881. A failed 1960's salvage attempt left a cable cut in the stern above the rudder. Visibility averages 7', which is good for Green Bay. The deck rises to a depth of about 128'. LORAN: 32176.11 / 48013.28, LAT/LON: 45.09.04 / 87.25.12

BRADLEY, CARL D. --- This 640', 31-year-old steel steamer rests in 365' of water five miles WNW of the Boulder Reef light in upper Lake Michigan. The ship reportedly broke in half in a storm on November 18, 1958, and sank with the loss of 33 of her 35 crew. This is the second-largest shipwreck in the Great Lakes (only the 729' *Edmund Fitzgerald* in Lake Superior is larger). This is an area of poor visibility, with "constant snow" existing below 300'. To date, no diver has explored this site. LORAN: 32427.2 / 49190.4, LAT/LON: 43.29.84 / 86.29.93

BYRON --- This little schooner, only 40' long and rising only about 3' off the lake bottom, is intact, with centerboard, fallen mast, attached tiller, and a capstan just off the wreck. The *Byron* sank in 135' of water off Sheboygan, Wisconsin, in a collision with the larger schooner, *Canton,* on May 8, 1867. This wreck is hard to find. Do not drag an anchor into any shipwreck while trying to locate it, particularly this fragile little beauty. Anchors cause damage. Using a knowledgeable local dive charter to visit this site is recommended. LORAN: 32736.4 / 48929.0, LAT/LON: 43.36.29 / 87.41.29

CHANNON, GRACE A. --- This 168' schooner sits in 198' of water on a sandy lake bottom 6.8 miles southeast of Oak Creek, WI. The *Grace A. Channon* sank after a collision with the steam barge, *Favorite,* put a large gash in her port side on August 2, 1877. The seven-year-old son of a co-owner, sleeping below deck, died in this sinking, while the *Favorite* rescued the others. The *Channon* is in remarkably good shape, with an intact cabin. This shipwreck was located by Kent Bellrichard and his team in April, 1985 after a long search. LORAN: 32963.2 / 49388.1, LAT/LON: 42.55.76 / 87.36.12

CONGRESS --- The 265' steamer, *Congress,* built at Cleveland in 1867, burned at South Manitou Island, Michigan, on October 4, 1904. The flaming steamer was cut loose from the dock and sank in the deepest part of the harbor. The wreck sits in 165', rising to about 135' of depth. There is usually very poor visibility at this dangerous site. The forward cabin area is penetrable and intact, since the fire was at the stern. Anchors, boilers, and engine machinery are still in place. LORAN: 31834.4 / 48330.5, LAT/LON: 45.01.49 / 86.05.46

DAVOCK, WILLIAM B. --- This 420' steel steamer, built at St. Clair, Michigan in 1907, lies in 210' of water off Pentwater, Michigan. The *Davock,* carrying a cargo of coal, sank in the severe Armistice Day Storm of November 11-12, 1940, with the loss of all 33 crewmembers. This shipwreck was located in 1982. Bow: LORAN: 32402.2 / 49065.9; Stern: LORAN: 32402.6 / 49066.0

EMBA --- Built in 1890 at West Bay City, Michigan, the three-masted schooner, *Emba,* (ex-*A.C. Tuxbury*) was converted to a twin-masted schooner-barge, a towed vessel often carrying lumber or coal. This ship was scuttled off Milwaukee's North Point in 1932. The shipwreck sits in 170' of water, broken from the scuttling. There are no penetration possibilities. LORAN: 32949.6 / 49271.6, LAT/LON: 43.03.80 / 87.53.06

FLORETTA --- This 134' schooner, built at Detroit in 1868, foundered in 181' of water with her iron ore cargo 11 miles southeast of Manitowoc, Wisconsin, at 9:00 A.M. on September 18, 1885. No lives were lost, the seven men on board reaching Manitowoc in their yawl. This $9,000 ship (she was worth $30,000 when new) was insured for $6,600, with the cargo fully insured. This ship-wreck is mostly intact, with three anchors at the bow. The stern is damaged. Visibility is usually poor and commercial fishing nets are snagged on this dangerous wreck. LORAN: 32576.4 / 48733.9, LAT/LON: 43.57.02 / 87.32.13

GALLINIPPER --- This early, 142-ton schooner, built in 1847, foundered in 1851 in 215' of water north of Sheboygan, Wisconsin. Beware of snagged fishing nets at this site! John Steele, who located this shipwreck, spent several dives cutting away as much of this dangerous netting as possible, but there is still plenty left.

HELVETIA --- This old ship's bare hull was purposely burned on Lake Michigan ten miles northeast of Sheboygan, Wisconsin, on September 10, 1921. She had outlived her usefulness after almost half a century of hauling bulk cargoes such as lumber around the Great Lakes. The 204' schooner was built at Tonawanda, New York, in 1873. This shipwreck, found in 1975, sits in 165' of water. Beware of commercial fishing nets snagged onto the hull. LORAN: 32650.7 / 48824.2, LAT/LON: 43.47.31 / 87.36.49

HOME, WILLIAM --- This 23-year-old, three-masted, 141' schooner, carrying 579 tons of pig iron, foundered in a storm off Seul Choix Point, Michigan, on September 25, 1894 with the loss of six lives. The sole survivor, a German sailor from Detroit named Anton Minga, washed ashore clinging to the battered yawl boat. The schooner was in tow of the steamer, *Buell,* along with two other schooners; these others survived the storm. The wreck sits in 165' of water. LORAN: 32585.5 / 48732.4, LAT/LON: 43.56.83 / 87.33.28

ISLAND CITY --- The captain, who lay unconscious at the bottom of the 9' yawl boat when it drifted ashore, was this wreck's sole survivor. The small, two-masted, 81' schooner, *Island City,* built in 1859 at St. Clair, Michigan, sank on April 8, 1894, with a load of lumber in 140' of water about 15 miles northeast of Milwaukee, Wisconsin. The other two men on board died. This shipwreck is badly broken up, with commercial fishing nets snagged on her pieces. LORAN: 32908.5 / 49138.1, LAT/LON: 43.14.38 / 87.50.71

LAKELAND --- This 280' iron steamer, launched at Cleveland in 1887, was the Great Lakes' first ship to be powered by a triple expansion steam engine. The *Lakeland* sprang a leak and foundered in a storm on December 4, 1924, with a cargo of 30 new Nash, Kissel, and Rollins automobiles. The crew was rescued by a passing steamer. A Rollins was raised from the wreck site in 1979. This shipwreck sits in 210' to 235' of water off Sturgeon Bay, Wisconsin. LORAN: 32219.3 / 48274.5, LAT/LON: 44.47.57 / 87.11.49

LAUREN CASTLE --- The 98' steel tug, *Lauren Castle,* built at Chester, Pennsylvania, in 1906, sank on November 5, 1980, in 392' of water in Grand Traverse Bay, Michigan, while assisting the tanker, *Amoco Wisconsin.* One life was lost in this sinking.

LORD, JARVIS --- This 178' wooden steamer, launched in 1872 at Marine City, Michigan, sank in Manitou Passage east of the Manitou Islands with an iron ore cargo after developing a leak on August 17, 1885. The shipwreck lies in 250' of water.

NORTHERNER --- The two-masted schooner, *Northerner,* only 78' in length, lies in 138' of water southeast of Port Washington, Wisconsin. Loaded with cord wood, the ship sprang a leak and sank on November 29, 1868. She was built in 1859 at Wells Island, Michigan. The wreck is upright and intact, with the bow rising to about 120' of depth. Items of interest include the railing, masthead, windlass, centerboard winch, bowsprit, anchor chain, and a figurehead resembling the one of the *Sandusky* in the Straits of Mackinac. LORAN: 32874.7·/ 49091.8, LAT/LON: 43.18.89 / 87.49.45

ROSINCO --- This 95', luxuriously equipped, $150,000 (in 1928 dollars) yacht sank in the middle of the night on April 18, 1928, about ten miles off Kenosha, Wisconsin, in 195' of water. The ship, dubbed "the most palatial on Lake Michigan," had left Milwaukee for Chicago at midnight, but struck some floating timber and sank within ten minutes. The seven people on board took to the lifeboat. The *Rosinco* was built at Wilmington, Delaware, in 1916. Upright and intact, the wreck is in immaculate condition, but with sections draped in dangerous fishnet. Her main cabin and outer rooms along the main deck can be penetrated by visiting divers. Many fine pieces of china and silverware were removed by early divers. Commercial fishermen first found this shipwreck in 1961. LORAN: 33088.9 / 49586.3, LAT/LON: 42.37.40 / 87.43.42

SILVER LAKE --- A 337', steel Pere Marquette Railroad carferry ran down and sank the 95', two-masted, scow schooner named the *Silver Lake* on May 28, 1900, nine miles northeast of Sheboygan, Wisconsin, in a heavy fog. The *Silver Lake,* loaded with lumber, was struck midship on the port side, cutting her almost in two. The cook lost his life. The wreck is upright and mostly intact, with the foremast rising to 138'. The *Silver Lake*, sitting in 209' of water, was found by John Steele's crew (consisting of John, Bill Cohrs, Steve Radovan, Jim Brotz, and Wally Bissonnette) on May 22, 1977. LORAN: 32637.5 / 48819.5, LAT/LON: 43.48.39 / 87.34.65

SIMMONS, ROUSE --- This three-masted, 127' schooner, built at Milwaukee in 1868, is the famous "Christmas Tree Ship," so-named because her last runs of the season always consisted of northern Michigan Christmas trees packed into her holds and on deck for the Chicago market. She was loaded with just such a cargo when she foundered in a violent blizzard off Kewaunee, Wisconsin, on November 23, 1912. All 16 people on board perished. The wreck, which sits upright and intact in 168' of water, with the deck at 155', was located by Kent Bellrichard in October, 1971. LORAN: 32437.7 / 48550.7, LAT/LON: 44.16.51 / 87.24.94

ST. ALBANS --- On January 30, 1881, ice in Lake Michigan pierced the hull of the 135', wooden steamer, *St. Albans,* and the ship sank in 178' of water off Milwaukee, WI. The crew of 21 and the six passengers made it through the ice-filled waters to the mainland in four lifeboats, with rescuers on shore playing dramatic parts. Built in 1868 at Cleveland, this vessel sits upright and intact, and was located by Kent Bellrichard and his team in late 1975, with team-mate Richard Zaleski making the first dive to this site on January 6, 1976. LORAN: 32951.7 / 49268.9, LAT/LON: 43.03.88 / 87.45.60

STONE BARGE (UNIDENTIFIED) lies in 200' of water off Milwaukee, Wisconsin. LORAN: 32943.8 / 49280.4, LAT/LON: 43.03.51 / 87.43.20

U-97 --- A 165' German World War I submarine lies at the bottom of Lake Michigan several miles off Chicago. In the summer of 1919, this sub was seen on the surface of Lake Michigan, convincing some people that World War I had not really ended. However, the *U-97* was a war prize, brought into the Great Lakes for exhibition purposes before being scuttled in 248' of water on June 7, 1921, when the *U.S.S. Wilmette* (ex-*Eastland,* infamous for overturning in Chicago harbor on July 24, 1915 and drowning 835 people) fired ten four-inch shells into the sub's hull. This is an unusual shipwreck site.

UGANDA --- This 291' wooden steamer sank in 207' of water after ice penetrated her hull in the western part of the Straits of Mackinac on April 19, 1913. Built at West Bay City, Michigan, in 1892, the *Uganda* was found by Stan Stock and Chuck and Jeri Feltner in 1983. The wreck sits upright and intact in a strong current, with anchors, chains, engine, boilers, and the midship cabin in place. LORAN: 31321.7 / 48047.2 LAT/LON: 45.50.50 / 85.02.99

VERNON --- Built in 1886 and lost in a gale on October 29, 1887, this 158' steamer sits in 210' of water off Manitowoc, Wisconsin. Of the 42 people on board, 41 of them died, the sole survivor clinging to a raft for two days. Kent Bellrichard located this shipwreck, which is upright and intact, on July 12, 1969. LORAN: 32461.6 / 49598.9, LAT/LON: 44.11.96 / 87.24.81

WARD, EBER --- This 213' wooden steamer, loaded with corn, sank in 142' of water in the Straits of Mackinac when ice holed her hull on April 9, 1909. Five lives were lost from the 16 on board. The ship was built at West Bay City, MI, in

1888. Her deck rises to a depth of 112', and three anchors are among the many items of interest. Chuck and Jeri Feltner located the *Eber Ward* in 1980. LORAN: 31253.7 / 48096.9, LAT/LON: 45.48.83 / 84.49.04

Deep Lake Superior Shipwrecks

ARCTIC --- This 237' sidewheel steamer sank on May 28, 1860 after stranding violently at Huron Island near Marquette, Michigan with a load of passengers and freight. The storm the following day destroyed any chance of salvaging the grounded vessel, but some of her machinery was recovered. The wreck lies quite scattered in depths of 5' to 150' along a steep, rocky slope. A large portion of the *Arctic's* bow lies in about 22' of water in the channel south of Lighthouse Island. This shipwreck is within the Marquette Underwater Preserve.

AURANIA --- The 352' steel steamer, *Aurania,* sits in about 440' of water off the south end of Isle Parisienne, Ontario, northwest of Sault Ste. Marie, in Whitefish Bay. This wreck was sunk by ice on April 29, 1909, with no loss of life. The 20 crewmembers made their way cautiously over several miles of treacherous ice to reach the safety of the steamer, *J.H. Bartow.* One scuba charter boat operator advertised this wreck in his scuba brochure (it is not known if he ever took any divers to this very deep site).

CHISHOLM, HENRY (ENGINE, 110'-140') --- The 256' wooden steamer, *Henry Chisholm,* built at Cleveland in 1880, sank at the Rock of Ages Reef at the western end of Isle Royale on October 20, 1898. Although intermingled with pieces of another shipwreck, the *Cumberland,* the main wreckage of the *Chisholm* lies in shallow water to 30' deep on one side of the rocky reef, with her engine and propeller in 140' and starboard fantail in 150' on the other side of that reef. That deep engine is often buoyed. This site lies within Isle Royale National Park. LORAN: 46068.0 / 31936.1 LAT/LON: 47.54.35 / 85.27.49

COMET --- This 181' wooden-arched steamer, launched at Cleveland in 1857, sank on Whitefish Bay on August 26, 1875, when, due to a failure to communicate, the sidewheel steamer, *Manitoba,* rammed the *Comet* at her forecastle. The *Comet* sank in less than two minutes in 240' of water, taking 10 of her 20 crew, as well as her cargo of pig iron ingots, copper ore, silver ore, and wool, with her. The deck sits at about 220', with the twin arches, with the name of the ship still painted on them, rising higher. The bow is detached and/or under silt and sand, while the exposed engine has the ship's name ornately painted on it (it was no problem identifying this wreck!). Caution: the wreck lies in the main shipping channel. This site is within Michigan's Whitefish Point Underwater Preserve. LORAN: 31111.1 / 47637.9

CONGDON, CHESTER A. (STERN) --- The fascinating bow half of this 532' steel steamer rests off Isle Royale within sport diving range, and is one of the "100 Best" described in detail in Volume II. However, the stern half sits in 60' to 212' of water and is infrequently explored. The ship stranded on Nov. 6, 1918 and subsequently broke in two on Congdon Shoal south of Canoe Rocks at the northeastern end of Isle Royale. The stern lies on a steep angle where the depth drops quickly to over 200'. The engine room and stern cabins are in this deep zone. The *Congdon* stern, like the *Kamloops,* is not buoyed, and diving on these sites is not encouraged by National Park authorities at Isle Royale. LORAN: 31717.3 / 46147.6, LAT/LON: 48.11.69/ 88.30.93

COWLE, JOHN B. --- This 420' steel steamer, loaded with 7,023 tons of iron ore, sank in a collision with the steel steamer, *Isaac M. Scott,* off Whitefish Point in thick fog on July 12, 1909, with 14 of the crew of 24 perishing. Coincidentally, the *Cowle* was located in the summer of 1972 by the same group of divers, Kent Bellrichard and his team, that later found the *Isaac M. Scott* in Lake Huron. The *Cowle,* launched at Port Huron, Michigan, in 1902, lies in a maximum of 220' of water in Michigan's Whitefish Point Underwater Preserve, with a portion of the wreck sitting shallower and rising to about 170'. The pilothouse is in place and in very good condition. The intact log was retrieved. LORAN: 31125.1 / 47579.4, LAT/LON: 46.44.435 / 84.57.875

EMPEROR (STERN) --- Launched at Collingwood, Ontario, in 1911, the 525' steel steamer, *Emperor,* stranded and sank at Isle Royale on June 4, 1947 with the loss of 12 men and women from the crew of 31. The shipwreck lies in 40' to 175' of water, with the forward, shallower half being a popular sport diver site. The deeper stern half has some portions which rise above 130' in depth, but the most interesting items, such as the stern cabins, propeller, rudder, and engine room, are deeper. This wreck lies in the northeast corner of Isle Royale National Park. Both bow and stern are usually buoyed. LORAN: 46150.0 / 31712.0, LAT/LON: 48.12.13 / 88.29.71

FITZGERALD, EDMUND --- The Mount Everest of Great Lakes shipwrecks lies broken in half in 529' of dark, cold water. All 29 men on board the 729' "Big Fitz," the largest vessel ever lost on the Great Lakes, died when a violent storm sank the ship on November 10, 1975. Several submersible and pressure suit explorations have reached the Edmund Fitzgerald, but only two scuba divers, Mike Zee and Terrence Tysall, using much training, planning, and tri-mix, and descending along a remote videocamera cable which kept the wreck in sight at all times to the boat captain above, did a brief eight-minute exploration of part of the wreck in a (total, in-water) three-hour dive in September, 1995. There is much controversy over further access to this famous shipwreck, with relatives of the lost crew requesting the site to be declared off limits. The wreck lies just inside Canadian waters off Whitefish Point. LAT/LON (old system): 46.59.9 / 85.06.6

GUNILDA --- Members of the Cousteau Great Lakes expedition in 1980, gazing at this wreck by means of a remote-operated video camera, declared the luxury yacht, *Gunilda,* to be the most beautiful shipwreck they had ever seen. This 177' ship, built in Scotland in 1897, stranded on a rock pinnacle named McGarvey Shoal in Lake Superior's Canadian north shore near Rossport, Ontario, on August 11, 1911. The *Gunilda's* rich owner, William Harkness, was too cheap a) to hire a local pilot in the first place to guide his ship through these dangerous waters, and b) to pay for TWO tugboats to tow his expensive toy off the rocks. The single tug he hired hauled the *Gunilda* off at such an angle that she capsized and sank in 260' of water at the base of the pinnacle. No passengers perished in this sinking, but two scuba divers have died at this deep, dangerous site. The wreck lies intact and upright, with virtually all of her lavish features, including her gold-trimmed carved wood at the bow, still in place. Although one man from Thunder Bay, Ontario, claims to have purchased the legal rights to this wreck, the province of Ontario asserts control over access, and the townspeople in Rossport keep careful eyes on the historic site, which has become a source of local pride, and call the police if they see any suspected diving or salvaging activity going on there. There is often a descent line to the wreck visible just below the surface of the water. The province of Ontario issued an archaeological license to Michigan diver Darryl Ertel (with partner Matt Turchi and other divers) to do survey work on the *Gunilda* in 1993 and 1994. Their subsequent report, photos, and videotape are astounding.

HART, JUDGE --- My jaw dropped in amazement when I first viewed photos in November, 1990, of the intact pilot house of the newly-discovered steel steamer, *Judge Hart,* complete with its ship's wheel, brass binnacle, and radio headphones sitting on the counter. The 253' *Judge Hart,* built at Cowes, England, in 1923, stranded with a load of grain on Simon's Reef in Ashburton Bay on Lake Superior's Canadian north shore on November 27, 1942. When the ship was released, she filled with water and sank in a maximum of 210' to the west of present-day Neys Provincial Park, Ontario. Parts of the wreck are in water about 35' shallower. The *Judge Hart* was located on June 16, 1990, by Minnesota diver Jerry Eliason and Wisconsin diver Kraig Smith, after about seven years of research and searching. The wreck lies in the vicinity of Fitzsimmons Rocks and Barclay Island, several miles from where historical resources and official reports indicate she sank. The province of Ontario issued an archaeological license to survey this shipwreck to Michigan diver Darryl Ertel (with partner Matt Turchi and other divers) in 1995 and 1996; as they had done earlier with the *Gunilda,* they again produced excellent photos and videotape on the *Judge Hart.*

KAMLOOPS --- The 250' steel steamer, *Kamloops,* is the deepest shipwreck at Isle Royale National Park, lying on her starboard side in 178' to 255' of water, bow deeper than the stern, near the northeast shore of the island. Built in England in 1924, the *Kamloops* went missing with all hands (22 people) and a cargo of general freight in a severe storm on December 7, 1927. The following spring, *Kamloops* bodies, as well as a badly damaged lifeboat and other loose items from the ship, were found on the island, indicating that survivors had reached land after the *Kamloops* stranded on the rocks and before the ship slid into deep water. These survivors starved or froze to death (a bottled note from Assistant Steward Alice Bettridge, whose body was found 300' on shore, read, "I am the last one alive, freezing and starving on Isle Royale. I just want Mom and Dad to know my fate." The port lifeboat is, indeed, missing from the wreck. The wreck of the *Kamloops* was picked up on a depth sounder on board the Isle Royale passenger/freight boat about 300' west of Twelve O'clock Point in 1977. Diver Ken Merriman was the first to explore and identify the *Kamloops* on August 21, 1977. LORAN: 46124.5 / 31786.1, LAT/LON: 48.05.24 / 88.46.14

The steamer, KAMLOOPS. ARTWORK © ROBERT McGREEVEY. Used with permission.

The shipwreck, KAMLOOPS. ARTWORK © ROBERT McGREEVEY. Used with permission.

MATHER, SAMUEL --- One of the best preserved and most intact deep wrecks off Whitefish Point is the 246' wooden steamer, *Samuel Mather,* sitting in 142' to 172' of water. Built at Cleveland in 1887, the *Mather,* downbound with a load of wheat, sank at 2:00 A.M., November 22, 1891, after being struck near the after-hatch on the starboard side by the newer steel steamer, *Brazil.* No lives were lost, but the ship and cargo, valued at $115,000 in 1891, were a complete loss. The wreck sits upright and intact, with penetration possible. The mast near the stern (early steamers carried them for emergency sail power) towers impressively upright off the deck. The rudder and four-bladed propeller are interesting sights. On-deck items include trumpet-shaped dorades, or air vents, and considerable rigging. This shipwreck, found by Tom Farnquist and his team in May, 1978, lies within Michigan's Whitefish Point Underwater Preserve. LORAN: 31086.7 / 47734.8, LAT/LON: 46.34.308 / 84.42.325

The propeller of the wooden steamer, SAMUEL MATHER, *examined here by Dr. Gary Elliott, sits in 171' of water in Whitefish Bay.*   PHOTO BY CRIS KOHL.

MITCHELL, JOHN --- The 420' steel steamer, built at St. Clair, Michigan, in 1907, sank within five minutes of a collision with the 354' steel steamer, *William H. Mack,* on July 9, 1911 off Vermilion Point, Michigan, in Whitefish Bay in 150' of water. Three lives were lost from the 34 on board the $300,000 *Mitchell.* The wreck, located by John Steele (and his crew of Bill Cohrs, Kent Bellrichard, and Tom Farnquist) in 1972, is upside-down, with the hull rising about 30' off the lake bottom. The bow lies buried in the sand at 150', with the propeller and rudder in about 120'. Inside, porcelain toilets hang from above, while the engine room and crew quarters are also accessible for the trained, experienced, and prepared divers visiting this site. LORAN: 31153.6 / 47545.6, LAT/LON: 46.50.05 / 85.04.81

MONARCH --- This 240' passenger and freight steamer, launched at Sarnia, Ontario, in 1890, stranded in a blinding blizzard at Blake Point, Isle Royale, on her last run of the season on December 6, 1906. One person from the total of 62 on board perished; the remainder spent four freezing days on the island before being rescued. The ship's emergency sails became a makeshift tent, and the only woman on board was given the sole blanket. In the 1960's, sport divers salvaged the capstan which is on display at Isle Royale National Park. This shipwreck is broken up in 10' to 150' of water. LORAN: 46171.3 / 31702.4, LAT/LON: 48.11.44 / 88.26.03

ONOKO --- The 299' iron steamer, *Onoko,* built in 1882 at Cleveland, sank on September 15, 1915, in 200' of water off Knife Island near Duluth, Minnesota, after her boiler exploded and the ship foundered. This shipwreck was located by Jerry Eliason and Kraig Smith in 1988.

OSBORN, JOHN M. --- In a fog-shrouded lake, the speeding 305' steel steamer, *Alberta,* collided with the 178' wooden steamer, *John M. Osborn,* off Whitefish Point on July 27, 1884, with the loss of four lives (three from the *Osborn* and one from the *Alberta).* The steel ship's bow sliced into the *Osborn's* hull just aft of the mizzen mast, puncturing the boiler. The two ships were wedged together long enough for most of the *Osborn's* crew to jump aboard the larger ship. The wrecked *Osborn,* which sank within five minutes, rests upright and incredibly intact in 150' to 170' of water. The *John M. Osborn* was located in the summer of 1984 by the Great Lakes Shipwreck Historical Society and the Odyssey Foundation of Lansing, Michigan. LORAN: 31149.5 / 47528.2, LAT/LON: 46.52.14 / 85.05.13

The bow of the wooden steamer, JOHN M. OSBORN, *in 150' of water off Whitefish Point, Michigan, is explored by technical diver Darryl Ertel.* PHOTO BY CRIS KOHL.

Twin anchors adorn the bow of the JOHN M. OSBORN. *An open hatch access near the engine/boiler at the stern will drop the visiting diver to 170'.* PHOTO BY CRIS KOHL.

SUPERIOR CITY --- This 429' steel steamer, launched at Lorain, Ohio, in 1898, sank with the loss of 29 of her 33 crewmembers in a collision with the 580' freighter, *Willis L. King,* at 9:00 P.M., August 20, 1920, about 4.5 miles southeast of Whitefish Point. In confusion over passing signals, the *King* pierced the port side, just aft of the midway point, of the ore-laden *Superior City,* which sank fast, especially after the cold water caused the boilers to explode, in 190' to 270' of water. The wreck, originally located by John Steele in 1972, is the deepest vessel in the Whitefish Point Underwater Preserve. LORAN: 31112.0 / 47633.5, LAT/LON: 46.43.51 / 84.52.37

VIENNA (BELOW DECK LEVEL) --- The full story of the steamer, *Vienna,* is covered in *The 100 Best Great Lakes Shipwrecks, Volume II.* Only the deck portion of this deep wreck is considered suitable for sport diving. The rest of the *Vienna,* which sits in 148' of water in Whitefish Bay, is excellent for penetration diving and around-the-hull exploring along the lake bottom by trained, experienced, and prepared deep divers. LORAN: 31135.8 / 47610.2, LAT/LON; 46.44.435 / 84.57.875

ZILLAH --- This 36-year-old, 202' wooden steamer, launched at West Bay City, Michigan, in 1890, carried a limestone cargo when a summer gale caused her to founder in 230' to 250' of water in Whitefish Bay on August 29, 1926. Her cargo shifted and she slowly capsized in heavy seas just after noon, but no lives were lost. This is another of the very deep shipwrecks within Michigan's Whitefish Point Underwater Preserve. LORAN: 31123.6 / 47624.3

Continued in
The 100 Best Great Lakes Shipwrecks, Volume II:

Appendix D: The 100 Most Hunted Great Lakes Shipwrecks

This appendix presents a compilation of 100 shipwrecks that have not yet been located, 20 from each of the five Great Lakes, with brief historical sketches of each. These ships are sought because of their strong dramatic and/or historic associations, or because the probability of intactness makes them appealing finds.

Appendix E: Shipwrecks in Great Lakes Parks and Preserves

This appendix relates briefly the shipwreck stories, the depths, and the locations (with Loran and/or GPS Lat/Lon co-ordinates) of approximately 200 shipwrecks in these 15 underwater parks or preserves:

Fathom Five National Marine Park at Lake Huron's Tobermory, Ontario
Eriequest Marine Park at Lake Erie's Point Pelee, Ontario
Isle Royale National Park in Lake Superior
Apostle Islands National Lakeshore, Wisconsin, in Lake Superior
Alger Underwater Preserve at Munising, Michigan on Lake Superior
DeTour Underwater Preserve (proposed) at DeTour, Michigan in Lake Huron
Keweenaw Underwater Preserve, Keweenaw Peninsula on Lake Superior
Manitou Passages Underwater Preserve in upper Lake Michigan
Marquette Underwater Preserve at Marquette, Michigan on Lake Superior
Sanilac Shores Underwater Preserve in lower Lake Huron
Southwest Michigan Underwater Preserve (proposed) in Lake Michigan
Straits of Mackinac Underwater Preserve, Michigan
Thumb Area Underwater Preserve in Michigan's lower Lake Huron
Thunder Bay Underwater Preserve at Alpena, Michigan on Lake Huron
Whitefish Point Underwater Preserve in Michigan on Lake Superior

Appendix F: 100 More Great Lakes Shipwrecks

This appendix presents thumbnail historical sketches, depths, and Loran and/or GPS Lat/Lon co-ordinates for 100 more Great Lakes shipwrecks that are a) not in the "100 best" list, b) not among the 100 deep shipwrecks, and c) not in an underwater park or preserve. (Incidentally, the fact that a shipwreck might not lie within an underwater park or preserve does not mean that it is open to removal of artifacts; the province of Ontario and the U.S. Great Lakes states have strict laws prohibiting such theft from *any* shipwreck in their waters.)

Plus a comprehensive, 14-page BIBLIOGRAPHY that covers both "100 Best" volumes, all in Volume II.

INDEX

TO VOLUME I

SHIPS' NAMES ARE IN *italics*.
AN ASTERISK [*] DENOTES A PHOTOGRAPH.

A & T Recovery, 153, 154
Aberdeen, 86
Ackerman, Capt., Murray, 11-12
Acme, 180
Admiral, 63, 65-68*
Albany, 196-198, 242
Alberta, 258
Allen, E.B., 247
Allen, Walter B., 249
Alpena, 182
Amadeus, James, 125
American Revolution, 62, 132
Amoco Wisconsin, 251
Anderson, Capt. Matthew, 79-80, 81
Antrim, 98
Arabia, 131, 135-138*
Arabian, 44
Arctic (sidewheeler), 253
Arctic (propeller), 242
Argus, 200, 205, 207, 242
Armistice Day Storm, 250
Asia, 133
Atlantic (propeller), 131, 139-142*
Atlantic (sidewheeler), 64, 139, 240-241
Aull, Capt., 38
Aurania, 253
Azov, 200*

Badger State, 230
Baker, Harris W., 150
Baker, William H., 202-204, 214
Barge No. 9, 242
Barney, F.T., 242
Barnum, William H., 131, 143-144
Bartow, J.H., 253
Baxter, Capt., 149-150
Becker, G.F., 242
Becker, William D., 86
Bell, Jenny (Jane), 249
Belle, Capt. Thomas, 78
Bellrichard, Kent, 243, 248, 249, 252, 254, 257

Bentley, James R., 236, 242
Bessemer, Sir Henry, 156
Betty and Jean, 72
Billson, Capt., 88
Biniecki, Gary, 174, 184, 209
Birtwhistle, John, 46
Bissonette, Wally, 252
Black Friday Storm, 96-97, 100, 102
Blodgett, Capt. C.C., 116
Boland, John J., Jr., 63, 69-72*
Bonanka, 175
Bradley, Carl D., 249
Bradstreet, Col., 1
Bramble, 216
Brandy 4, 242
Brazil, 257
Bristol, Robert, 52
Briton, 100, 156
Bronson, Tracy J., 242
Brookdale, 166
Brooke-Lauren, 15
Brotz, Jim, 252
Brûlé, Étienne, xiii, 1, 129
Brunswick, 63, 73-75*, 76-77
Brusate, Wayne, 174, 209, 218
Buell, 250
Burns, Capt. George C., 182
Butters, Marshall F., 97
Byron, 249

Cadillac, Antoine de la Mothe, 62
Caldera, 245
Calumet, 117
Canton, 249
Carlingford, 63, 73-75, 76-77
Caroline Rose, 134
Carruthers, James, 200, 205, 207
Carson, Barbara, 13, 20, 24
Cartwright, Capt. D.L., 191
Cayuga, 20

Cedarville, 131, 145-148*
Chamberlain, Capt. C., 73-74
Champlain, Samuel de, xiii, 1, 129
Channon, Grace A., 249
Checotah, 184
Chicora, 231
Chisholm, Henry, 253
Clarion, 63, 78-83*
Clement, Norman P., 242
Cleveco, 66-68
Cleveland, City of, 131, 149-151*
Cobourg, 18
Codorus, 118
Coe, S.S., 109
Cohrs, Bill, 252, 257
Colgate, James B., 97
Columbus, Christopher, 232
Comet (Lake Ontario), 3, 5-8*
Comet (Lake Superior), 253
Concord, City of, 198
Congdon, Chester A., 253-254
Congress, 249-250
Cormorant, 240
Courtland, 105, 109
Cousteau Great Lakes Expedition, 254
Cowle, John B., 254
Cranage, Thomas, 231
Crusader, 144
Cumberland, 253
Curran, James W., 242

Danforth, F.L., 123
Davis, Lyman, M., 240
Davock, William B., 250
Dean, Roger, 186
Deepstar Enterprises, 52
Detroit, 243
Detroit, City of, 124
Dix, Capt., 36
Dixon, H.R., 149-150
Dolphin I, 178
Donaldson, J.P., 91

Donnelly Wrecking Company, 18
Donnelly, Edward, 24
Dorr, E.P., 243
Doty, L.R., 51-52
Douville, Capt. Henry, 135
Dows, David, 151
Dufferin, Lady, 243
Dundee, 63, 84-87*
Dunderberg, 236, 243
Durant, Capt. Homer, 76-77

E *astland*, 252
Eddy, Newell A., 244
Ehorn, Paul, 247, 248-249
Eliason, Jerry, 255, 258
Elliott, Dr. Gary, 257*
Ellison, Ed, 244
Elma, 116
Elven, Capt. Martin, 86
Emba, 250
Emerald, 171*
Emperor, 254
Empire State, 243
Enterprise, 180
Equinox, 123
Erie, 64
Erie, Lake, 61-128*
Ertel, Darryl, 244, 255, 258*
Exchange, 5, 6

F *alconer, Annie*, 3, 9-14*, 180
Farnquist, Tom, 257
Fathom Five National Marine Park, 134, 151, 219, 243
Favorite, 249
Feltner, Chuck and Jeri, 147, 252-253
Filer, D.L., 97
Finglo, 100
Fitzgerald, Edmund, 249, 254
Floretta, 250
Florida, 244
Forest City, 244
Forsberg, Joan, 3, 63, 130-131, 215*, 216*, 221*, 246*
Franz, W.C., 248
Fritz, David, 178
Frontenac (tug), 3, 15-18*
Frontenac (schooner), 4
Frontenac (steamer), 4

G *ale, Steven F.*, 63, 88-90
Gallinipper, 250

Galvin, Capt. Michael, 186
Gee, 116
German, 156
Germanic, 226
Gilbert, W.H., 245
Glidden, John N., 86
Goshawk, 131, 152-155*
Gotham, 66
Gould, Jay, 64
Grantham, 112
Great Storm of Nov., 1913, 134, 174, 200-206*, 207-212, 214
Great Western, 36
Grecian, 131, 156-157*
Griffin, Capt. John, 49-50
Griffith, G.P., 64
Griffon, 3, 62, 132-133
Gunilda, 254-255

H *ale, Dennis*, 245, 247*
Hamilton, 4, 236, 240
Hamilton, Capt. Robert, 112
Hammond, Richard, 226
Hanna, D.R., 244-245
Hanna, Leonard C., 79-80, 81
Harrison, J.C., 123
Hart, Judge, 255
Harvey, A.F., 145, 148
Haskell, William A., 160, 161
Hattie, 116
Hawman, Capt. E.C., 71-72
Hayward, Joyce, x-xi, xviii, 243*
Hebard, 116
Helen, 120
Helvetia, 250
Henley, Adam, 12, 30, 33, 39, 43, 57, 114, 137, 141, 169, 173
Henry, Alexander, 54
Herbert, Capt. Jim, 115
Home, William, 250
Hughes, Ronald, 46
Hunter, 179
Hurd, Joseph L., 20
Huron, Lake, 129-226*
Hydrus, 200, 205, 207

I *daho*, 241
Illinois, 120
India, 131, 158-159*
Iron Chief, 245
Island City, 250-251

J *ack*, 247
Jackson, Larry, 97
Jackson, Rick, 170

Jenness, B.W., 116
Jessie, 219
Johnson, Henry J., 245
Johnson, Levi, 109
Jolliet, Louis, xiii, 61
Jones, Capt. Harry L., 100
Jones, Elizabeth, 126-127
Joppich, Capt. Martin, 145-148
Joyland, 131, 160-164*
Juhl, Tim, 184

K *amloops*, 254, 255-256
Keewatin, 49
Ketchum, J.L., 91
Ketchum, V.H., 248
Kewaunee, 79
King, Willis L., 259
Knight Templar, 180
Kozak, Gary, 77, 121

L *abadie, C. Patrick*, 186
Lakeland, 251
Lansdowne, 82
LaSalle, R.R.C. de, 4
Lauren Castle, 251
Laurentian, 244
Lee, Dani, 8*, 28*
Lee, Fred, 245
Lester, T.G., 91, 92
Linn, William R., 247
Little Wissahickon, 63, 91-95*
Lomox, 175
Lord, Jarvis, 251
Loudon, Capt. James W., 106
Lowden, Gerry, 170
Lyon, John B., 86
Lyons, Kate, 90*

M *ack, William H.*, 257
Maddock, Capt. James, 224
Mallen, Capt., 18
Manitoba, 253
Manitoulin, 139, 140
Manola, 3, 19-22*, 165, 166
Mapledawn, xvi, 20, 131, 165-169*
maps, xv, 3, 63, 130-131
Mareci, Sam, 180
Marquette and Bessemer #2, 80
Marquette, 131, 170-173*
Marsh, George A., 3, 23-30*
Marshall, Barb, 7

Mary Alice B., 131, 174-178*, 209, 218
Massey, Capt. S.B., 118
Mather, Samuel (steamer) 257*
Mather, Samuel (freighter), 187
Maxwell, A.C., 112*
Mayflower, 5, 6
McCaldon, Dr. Robert, 7
McClellan, Stan, 136
McConkey, Capt. Edward, 209
McCready, Jim, 7
McCready, Norm, 144
McDonald, Capt. Edward, 44
McElmon, Marcy, 13*, 34*, 35*, 55*, 58*, 59*, 60*
McFarlane, Capt., 116
McGean, John A., 200, 205, 245
McGreevy, Robert, 256
McKay, Capt. George, 92
McKay, Capt. William, 108
McLeod, Ken, 170
McPhail, John A., 245
McRady, James, 46
Merida, 63, 96-104*
Merrill, John B., 131, 179-180
Merriman, Ken, 255-256
Metcalfe, Willis, 38
Meteor, 133, 248
Meyer, W.H., 65
Michigan, 111-112
Miller, Capt. Alfred, 124-125
Millhouser, David and Susan, 72
Milwaukee, City of, 236-245
Minnedosa, 31-32, 133, 245
Minnehaha, 179
Misener, Capt. R. Scott, 69
Mitchell, John, 257
Monarch, 258
Monguagon, 82
Monrovia, 245
Montana, 131, 181-183*, 236
Morning Star, 63, 105-110
Morrell, Daniel J., 245-247*
Morton, Capt. Edward, 152
Mullings, Ken, 14
Munro, Josiah C., 79
Munson, 3, 31-35*
Munson, Emma, 32
Murray, H.P., 36

Myron, 234

Naples, City of, 119
Narragansett, 94*
Nemesis, 186
New Orleans, 247
New York, 131, 184-186
Nicolet, Jean, xiii
Nielsen, Emma L., 247
Nimrod, 63, 111-113*
Nordmeer, 131, 175, 187-189*
Norman, 156, 247, 249
Noronic, 4
North Star (sidewheeler), 230
North Star (propeller), 131, 190-193*, 194
North Wind, 131, 190, 194-195*, 222
Northern King, 190, 194
Northern Light, 190, 192, 194
Northern Queen, 190, 191, 194
Northern Wave, 190, 194
Northerner, 236, 251
Nucleus, 243

O'Connor, Frank, 119
Ocean Wave (steamer), 240
Ocean Wave (schooner), 36
Ocean, 105
Ogdensburg, 64
Ohio, 241
Olson-van Heest, Valerie, 153
Olive Branch, 3, 36-40*
Oneida, 241
Onoko, 258
Ontario Underwater Council, 136, 2
Ontario (sloop), 4
Ontario (schooner), 2
Ontario (steamer), 4
Ontario, Lake, 1-60*
Ormidale, 248
Osborn, John M., 258-259*
Ossipee, 66
Ostifichuk, David, 195
Oswego, 4
Ottawa Maybrook, 53
Ottenhof, Peter, 46

Pabst, Fred, 245
Paisley, 86
Palmer, Richard, 27
Passaic, 63, 115-116
Patterson, Capt. Francis, 6
Perry, Oliver Hazard, 62

Persian, 241-247
Pettingill, Doug, 13, 20, 21*, 22*, 45*
Pewabic, 133, 248
Philadelphia, 131, 196-199*
Pickering, Roy, 103*, 104*, 128, 138*, 189*
Pollock, William G., 191
Preserve Our Wrecks (P.O.W.), 4, 14, 20, 24, 32
Price, Charles S., 131, 200-206*, 207, 208, 209, 214
Prindiville, 181
Proctor, 50
Purvis, George, 164

Queen of the West, 63, 117-118*
Quintus, 174, 175

Radovan, Steve, 252
Ralph, P.J., 154
Regina, 131, 174, 200, 205, 207-212*, 218
Remick, Walter, 68
Rescue, 123
Rice, R.N., 106*, 108-109
Richards, May, 117
Richardson (schooner), 36-37
Richardson, W.C., 80
Richmond, Dean, 63, 77, 115, 119-121*, 179
Rindlisbacher, Peter, 128
Rival, 18
Roberts, Ralph, 11, 85
Roby, George W., 244
Roman, 156
Rosinco, 251
Royalton, 245
Rushbrook, Audrey, 13

Sage, H.W., 117
Sandusky, 236, 251
Sanilac Shores Underwater Preserve, 178
Sarniadoc, 18
Save Ontario Shipwrecks (S.O.S.), 4, 95, 170
Savidge, Hunter, 248
Sawyer, James D., 179
Saxon, 156
Schoger, Michael, 127
"Schooner X", 241
Scott, Capt. William, 48-49
Scott, Isaac M., 200, 205, 207, 248, 254
Scott, Thomas, 248
Scourge, 4, 236, 240

Seven Years' War, 1,
132
Sevona, xvi
Shales, Lloyd, 46
Shannon, 5
Shaw, Quincy A., 244
Sheboygan, City of, 3, 41-
46*
Sheffield, Charles J., 190
Shoniker, Spencer, 15-
16, 18
Short, Scott, 244
Shupe, William, 154
Silver Lake, 251-252
Simmons, Rouse, 127*,
252
Slauson, Minnie, 77*
Smith, 241
Smith, Capt. Albert, 136
Smith, Capt. John
Wesley, 24, 26-29
Smith, Capt. Oscar B., 76
Smith, Capt. William,
143-144
Smith, Capt. William H.,
66
Smith, Governor, 248
Smith, Kraig, 255, 258
Spinner, F.E., 179
Sport, 131, 174, 213-218*
St. Albans, 252
St. Peter, 3, 47-52
Stayer, Jim and Pat, 176,
177*, 178, 184, 185,
193, 199*, 210, 217
Steele, John, 148, 180,
192, 198, 242, 247,
248-249, 250, 252,
257, 259
Stevens, J.H., 37*
Stock, Stan, 242, 245
Stoddard, Capt. George
W., 120
Stone barge
(unidentified), 252
Straits Underwater
Preserve, 144, 148
Suchy, Joseph, 118
Sullivan, James, 11
Superior City, 259
Superior, 116
Swanson, Capt. John O.,
66, 68
Sweepstakes, 131, 219-
221*
Symonds, Ted, 24

*T*aylor, James, 29*
Thompson, Capt.
Merwin Stone, 149
Thompson, Capt. Robert,
202-204, 213, 218
Thompson, Emma E.,
131, 222-226*
Thumb Underwater
Preserve, 198

Thunder Bay
Underwater Preserve,
157, 183
Tioga, 116
Titanic, 50, 74, 166
Tonawanda, 63, 122-123
Topdalsfjord, 146
Tower, Charlemagne, Jr.,
86
Trotter, David, 134, 242,
243, 245, 247
Troxell, Frank, 113*
Troxell, Sharon, 148*
Turchi, Matt, 244, 255
Tuscarora, 91
Tuxbury, A.C., 250
Two Fannies, 63, 124-
125*
Tyneville, 69-70
Typo, 248
Tysall, Terrence, 254

U-97, 252
Uganda, 252
Unicorn, 5
Uranus, 248

*V*an der Linden, Rev.
Peter, 21
Vandalia, 4
Verbrugge, Mike, 112
Vernon, 252
Viator, 248
Vienna, 238, 259
Viger, Capt. Edward R.,
106
Volunteer, 180

*W*alk-in-the-Water,
64, 230
Walton, George, 67-68
War of 1812, 2, 62, 132
Ward, Eber, 252-253
Weissenberg, 145-148
Wernthaler, Guenter, 38
Wesley, John, 48*
Western Reserve, 231
Wexford, 200, 205, 207
White Oak, 36
Whitefish Point
Underwater Preserve,
253, 254, 257, 258-259
Wilcox, Capt. F.H., 112
Willis, 63, 73, 126-128*
Wilmette, U.S.S., 252
Windiate, Cornelia B.,
247, 248-249
Witherspoon, Colette,
218
Wocoken, 179
Wolfe Islander II, 3, 4,
53-60*
Wolfe Islander III, 54

World War I, 20, 29, 41,
165
World War II, 166
Wright, A.W., 91
Wright, Dr. Richard, 171

*Z*aleski, Richard, 252
zebra mussels, 8, 24,
58*, 59*, 83, 112-113,
123
Zee, Mike, 254
Zillah, 259

IMPORTANT CONTACTS

for the Lake Ontario, Lake Erie, and Lake Huron region

Hyperbaric Chambers:

D.A.N. (Divers Alert Network): (919) 684-8111 or (919) 684-2948

Tobermory, Ontario, Hyperbaric Facility: (519) 596-2305

Toronto, Ontario, General Hyperbaric: (416) 340-4131
After hours: (416) 340-3155

McMaster Hospital, Hamilton, Ontario: (905) 521-2100

Bronson Methodist Hospital, Kalamazoo, Michigan: (616) 341-7654
or (616) 341-7778

Parks and Preserves:

DeTour Underwater Preserve, (proposed), c/o DeTour Area Chamber of Commerce, DETOUR, MI 49725

Erie Quest Marine Park, c/o Leamington (Ontario) & Area Tourist Information Council, 1-800-250-3336

Fathom Five National Marine Park, P.O. Box 189, TOBERMORY, Ontario N0H 2R0. Telephone: (519) 596-2233

Michigan Underwater Preserve Council, Inc., 560 N. State Street, ST. IGNACE, MI 49781

Sanilac Shores Underwater Preserve, P.O. Box 47, PORT SANILAC, MI 48469

Straits Underwater Preserve, c/o St. Ignace Chamber of Commerce, 560 N. State St., ST. IGNACE, MI 49871. Tel.: 1-800-338-6660

Thumb Area Underwater Preserve, Lighthouse County Park, 7320 Lighthouse Road, PORT HOPE, MI 49468. (517) 428-4749

Thunder Bay Underwater Preserve, P.O. Box 65, ALPENA, MI 49707

Periodicals:

The only glossy scuba diving magazine which has consistently, since the mid-1970's, printed articles about shipwrecks in the Great Lakes is DIVER Magazine, #230--11780 Hammersmith Way, RICHMOND, B.C., Canada V7A 5E3. Telephone: (604) 274-4333. Fax: (604) 274-4366. Website: Http://medianetcom.com/divermag/ E-mail: divermag@axionet.com

General:

Cris Kohl can be contacted through his publisher, Seawolf Communications, Inc., P.O. Box 66, West Chicago, IL 60186, telephone (630) 293-8996, fax: (630) 293-8837, e-mail: SeawolfRex@aol.com or Cris Kohl's e-mail: criskohl@aol.com

ABOUT THE AUTHOR

Cris Kohl first became intrigued by shipwrecks and the stories behind them after his initial exposure to the underwater world in Bermuda and the Florida Keys in 1974. Hailing from Windsor, Ontario, Canada, his three university degrees include a Master's degree in History, specializing in Great Lakes maritime history. He published his first Great Lakes scuba dive book in 1985. He has written seven books and, since 1982, hundreds of articles about Great Lakes shipwrecks and scuba diving in a variety of magazines, journals, and newsletters. A certified Divemaster, Master Diver, Nitrox, and Full Cave Diver, he has more training in his plans.

Cris Kohl's intense research, award-winning photography, enthusiasm, vigor, and sense of drama have made him a popular speaker at local historical societies, dive club meetings, and major scuba shows. In recent years, he has presented often at such annual shows as Our World--Underwater in Chicago, New York City's Beneath the Sea Show, Underwater Canada in Toronto, the Great Lakes Shipwreck Festival in Dearborn, Michigan, the annual Shipwrecks show in Ontario's Niagara region, the scuba show in Montreal, and the Boston Sea Rovers' annual clinic.

Cris Kohl, a firm supporter of diver access to shipwrecks and shipwreck information, is also a staunch marine conservationist and globetrotter, fully aware that the shipwrecks in our Great Lakes are the best preserved shipwrecks in the world!

MORE GREAT LAKES SHIPWRECKS BOOKS

Shipwreck books by Cris Kohl are available at bookstores and scuba dive shops, or they may be ordered through the mail. The following titles are available at press time:
DIVE ONTARIO! THE GUIDE TO SHIPWRECKS & SCUBA IN ONT. $29.95 U.S.
DIVE ONTARIO TWO! MORE ONTARIO SHIPWRECK STORIES.... $24.95 U.S.
TREACHEROUS WATERS: KINGSTON'S SHIPWRECKS............ $17.95 U.S.
THE 100 BEST GREAT LAKES SHIPWRECKS, VOL. I (EAST)..... $21.95 U.S.
THE 100 BEST GREAT LAKES SHIPWRECKS, VOL. II (WEST) ... $21.95 U.S.
Add postage & handling: $2.00 for 1st book, and $1.00 for each additional book.
Illinois orders please add 6.75% sales tax.
Mail check or money order, made out to Seawolf Communications, Inc., to:
Seawolf Communications, Inc., P.O. Box 66, West Chicago, IL 60186.